OUR WAY OF LIFE

Edited by Desmond Gillmor

CONTRIBUTORS

FREDERICK AALEN · ROY ALEXANDER
MARY CAWLEY · DAVID DREW · ANNE O'DOWD
JIM HOURIHAN

Heritage
Wildlife
Countryside
People

Wolfhound Press

This edition published 1993

© Wolfhound Press 1993, 1990, 1989
Individual texts © Desmond Gillmor, David Drew,
Roy Alexander, Frederick Aalen, Anne O'Dowd, Mary Cawley.
Illustrations © Contributors and listed sources.
Colour photographs © Jim Hourihan.

ISBN 0 86327 331 9
WOLFHOUND PRESS,
68 Mountjoy Square, Dublin 1.

First published in 1989 by Wolfhound Press as *The Irish Countryside*. This new edition has
been re-designed to a larger format and contains colour plates not included in the original
edition with some new black and white photographs, and a specially commissioned series
of line illustrations by Jeanette Dunne.

Cover design: Jan de Fouw.
Typesetting: Redsetter Ltd., Dublin.
Cover separations: Graphic Reproductions Ltd., Dublin.
Printed and bound by Techman Ltd., Dublin.

OUR WAY OF
LIFE

Glenmalure, Co. Wicklow. (photo: Hunting Aerofilms)

CONTENTS

Preface   *page* 6

1 Introduction · DESMOND GILLMOR   7

2 The Shape of the Land · DAVID DREW   13
The elements of the landscape; rocks; landscape forming agencies; (limestone
country; downslope movement; rivers; ice; coastline), the veneer on the land;
Irish landscapes; scenery and conservation.

3 Wildlife in the Countryside · ROY ALEXANDER   41
Wildlife past and present; boglands; uplands (plants; animals); lowlands
(woodland; hedgerows; grassland); fresh water; coast.

4 Imprint of the Past · FREDERICK AALEN   72
Landscape study; earliest human impact; prehistoric farm landscapes;
Christianity and the landscape; medieval and early modern landscape; the
making of the modern landscape; (economic expansion and landscape
development; land reclamation and settlement expansion; mining and
quarrying; domestic industry; communications; rural buildings); placenames;
threats to the historical heritage.

5 Folklife and Folk Traditions · ANNE O'DOWD   109
Farming practices (agricultural innovations; cultivation; harvesting); the
business life of the countryside (fairs and markets; industries and trades), social
life (storytelling, singing and dancing; patterns and pilgrimages; calendar
customs); home life (the house; food and drink; furnishings), museums.

6 Land, Work and Recreation · DESMOND GILLMOR   146
Land use; land ownership; employment; changes in farming; agriculture and the
environment; forestry; fishing; extractive industries; recreation (parks and forest
recreation; some problems in recreation).

7 Rural People and Services · MARY CAWLEY   175
The changing countryside; rural population change; physical planning in the
countryside; welfare issues; service needs and provision; community
development; rural social organisations; territoriality in rural Ireland; impacts
of change.

8 Management of the Countryside · DESMOND GILLMOR   200
Rural development; countryside conservation; integrated management

SELECTED FURTHER READING   212

INDEX   214

PREFACE

The landscape and people of the Irish countryside figure prominently in popular perceptions of Ireland, which remains one of the most rural countries in Europe. The high quality environment, rich historical heritage and distinctive society of the countryside are of great importance in Irish life, and even in the broader context of an urbanised Europe. Thus it is particularly appropriate that this book on the Irish countryside was selected for inclusion in the recent 'Irish Life Classic Collection'.

The new readership and the enlarged format made possible by inclusion in that collection are greatly welcomed. The initial aim of having such a format could not be achieved in the original version of the book. The very favourable reception which nonetheless was given to *The Irish Countryside* was most gratifying. It is hoped that the improvements in presentation will further enhance the appeal and value of the book for its enlarged readership. The addition of colour photographs is a notable feature and I am very grateful to James Hourihan for the provision and selection of these. This is in addition to the debt owed to my co-author geographers and to the publishers for making the book possible.

Desmond Gillmor,
Department of Geography,
Trinity College Dublin.

CONTRIBUTORS

DESMOND GILLMOR · Department of Geography, Trinity College, Dublin.
FREDERICK AALEN · Department of Geography, Trinity College, Dublin.
ROY ALEXANDER · Department of Geography, Chester College, Chester.
MARY CAWLEY · Department of Geography, University College, Galway.
DAVID DREW · Department of Geography, Trinity College, Dublin.
ANNE O'DOWD · Irish Folklife Section, National Museum of Ireland, Dublin.
JIM HOURIHAN · Department of Geography, St. Patrick's College, Drumcondra.

Introduction

DESMOND GILLMOR

The Irish countryside is often perceived to be the real Ireland, in that its landscapes and people are taken to epitomise those physical and human characteristics which are considered to represent Ireland and embody its ethos. It is no longer true to regard Ireland as rural, in that two-thirds of its population may be classified as urban, but yet the Irish countryside is of immense importance and constitutes a priceless asset.

About 97 per cent of the area of Ireland remains rural land. Outside of the few main urban concentrations the majority of the people reside in the open countryside and villages. Even many of those living in the towns and cities are only one or two generations removed from the land. Rural issues retain a strong influence in national affairs and Irish rural areas have a more important economic role than in most European countries. The countryside not only supplies the population with much of its food and water but its produce provides substantial employment in processing and is a major sector of export trade. The Irish countryside has a rich and diversified heritage of landscape, wildlife and historical features, much of it being relatively unspoiled. It functions as a vital recreational resource, which is highly accessible to the urban population and attracts large numbers of visitors from overseas. The extent to which the countryside is used in the advertising of varied products indicates its perceived appeal and it has provided the inspiration for much Irish literature, art and music.

Although it has developed later than in many countries, within Ireland there is an increasing public interest in the countryside as society has become more urbanised, leisured and educated. This book has been written for those people with general interests in rural Ireland, whether Irish residents, visitors or others. Its purpose is to provide the general information on and explanation of different aspects of the countryside necessary for a broad understanding and fuller appreciation of it. It is not intended that the book should be a guide to individual objects in the country but the treatment should enable the main features to be put in their proper contexts. It is hoped that the book will reinforce and stimulate interest in rural Ireland and that it will enhance the enormous pleasure to be derived from the countryside. Greater understanding and appreciation should contribute to fuller discussion about the Irish countryside and to concern and action about its future.

The arrangement and content of the book are based on the conviction that there is a need for a general work which investigates the main facets of the Irish countryside. Books on the countryside of other countries usually focus on nature or history or combine these but the countryside is much more than a nature reserve and a museum; it is a living working countryside. Its landscape reflects the work of modern forces as well as being shaped by nature and fashioned by earlier habitats throughout human history. Thus aspects of contemporary rural society and its livelihoods are considered in addition to nature and history. It is hoped that a balanced view of the totality of the Irish countryside emerges from this approach.

Nature is explored in two chapters which are concerned with the development of the physical landscape and with its wild plant and animal life. In chapter 2, the rocks of varied age and type from which the landscape of the countryside has been sculptured are considered first. Then much of the chapter is devoted to the ways in which the land has been shaped by limestone weathering, gravity, rivers, ice and sea, and to the landforms resulting from these processes. The evolution and character of the wildlife of the countryside are outlined at the beginning of chapter 3. Discussion then focuses on the plants and animals of the different wildlife habitats, comprising the boglands, uplands, lowlands (woodlands, hedgerows, grassland), fresh water and the coast. The great diversity of nature encompassed within the small area of Ireland is emphasised in these two chapters.

The rich historical heritage of landscape features and of folk traditions and materials associated with the Irish countryside is evident in the next two chapters. In chapter 4, the evolution of the human landscape is traced in sequence from the arrival of the first settlers, emphasising the features which remain. Particular attention is given to developments since the seventeenth century, the period from which much of the present landscape dates. The varied folklife and folk traditions of the countryside are investigated in chapter 5 in the contexts of farming practices, business life, social life and home life. Much folk tradition has ceased but surviving elements are noted. The need to preserve the historical legacy in the landscape and in museums is emphasised.

Attention then turns to economic and social aspects of the contemporary countryside. In chapter 6, after consideration of land use, land ownership and employment, the activities of agriculture, forestry, fishing, extractive industry and recreation are discussed. Particular emphasis is placed on farming because of its importance in the economy and appearance of the countryside. The nature and changing character of rural society and the effects which these changes are having are investigated in chapter 7, especially with regard to population, physical planning, welfare, services, community development, social organisations and territoriality. Problems of both development and conservation arise and these are outlined in the concluding chapter.

It is evident that in the presentation of such an overview of the multi-faceted countryside not every feature could be covered and only a broad outline of any one aspect can be given. Thus the reader with a specialist interest and knowledge of one sphere of the Irish countryside may have little to learn from the treatment of that topic. However, such a person should discover that there are other fascinating aspects of the countryside and it is beneficial to see one's specialism within the context of the whole countryside. The difficulties in resolving the problems of the countryside lie partly in unfamiliarity with other aspects and in the failure of people to give adequate recognition to other interests and viewpoints.

It is hoped also that the book will stimulate the reader to undertake further and deeper investigation. A selected list of books for further reading is given

Figure 1.1
Locations of counties and provinces in Northern Ireland and in the Republic of Ireland.

Hillsborough, an estate village, Co. Down. (photo: Northern Ireland Tourist Board)

at the end. Many of these works contain references to the more detailed literature on particular topics in periodicals and elsewhere. Even more pleasurable and rewarding are exploration and investigation of the Irish countryside in its many aspects at first hand. The regional variations over short distances add greatly to its inherent interest. It is important to visit also the areas which are not considered to be the most scenic and popular, as all places have their interests and attractions. It is particularly satisfying to get to know and understand a locality in depth. The sense of discovery can be heightened by the fact that many features of the Irish countryside are far from being fully understood.

Because of the multidimensional nature of the countryside, the geographical perspective seems an appropriate approach to adopt in this book. Geography is to some extent a generalist and multidisciplinary field of study but individual geographers have their own areas of expertise within the discipline as a whole. Thus each of the contributors to the book was trained as a geographer and has that perspective but is here writing on her or his own field of interest within the Irish countryside. Geography is concerned with the nature and regional variations of the physical environment and of human features and with the interrelationships between the physical and human elements. Thus it is very relevant to the subject matter of the countryside, which reflects both natural conditions and the effects of past and present human activity.

While the subject of this book is the Irish countryside, it is not intended to imply that rural and urban areas are unrelated, that they are distinctly different in all respects or that the boundary between them is readily and precisely identifiable in the landscape. Town and country are closely interrelated, as is indicated by the extent to which there are flows of goods, services, information, money and people between them. They are both integral parts of the same regional, national and international systems and the welfare of one depends in part on the welfare of the other.

There is no simple definition and delimitation of what constitutes countryside. It is here taken as comprising those parts of Ireland in which the extensive land uses of agriculture and forestry and undeveloped land dominate, as compared with urban areas in which the more intensive manufacturing, service and residential uses predominate. Associated with these differences in land use, the population tends to be of lower density and more dispersed pattern in rural areas. There is thus a visual distinction in the landscape which is generally evident, especially at the extremes, but it is in intermediate areas that there may be uncertainties and ambiguities. With regard to people, it can be argued that socially the distinction has diminished or disappeared with urbanisation of the countryside, the process whereby urban influences are introduced to rural areas.

As these features imply, there is gradation and differentiation within the countryside. At one end of the scale are the urban fringe areas, where the town is encroaching into the countryside, so that agriculture and woodland are giving way to housing, industrial and recreational use. Although the extensive uses still occupy the majority of the land, the population is strongly urban oriented, especially through commuting. At the other end of the gradation are those places which may be said to have a high degree of rural-ity and are likely to be the most remote from urban centres. This rurality gradation is mainly in human terms but within the visual landscape of the countryside it is possible to make a twofold differentiation between what may be termed farmscape and wildscape. The farmscape is that part comprised mainly of fields enclosed by hedgerows, walls and fences and with a network of roads and lanes along which are villages but predomin-antly dispersed houses and other buildings. The wildscape is the unimproved and generally unenclosed land, mainly rough grazing, bog, heath and rock, where there are much fewer roads and little human settle-ment. Both types of area and transitional places constitute the Irish countryside of this book.

Figure 2.1.
The landscape:
Relief and Drainage

100 km

Height of land above sea level

300 metres

150 metres

Rivers

R Foyle
R Bann
Lough Neagh
R Lagan
River Erne
Lower Lough Erne
Upper Lough Erne
R Bann
L Conn
R Moy
Lough Allen
R Shannon
R Suck
Inny R
Lough Ree
R Boyne
R Liffey
Lough Mask
Lough Corrib
R.Corrib
R Brosna
Lough Derg
R Barrow
R Shannon
R Nore
R Slaney
R Suir
R Blackwater
R Lee
R Bandon

The Giant's Causeway, Co. Antrim. (photo: Northern Ireland Tourist Board)

The Shape of the Land

DAVID DREW

he Irish countryside is famous for the beauty of its landscape. It is an unspoiled beauty in large part, particularly when compared with the more densely populated
industrialised regions of Europe. More remarkable
still is the diversity of scenery within the island. The
regions of upland and lowland, crag and pasture, shoreline and lakeside, are
compressed into so small a compass as to accentuate the contrasts.

These differences between one place and another are not of course wholly
natural; human activities, or lack of activities, may accentuate or lessen the contrast. Landscape is not simply 'scenery' for recreational use but also the place in
which people live and work. To the dweller in Belfast or Dublin the 'countryside' may impinge only as a distant glimpse of Cave Hill or the Dublin
Mountains, or as a place to be visited at weekends or on holidays. To the rural
dweller the landscape of the countryside has a more fundamental and
immediate relevance. For example the type of agriculture practised in particular areas of Ireland is to some degree influenced by the nature of the rocks
and soil and by the form of the land. Dairy farming, for instance, is most widespread on gentle lowlands underlain by limestone rock and a thick soil. Such
terrain can yield an abundant growth of sweet grass in Ireland's damp climate.
The location of rural settlements is or was affected by the character of the landscape; in a negative manner by the avoidance of barren, ill-drained or
mountainous regions and in a positive sense perhaps by proximity to fertile
land or a good harbour. Economic activity is even more closely related to the
natural landscape where the exploitation of natural resources is concerned.
Whether the resource be metallic ore, fossil fuel, sand and gravel, building
stone or underground water, the occurrence and abundance is determined
by the makeup and history through geological time of the area.

THE ELEMENTS OF THE LANDSCAPE

Every landscape has a skeleton of rock. In some places the bones project
above the surface, as in the sea cliffs of Moher or Slieve League or in the bare

limestone of the Burren. Elsewhere the solid rocks may be mantled by soils, by bog, or even by thick layers of broken rock, sands and clays laid down by glaciers in the past.

Rocks are not immutable unchanging facets of nature, however. Rock strata at or close to the land surface are subjected to a host of natural and human influences that modify, to a greater or lesser extent, their original character. Some of these forces eventually weaken the rock fabric, fragmenting it into boulders, stones or grains according to the character of the rock. Any old building made of natural stone shows this process of rock disintegration taking place as discolouration of the rock is followed by flaking and crumbling of the surface of the stone. More dramatic is the work of rivers, carving valleys into the rocks and carrying debris from the valley slopes downstream, ultimately to the sea. In the past other natural forces, for example glaciers capable of sculpting and moulding the land, were active in Ireland. Thus the familiar landscape of today has a long history. The landscape has evolved through time as myriad natural forces altered the fundamental building blocks of the land, the rocks. No two places have had exactly the same array of forces acting upon exactly the same type of rocks for exactly the same length of time, so that no two landscapes are exactly alike.

In this chapter it will be attempted to make sense of aspects of the landscapes of the Irish countryside in terms of the rocks that underlie the terrain and in terms of the forces that operate or have operated in the past to fashion the rocks into particular forms. Often the history of a landscape is so complicated as to be almost impossible to unravel with any certainty, and in many parts of Ireland the events of recent geological time have all but obliterated that which went before. This occurs over the midlands where the imprint of the Ice Age dominates the countryside. In this instance a particular natural agency has been so powerful as to largely negate the influence of rock type. Likewise there are localities in which a rock type or rock structure is of overwhelming importance in the landscape. Thus it is perhaps useful to begin the investigation of the shape of the land by looking at landforms dominated by one particular rock or formative agency.

THE ROCKS

The youngest rocks that are exposed at the surface in Ireland are approximately 15,000 years old, though they are rocks only in the eyes of the geologist, consisting of the mounds of sands, gravels and clays deposited by the ice sheets that covered the country at that time. Surrounded by such 'young' glacial debris are rock outcrops at Kilmore Quay in Co. Wexford that are thought to be some 2,500 million years old, an unimaginable antiquity and the oldest in Ireland. As with human history so with geological history, much more is known about the recent past than about distant times. For hundreds of millions of years the geological record for Ireland is scanty and incomplete. It is certain, however, that the land area now known as Ireland has in the past been submerged beneath the sea on more than one occasion, has boasted mountain ranges of Himalayan proportions, and has been desert, ice cap and tropical forest. Ireland has seen mountains built and destroyed and has experienced earthquakes and volcanoes. It is difficult to reconcile such excitements and extremes with the gentle and (geologically!) uneventful land of today, until we consider the vast time scale over which these events took place. For every year that Ireland has been inhabited by humans, there have been 250,000 years during which the geological dramas had no human audience.

The most widespread rock type in Ireland is limestone, extending over much of the midlands and reaching from east to west coasts between Dublin and Galway (Figure 2.1). Extensive though the limestones are, they are inconspicuous over much of their outcrop in the midlands. Over millions of years they have been worn down close to sea level and then overlain with the material deposited by glaciers. Although knolls and hillocks of limestone rise above the undulating countryside of the midlands in places, the Ben of Fore and other steep hills nearby in Westmeath for example, the limestones form dramatic landforms only where they remain as plateaux elevated above the surrounding countryside, as in Clare, Sligo and Fermanagh-Cavan.

Limestones formed as deposits of shells and other lifeforms on the floor of a warm clear sea that existed about 340 million years ago. The marine origin is obvious to the most casual observer of an exposure of limestone rock in a cliff or a quarry. Fossil shells and fragments of other marine organisms, including corals, are common. In some instances the limestone consists entirely of a jumble of fossil remains, cemented together to form a hard rock.

In the south and southwest of the country sandstone rather than limestone is the predominant rock. These rocks were formed earlier than the limestone by the compaction of sands and other grains accumulating under the desert conditions that characterised Ireland at that time. Being formed through accumulation of loose sediment, such rocks are termed sedimentary, as is limestone. Subsequent to the formation of both the limestones and sandstones, earth movements distorted the rocks of the southwest from their original horizontal condition into a series of parallel upfolds called anticlines, separated by downfolds known as synclines. Now, millions of years later, those same folds find expression as the parallel hill ranges (Knockmealdowns, Nagles, Boggeragh for example) and valleys (Lee, Blackwater,

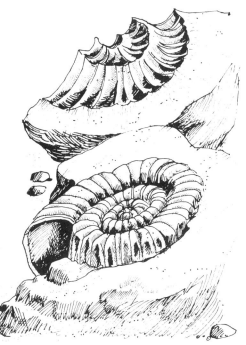

Kenmare for example) all oriented west to east, that are such an outstanding feature of Kerry and Cork in particular. The limestone has long ago been eroded from the mountains and now remains only in the valley floors as thin slivers surrounded by the sandstone.

Older still are some of the rocks of west Connacht as in the Sheffry Hills, those of the triangle of land between Belfast, Longford and Drogheda, and those of Wicklow-Wexford. Despite their great age it is often still possible to visualise how these rocks originated; the type of material from which they are made is unaltered and the life forms which existed at the time and which were incorporated into the rock fabric as fossils are preserved. The fossils consist almost entirely of marine creatures as life on land evolved only late on in this period. Rock types include claystones, shales and slates, for which the original sediments accumulated in a muddy sea. There is also limestone, for example that exposed in the cliffs near Tramore, Co. Waterford, the product of clear warm water.

Oldest of all are what are termed the basement rocks of Ireland, upon which all the subsequent rock formations lie. Over most of the country the basement rocks are buried hundreds or thousands of metres below the ground, but on the northwestern and southeastern margins of Ireland, they break surface. Much of Donegal and parts of Mayo and Galway, as well as the small area in Wexford already mentioned, are underlain by these ancient rocks. Almost all of these rocks have been radically altered from their original state by being subjected to extreme pressure and heat at some stage in their history; they are termed metamorphic rocks because of their changed form. Thus limestones have become marbles, mudstones have turned to hard but brittle slates, sandstones have mutated into the rock type called quartzite. Traces of former lifeforms as fossils are rare in such rocks, as presumably any remains in the original rocks were destroyed by the heat and pressure they later experienced.

Almost all of these altered rocks are more compact and resistant to erosion than their original counterparts and so commonly form uplands or individual mountains. Quartzite, the altered form of sandstone, is a good example of this resistance to the elements; some of Ireland's most spectacular mountains are composed of the rock, Errigal, the Great Sugar Loaf, Croagh Patrick and the Twelve Bens for example. A further distinctive characteristic of these mountains is the bleached appearance of the rock, again due to the quartzite which is composed almost entirely of the grey-white mineral called silica.

Rocks younger than the limestones are comparatively uncommon in Ireland, though west Clare, the Castlecomer plateau of Carlow-Kilkenny and the uplands of Leitrim and Fermanagh are largely composed of shales or sandstones, and sometimes coal seams, that rest directly upon the limestones and are therefore younger. Younger still, infants in geological terms, are the rocks in the extreme northeastern corner of the island, in particular north and east of Dungannon. These include sandstones in the Lagan valley some 200 million years old, volcanic rocks and chalk in Antrim and, 60 million years old and youngest of all, clays laid down on the bed of what was formerly a much more extensive Lough Neagh, in south Tyrone.

Finally there is a group of rocks that did not originate as mineral fragments laid down on land or sea but rather by the cooling and solidification of a broth of liquid rock containing a variety of elements. This magma originated deep beneath the surface of the earth. Some of it reached the surface as a volcanic eruption or lava flow and some cooled down gradually at depth, being exposed only when the overlying rocks had been removed by erosion, perhaps millions of years later. Some of the youngest rocks to be found in Ireland are of this type, for example the dark, fine-grained basalts that form the Antrim plateau and the Giant's Causeway. The basalts originated as a succession of lava flows oozing from fissures and blanketing the land for hundreds of square kilometres. The lavas cooled rapidly and because of this the individual crystals in the rock are tiny. By contrast, granite is an example of a rock that solidified very slowly, insulated deep beneath the surface. Its crystals are large and distinct, with black, white and pink crystals being common. Granite rocks form the Wicklow Mountains and the Mourne Mountains but also the wild lowland terrain west of Galway city. There have been several periods during which these igneous rocks or 'fire-rocks' were created, periods during which the earth's crust was unstable in Ireland, but periods separated by many millions of years of relative quiescence.

Volcanic rocks often form distinctive local as well as regional landforms, usually because they have proved more resistant to erosion than the neighbouring rocks. Slieve Gullion and the Carlingford Mountains of Armagh-Louth are ancient isolated volcanic rocks. East of Lough Gur in Co. Limerick, conspicuous isolated hills such as Killteely Hill are former volcanic openings rising above the limestone plain.

Some indication as to the rock type underlying an area may be obtained where it is used as a building stone and this can contribute to the regional character of a landscape. Traditionally, local stone was used for construction and so over much of Ireland the grey limestone is the commonest natural building material. Sandstone, warmer and softer, has been used widely in southwest Ireland and in the Belfast region. Wicklow and Mourne villages and farmhouses may be built of speckled blocks of granite. This use of stone, however, is now the exception rather than the rule; the undistinguished concrete block, though admittedly largely originating from limestone, rules supreme. Similarly with field boundaries of rocks, the characteristic limestone

The Galtee Mountains, formed of sandstone, are the backbone to the pastoral landscapes of the Glen of Aherlow. (photo: Bord Failte)

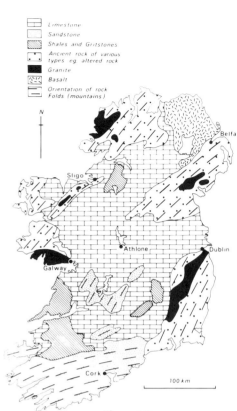

Figure 2.2
The principal types of rocks.

Legend for Figure 2.2:
- Limestone
- Sandstone
- Shales and Gritstones
- Ancient rock of various types eg. altered rock
- Granite
- Basalt
- Orientation of rock Folds (mountains)

Human imprint on the landscape: scattered farmhouses and fields near Taghmon, Co. Wexford. (photo: Cambridge University Collection of air photographs)

Figure 2.3
Features of glaciation of the landscape.

Legend for Figure 2.3:
- Areas covered only by earlier ice sheet
- Drumlins
- Kames (gravel mounds)
- Eskers (gravel ridges)
- Direction of ice movement

stone walls or eccentric slabs walls of flagstones in Co. Clare are gradually yielding to the efficient unromantic wire fence.

Sometimes it is true to say that a particular rock type is associated with a distinct landscape type in Ireland. Shale lands, west Clare for example, are regions of gentle slopes and boggy fields; granites yield a thin soil, a stony or peaty landscape of broad swelling slopes; upland limestones give dramatic rocky scenery of green and grey. Sometimes it is true to say . . . but in Ireland often not, the rocks are only one of the elements that go to create the landscape.

LANDSCAPE FORMING AGENCIES

In emphasising the importance of the rocks in the shaping of the landscape, reference is often made to large-scale extensive, perhaps regional, landscapes, for example Slieve Aughty and the Mourne Mountains, composed of one or a group of similar rocks. To understand landscapes on a more modest local scale requires a different approach. The panorama from a hilltop, the prospect of headland and bay from a cliff, or the slopes, hillocks and hollows that surround a rural community can be explained only with reference to the modifications, transmutations and rearrangements that have been imposed on the rock fabric. Earlier, the great variety of Irish landscape was referred to:

> Lush Kildare of scented meadows,
> Roscommon, thin in ash-tree shadows
> And Westmeath the lake-reflected,
> Spreading Leix the hill-protected
> Kneeling all in silver haze?
>
> Stony seaboard, far and foreign
> Stony hills poured over space,
> Stony outcrops of the Burren,
> Stones in every fertile place.
>
> (John Betjeman, 'Ireland with Emily')

More prosaically, the landscapes described above are very different one from another but all are developed on limestone rock; clearly one rock type need not have a predestined landscape.

Rocks are transformed into 'landforms' via several steps. If the rocks are to be rearranged they must first be broken down into manageable and moveable fragments. Whole mountains cannot be moved except by the mighty earth forces that build mountains. Secondly the fragmented rock must be moved from its original position and finally it must be deposited, either elsewhere on land or, eventually, in the sea. Initially therefore, the fabric of the rock must be weakened, allowing particles to be prised free. The particles may be bus-sized boulders, sand grains or molecules; it all depends on the character of the rock and the character of the agency responsible for the attack.

In Ireland today rock decay is gradual and its results unspectacular; it is largely a process of chemical rotting of solid rock beneath the blanket of soil. The disintegration is accomplished by natural acids in the soil and even by rainwater itself. In specific localities more obvious forces may be at work, destroying the rock with physical rather than chemical weapons. The scree slopes of rocks and boulders in the higher mountains have largely been produced by frost action plucking loose rock lumps. Sea cliffs crumble under the onslaught of waves, whilst mountain rivers in flood batter their rock bed and banks with an armoury of bouncing boulders. These forces can operate only where rock is at or near the surface, an unusual condition in Ireland, and so their effect is restricted to a few areas of the country. Some rocks resist attack by the forces of decay; this includes quartzite which is an almost indestructible rock under Irish conditions, as is slate. On the other hand, limestone, the most commonly occurring rock in Ireland, despite its solid appearance, surrenders without a murmur to the assault of rainwater, a fluid rarely lacking in Ireland. When an acid, vinegar for example, comes into contact with limestone, some of the rock is dissolved, accompanied by bubbling and fizzing if the acid is strong. Almost all rain and river water is slightly acidic naturally and so able to dissolve some lime. Thus, in the damp Irish climate limestones are very vulnerable to being, in effect, washed away. Because of this, much of the Irish limestone forms lowland, notably the central plain of the country. The hill ranges that rise above the plain, Slieve Bloom and the Knockmealdowns for example, are composed of almost insoluble sandstone.

LIMESTONE COUNTRY

Around the western and northern periphery of the central plain there are some elevated limestone regions, commonly comprising steep-sided plateaux. These areas, including the Burren, the Marble Arch area and Benbulben-Truskmore, exhibit some remarkable landforms.

One feature typical of such upland limestone areas, or karsts as they are sometimes termed, is an absence of water at the surface of the land. Lacking rivers, streams or lakes and dry a short time after rain ceases to fall, they are almost deserts in a damp climate. Over millennia the rainwater enlarges fissures and cracks in the limestone by the process of dissolution, until eventually the openings are sufficiently large and numerous to engulf rainwater and to carry it off underground. In some limestone areas these enlarged fissures are exposed at the surface, particularly if there is no covering of soil. The bare limestone surface is thus sectioned into blocks separated by the deep fissures called grikes. Because it is into these grikes that rainwater finds its way and because they provide a sheltered shaded humid refuge from the barren rock 'pavement' above, they are densely vegetated, constituting long narrow gardens in the desert. The Burren plateau in Co. Clare is one of the finest such barren karstlands in western Europe. The bleached rock stretches in every direction, cliffs and terraces forming natural giant staircases on the hillsides. The lack of rivers on the limestone means that there are no true valleys. Instead, the Irish karstlands are pitted by innumerable hollows, and trenches, sections of gorge and canyon.

If the geological conditions are suitable, then complete streams or even rivers may disappear underground in limestone terrain. This might be the case where, for example, a river, flowing over an insoluble, non-limestone rock, passes on to the limestone. The corrosive energy of the river water causes concentrated erosion of the limestone at the boundary between the two rock types and eventually a sinkhole or swallowhole is created, engulfing all the flow.

To the north of Drumshanbo in Co. Leitrim and extending some 50 km into Co. Fermanagh and Co. Cavan, there is a bleak boggy upland formed of shales, sandstones and coal measure rocks. The area reaches its highest point at Cuilcagh Mountain (687 metres) and the slopes of Cuilcagh generate the series of small streams that flow into Lough Allen and form the headwaters of the River Shannon. The Shannon itself remains on the surface of the land but not so many of the other streams of this upland, for the watertight rocks of Cuilcagh are surrounded on all sides by a rim of limestone. When the streams reach the edge of the limestone they disappear underground to re-emerge from springs that may be many kilometres distant. The point at which the water sinks underground may be an unappealing boggy hollow, as with the series of disappearing streams in the Geevagh area of Co. Sligo.

Alternatively the engulfment may be dramatic. South of the Marble Arch caves near Belcoo in Co. Fermanagh, the Owenbrean (Monastir) River flows down the northern flank of Cuilcagh in an ever deepening gorge. Finally the river slides away into the darkness at the base of a 40 metres high limestone cliff. In flood, the underground passageways cannot cope with the great quantities of peat-stained water and the valley upstream of the cliff becomes a deep silent lake with an underwater outlet. The water sinking here reappears, greatly augmented by other underground rivers, at the base of another spectacular cliff, a kilometre away at the Marble Arch caves, there to form the Claddagh River.

Elsewhere in Ireland, sometimes in unlikely locations, are other 'lost rivers'. On the sodden boggy lowlands of Mayo near the village of Bellaburke to the east of Westport, the course of the Aille River terminates abruptly at the foot of a long cliff. Banks of mud on either side testify to violent flooding when the underground fissures cannot cope with the river in spate. Most singular of all perhaps is the engulfment of the waters of Lough Mask. Lough Mask in Co. Mayo and Lough Corrib in Co. Galway are separated by a narrow neck of land on which is located the town of Cong. The famous Cong Canal was built to link the lakes in the nineteenth century, both to lower the water levels in the higher Lough Mask and also to allow for navigation between the lakes as there is no natural connection on the surface. Yet the lakes are connected, but subterraneously rather than by a surface river. On the lonely southeastern shore of Lough Mask amid strangely sculpted lime-stones, are dozens of fissures into which the waters of the lake slide or tumble. Five kilometres away the waters return to the surface from huge springs that almost encircle Cong, before uniting to form the short Cong River which flows into Lough Corrib. A walk in the scrub and forest that covers much of the isthmus between the lakes leaves no doubt in the mind but that this is a hollow landscape. Clefts and potholes are everywhere, water is glimpsed at the base of shafts emerging from the darkness and disappearing after a few metres or forming still black pools tens of metres in depth. A strange but secret limestone landscape.

More secret still to all but a few enthusiasts, are another feature of many of Ireland's limestone areas – caves, or potholes as they are sometimes called. As underground streams flow from their sinkholes to the springs, they dissolve and enlarge the rock fissures that they traverse. Over thousands or millions of years these underground river channels become sufficiently roomy for humans to enter, should they so choose. There are many groups of cave explorers in Ireland, and the only sensible way to visit the majority of Irish caves is by joining such a group. However, even an ordinary non-athletic person can glimpse the underworld of Ireland in one of the caves that have been made accessible to the general public. The Marble Arch caves of Co. Fermanagh previously referred to, may be visited, and allow a glimpse of an underground river flowing in the great tunnel it has carved for itself in the limestone massif.

Eventually the cave river abandons the route it carves for itself, perhaps to adopt another course at a lower level in the limestone. If this happens then the original cave becomes fossil, it no longer functions to carry water and gradually it decays and collapses. However, fossil caves are often places of great beauty because under the quiet water-free conditions stalactites and stalagmites can form. These are columns of the pure mineral calcite, of which the limestone rock is made, deposited as crystals on the roof and floor respectively of the caverns. They grow slowly, a centimetre every few centuries perhaps, but given the vast scale of geological time, they may form elegant tapering columns and pillars several metres in length. The cave of Pol-an-Ionain in the Burren contains a stalactite seven metres in length. Other caves, such as Dunmore near Kilkenny and Mitchelstown in Co. Tipperary, contain great numbers of such features, often tinted red, black or bronze by impurities in the rock.

DOWNSLOPE MOVEMENT

The hidden landscape of Ireland is confined to the limestone rocks. Elsewhere, where the rocks are not easily dissolved, much of the rainfall remains on the surface of the land. Again, unlike the limestone regions where the rainwater both dissolves the lime and carries it away invisibly, other rocks which have been fragmented by chemical decomposition or weakened perhaps by ice action need some other agency to move them over the landscape. In desert regions of the world, with no vegetation to anchor down the soil and rock fragments, wind might readily move the material. Not so in Ireland; here, gravity and running water are the effective mechanisms. Gravity, usually a muted modifier of landscape, is ubiquitous; running water (in effect, rivers) has a much more localised effect.

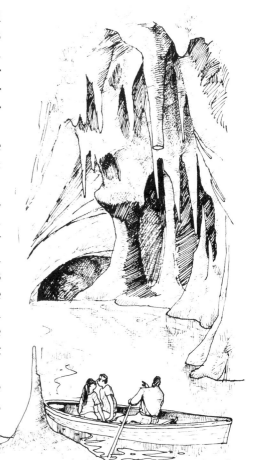

It is gravity that causes the broken weathered rocks and soil on a slope, however gentle, to move downwards to the lowest points in the landscape. Under Irish conditions such downslope movement of material is usually imperceptibly slow and its existence can be inferred only from the longterm effects that it may produce. For example, if a wall or other barrier runs across a slope, the upslope side of the wall is normally of lesser height than the downslope side. Loose material moving downslope has its progress impeded by the barrier and banks up against it, whilst downslope of the wall the loose material moves downwards unhindered. Such processes are so slow that individual particles might take decades to inch their way to the foot of a slope.

Under particular conditions this movement of material can be much more rapid, in some instances to the extent of being a catastrophic event, landslips rather than soil creeps. The Antrim coast road north of Larne is flanked by scars on the hillsides where huge masses of rock and soil have slipped downslope, often following very heavy rains. In the steep-sided valleys near Sligo, Glencar and Glenade for example, weak shale rocks beneath strong limestone have collapsed on many occasions at many places in the past. This has created a steep cliff above and a chaos of hummocks and hollows below where the slipped material has come to rest.

Massive movements can take place even on relatively gentle slopes. Whole sections of peat bog can simply detach themselves and flow, like a brown syrupy river, downslope. Such bog-flows are reported regularly from the uplands and even the low-level bogs of Ireland. In 1984 a 'bog-burst' took place near Geevagh in Co. Sligo. A mass of waterlogged peat flowed for five kilometres along a broad declivity at speeds of up to 20 kph before coming to rest and blanketing 40 hectares of farmland and the local GAA pitch with a metre of liquid peat!

THE WORK OF RIVERS

If the material, be it peat, boulders or sand grains, is to be moved any further across the landscape, it is rivers that must in both senses, pick up the pieces. All rivers have energy which they can use to carry along loose particles. In mountain streams, although the streams may not be large, the gradients are steep with waterfalls and cascades as typical features. The beds of such streams, in the Kerry or Connemara mountains perhaps, are a jumble of boulders and stones. For most of the time the stream is quite incapable of moving such large objects and it is only following heavy rain that the ability of the stream to transport great rocks becomes apparent. With its flow swollen perhaps ten or one hundred fold, the torrent can carry the smaller stones and bounce the largest along its bed. As the material is manhandled downstream in this manner so it becomes abraded, its sharp projections are rounded off and its size diminishes. It is interesting to walk down the course of such a stream in dry weather to observe how the material in the bed becomes smaller and rounder downstream. Often it is possible to distinguish between different rock types by noting the different shapes to which they are weathered by the river abrasion, shales and slates become thin flat plates, granites often become almost spherical pebbles and so forth.

When they reach the lowland, rivers take on a more placid aspect. They are still transporting fragments of rock or soil as the typically brown colour of lowland rivers testifies and the quantity thus transported again increases greatly in flood periods. They also deposit some of this material. If flows are

Above: Inis Oírr, The Aran Islands, Co. Galway. The little soil on these limestone islands has been made by people over many years from seaweed. The stone walls are very typical of the islands.

Right: High up in the Wicklow Mountains, an ox-bow lake and meanders make a striking pattern against the background of marginal soils and coniferous forestry.

PREVIOUS PAGE.
East Town, Tory Island, Co. Donegal. A former clachan settlement where people lived in a village-type community. Notice the field pattern radiating from the houses.

People continually change the countryside. In this landscape in Co. Wexford, people have created field patterns strongly evocative of Dutch polder-lands.

OVERLEAF:
Much of the west of Ireland landscape is virtually unchanged for the last few centuries. Notice the linear settlement pattern and field system near Slieve League in Co. Donegal.

sufficiently great, the river overspills its banks and floods the surrounding area; this is often a disaster for people living nearby but it is a wholly natural part of the behaviour of a river. When the floodwaters subside the material that was being carried along by that water is simply dropped. The sight of the muddy squalor in any village or town from which floodwaters have just receded leaves no doubt in the mind as to the amount of debris that even a small river can carry. Over long periods of time countless inundations can allow extensive flood-lain sediments to build up, so developing the very flat, and often very fertile, land on either side of a river channel. The middle course of the Liffey, the River Main upstream of Ballymena and many of the rivers tributary to the Shannon all exhibit lazy rivers winding their way over the deposits they themselves lay down in times of high water. One of the purposes of the programme of arterial drainage carried out in Ireland has been to minimise the number of occasions on which rivers overflow their banks, by straightening river courses, by embanking the channels and by creating uniform channel gradients. Such schemes are effective, but do little for the aesthetic appeal of the particular river valley. The overall effect of deposition by rivers is one of smoothing the angularities of landscape, of infilling, blanketing and creating gentle slopes or flats; this in contrast with the erosive work of rivers engaged in eroding valleys and removing material from the base of slopes.

Previously it was remarked that rivers cut their valleys, that valleys are simply the long hollows remaining when the river has carried away the broken-down rock. This is obviously the case with mountain streams flowing in deep clefts gouged into the hillside, the stream commonly occupying almost all of the flat ground at the foot of the valley slopes. Hundreds of such rivers pursue short turbulent courses to the sea wherever uplands abut the coast on the periphery of Ireland. However, many of Ireland's largest rivers scarcely seem to flow in a valley at all. The Shannon seems more a string of lakes linked by sections of sluggish channels than a proper river over much of its course, whilst the same is true to an even greater extent of the River Erne. How can great rivers such as these have failed to carve valleys? At the other extreme there are, in many of the upland areas of Ireland, great straight trench-like valleys, flat-floored and steep-sided, occupied by a small stream, insignificant when compared with its valley. Valleys such as Glenmalure in Wicklow and the Sneem valley in Co. Kerry are such features. How did such valleys come to be? In fact the explanation for these and for many other Irish landforms lies in the past rather than the present. The natural forces responsible are no longer operative but their legacy remains. In Ireland the events of greatest importance in the recent past were those associated with ice, snow and the melting of ice and snow.

THE ACTION OF ICE

For tens of thousands of years on at least two occasions during the past 1½-2 million years, Ireland must have looked much as do Greenland and Antarctica at the present day. Not just Ireland was affected of course; the climate of the Earth must have cooled, allowing snow and ice to accumulate over great areas, particularly of northern Europe, Asia and North America. The cause is uncertain but it is known that the climate has oscillated between polar and warm-temperate in Ireland at irregular intervals. The last major cold episode ended only some 10,000 years ago having lasted, with warmer intervals, for approximately 60,000 years. A warmer episode of about the same duration preceded this last great freeze, it, in turn, following an earlier prolonged polar climatic phase. Almost certainly there were other violent fluctuations in temperature at still earlier times but knowledge of them is still scanty and confused. During some of these periods of cold the whole of Ireland was buried beneath ice and snow, as was what is now the surrounding sea. At other times ice thicknesses were less and the tops of the higher mountains projected above the white expanses. For perhaps longer periods still, the Irish climate was dry and very cold, similar to the high tundra of Canada and Siberia today, with intensely cold snowy winters but no permanent cover of snow.

As the climate cooled at the beginning of each of the episodes of polar climate, so the snows of winter would linger on later into the year until there came a time when one season's snow had not melted before the next winter's accumulation began. Thus the snow cover became deeper and deeper year by year. Eventually the thickness of snow would be so great that the underlying layers would be compacted into ice, as happens for example when vehicles drive over snowy roads and create icy ruts. The thicknesses of snow were prodigious, hundreds and perhaps thousands of metres in depth. All but the topmost layer was composed of ice as compact and unyielding as rock, the product of thousands of years of accumulation.

Inevitably it was on the highest mountains that such ice masses first began to form, and much later they were the last places from which the ice would disappear. Upland massifs such as the mountains of Wicklow, Mourne, Donegal, Kerry and west Galway and Mayo all developed their own ice caps or glaciers. As the cold persisted, so ice deepened on the lowlands also and eventually great ice domes formed, the largest of which was probably centred in the midlands, west of what is now the Shannon. When pressures at the base of the ice became sufficiently great, it behaved as a very thick treacly liquid, rather than a solid, and the ice masses began to ooze outwards

OPPOSITE PAGE :
Esker on the plains of Co. Meath. (photo: Cambridge University Collection of air photographs)

in all directions from their core area. The movement was slow, almost imperceptible perhaps, but the immense mass of the ice made it an irresistible force as it advanced over the land. Any loose rocks and soil would be swept along at the base of the ice, and indeed would be used as tools to abrade and pluck at more resistant obstacles – a gigantic rasp scouring the surface, leaving only the strongest landforms surviving.

Unless the ice met an impassable obstacle, another ice sheet or very high mountains for example, its outward seepage continued, all the while moving eroded material along at its base. At the limit of expansion of the ice, where temperatures were above freezing and the ice melted at the same rate as it was advancing, the ice front stood still, even though fresh ice with its accompanying debris still replaced the melted ice. Thus the ice functioned as a one-way conveyor belt, bringing eroded material to the edge of the ice sheet and dropping it as the ice melted away. The edge of an ice sheet is often marked by a zone of accumulation of such debris, called a moraine.

As was remarked previously, the effects of the Ice Age upon the Irish landscape were profound. In the fifteen thousand or so years since ice melted from the lowlands and the mere ten thousand years since the last of the mountain glaciers disappeared, there has simply not been time for the landforms to recover from the glaciers' advance. Much of the Irish landscape remains bruised and battered from the onslaught of the ice.

The last ice sheet did not envelope the whole of Ireland but reached only as far south as, roughly, a line between the Shannon estuary and south Wicklow. Ice centred over the Cork-Kerry uplands covered the extreme southwest, but in between was a strip of land which had no ice cover and which experienced the fierce subarctic climate associated with regions adjacent to ice sheets (Figure 2.2). This area, which includes parts of Wexford, Waterford, Cork and north Kerry, thus avoided the imprint of the last glacial episode and its landscape has therefore recovered to a greater degree than the area to the north. River systems are better organised, there are few hummocks and marshy hollows, and slopes are smoother and more rounded, so that in a sense the landscape is 'older' than in those areas that were covered by ice more recently.

The work done by ice has two opposed facets – destruction and construction. The destructive action involves the erosion and removal of any rock or other material unable to withstand the abrasive power of ice armed with stones and boulders. By definition the process usually destroys the evidence, so that the landforms due to glacial erosion are mainly negative features, comprising hollows, grooves, trenches and smoothed rocks. In lowland areas many of these features may subsequently be infilled by material carried by the glaciers and it is in upland regions that the erosive effect of ice leaves its most obvious imprint.

Most of the hill ranges of Ireland above 500 metres show landforms that are the product of ice-sculpting. In many uplands the ice moved outwards from the centre of the massif along natural lines of weakness, parts of the pre-existing valleys in particular. Rock erosion was thus concentrated along the line of the valleys, causing them to be scoured, deepened and straightened, whilst the higher land remained relatively unscathed. When the ice finally melted, the original narrow winding mountain valley had been reshaped into impressive flat-floored steep-sided trenches, such as Glenmalure in Co. Wicklow and the Gaddagh valley beneath Carrauntoohill in Co. Kerry. Killary Harbour on the border between Mayo and Galway and Lough Swilly in Co. Donegal are similar valleys gouged by ice, but which have later been flooded by the sea to give the long cliffed sea inlets termed fiords. Rarely are the floors of upland glaciated valleys smooth. Often they contain rock hollows excavated by the ice or partial barriers due to mounds of material laid down by the ice. In either instance, these may become lakes, interrupting the course of the present river, for example the lakes of Gleninagh in Co. Galway.

Other lakes are found high in glaciated mountains in the base of the great amphitheatre-like bites out of the mountain that are called corries. Corries were the last retreats of the ice in Ireland and are usually located on the sunless northern and northeastern slopes of the hills. They were formed again by glacial erosion and may occur at the upper end of a glacial trough. Coumshingaun in the Comeragh Mountains of Co. Waterford, with its 400 metres high headwall, is the finest example of a corrie in Ireland. Coomasaharn in Kerry, Lough Bray in Wicklow and the fretted northern slope of Slieve Corragh in the Mourne Mountains are also spectacular corrie landforms.

The action of ice in the mountains produced stark and dramatic landscapes. On the lowlands, though they are much greater in extent, the impact of ice, while unmistakable, is more subdued. Erosive effects are less visible and the dominant landforms are those created by the deposition of the rocks, clays and sands carried along by the glaciers. Material removed from the uplands came to rest in the lowlands, material removed from one part of the lowlands was laid down in another. On the south coast of Co. Wexford are sea cliffs cut into glacially deposited material. They contain boulders of granite derived from the Blackstairs Mountains 30 km to the north, limestone rocks from Co. Kilkenny and volcanic rock fragments from the New Ross area; it is clear that the ice must have come from the north to have acquired this collection of debris. A few kilometres away to the east, and particularly to the north of Wexford town, are equally thick deposits of material laid down by the glaciers. However, the material itself is wholly different, consisting of sand containing many shells. The ice scoured this material from the bed of what is now the Irish Sea. Glacial deposits, or tills as they are called, are visible everywhere in Ireland. They occur not just in sea cliffs, but in river banks, road and rail cuttings and practically every excavation. It is interesting to note the material of which they are made, often large stones or boulders in a matrix of much finer clay or sand, and to try to identify the rock types that occur at a particular location. The arrows on the glacial map of Ireland suggest the general directions of ice movement and so where particular till materials may have originated (Figure 2.2).

It has been demonstrated that when the ice melts it must deposit whatever rock debris it had been carrying and that if the ice front stands still for a long period, ridges of such material may accumulate. Behind the ice front, however, the final melting of the ice sheet may be a complicated business. Over large areas of lowland Ireland, the melting ice simply dropped the material it was carrying. The result is the flat or undulating terrain so common in the midlands, sometimes badly drained, sometimes well drained, according to the underlying material. This material might be large boulders, compact clay, sand or any permutation thereof; glaciers are not selective, they pick up, carry along and mix together any material that they are able to erode.

In some areas more distinct landforms are found, small hummocks and hollows may pimple the landscape. The hummocks are called kames and are rarely more than 10-15 metres in height. Often they are made of sands or gravels and probably formed where heaps of material lying on the surface of the ice sheet were lowered to the ground as the ice beneath melted away. The hollows may be the location of former 'icebergs', buried in the deposited material but which later melted away to leave a hollow, which is now often a marshy hollow or a pool. The areas in which this curious topography is widespread are shown on Figure 2.2.

More curious still are the remnants of glacier-rivers that are still preserved in the Irish landscape, river channels that are now ridges. These ridges, or eskers, were originally the beds of rivers flowing in tunnels beneath the glaciers and carrying away waters from the melting ice. Eventually these ice caves emerged at the edge of the ice but upstream whole networks of tunnels might extend for kilometres beneath the ice. The icy fast-flowing waters carried along great masses of rocks and other debris, just as do mountain streams today. When all of the ice finally melted away, the stony former beds of these rivers remained as narrow twisting ridges, snaking across the countryside. As Figure 2.2 indicates, eskers are found in a broad band across the country from Dublin to Galway and in a second strip northwards from

Galway into south Mayo. They are unmistakable landforms; dry, well-drained ribbons wend their way through bog or sticky clay lands, sometimes being the preferred routes for roads. Their steep sides and very limited extent have meant that often they are neglected by farmers. Many are clothed in trees or furze, distinctive linear woods in a sea of pasture. However, they have not been neglected entirely. Because they are formed of water-lain materials, they are usually composed of well-defined layers of sands and gravels. Thus many eskers, in the area around Tuam in Co. Galway for example, have been eaten into by sand and gravel pits, small-scale enterprises usually, but sufficiently numerous to reduce some eskers to a series of stony hillocks.

One other feature of the landscape figures prominently on the glacial map of Ireland, the drumlin. Drumlins are mounds but unlike kames they are usually oval in plan view. They have a distinctive blunt end and a tapering end, the tapering end pointing in the direction to which the ice moved. They are larger than kames, attaining lengths of up to 500 metres and heights of up to 30 metres. Drumlins are gregarious. They occur in swarms of dozens or hundreds rather than singly; so much so indeed, that Ireland is said to have a 'drumlin belt', very apparent on the map, stretching from Co. Down through Armagh, Monaghan, Cavan, Leitrim and Sligo to Mayo. At either extreme, Clew Bay in the west and Strangford Lough in the east, the drumlins extend even into the sea as islets created by a rise in sea level.

The great concentration of drumlins is to be found to the north (up-ice) of the line marking the very final prolonged standstill of melting ice as it retreated northwards across Ireland. Journeying northwards or northwestwards from Dublin, the traveller crosses this line in the landscape in the vicinity of Dundalk-Kells-Longford. The landscape becomes one of endless small rounded drumlin hills separated by rushy hollows, views are limited, roads twist and undulate, farm-holdings are small and the land is poor:

> "From Cavan and from Leitrim and from Mayo
> From all the thin-faced parishes where hills
> Are perished noses running peaty water"
>   Patrick Kavanagh, 'Lough Derg'

A less than flattering picture yet not unrecognisable as the cramped terrain of the drumlin swarms. The River Erne was mentioned as a river without a valley; a major reason is that it pursues its course and has its headwaters amongst the drumlins, within that part of Ireland where the heritage from the glaciers is freshest. The Erne, and also many other Irish rivers, is merely the overspill route by which the rains that fall inland reach the sea.

THE COASTLINE

The scenery of the Irish coast is not wholly explicable in terms of any of the natural agencies thus far mentioned. In one sense, coastal landforms are extensive in Ireland, in that there are more than 3,000 km of coastline. In another sense, they are very restricted, as they are a few hundreds of metres in width at most and, in the case of seacliffs, have no horizontal extent at all! Yet the importance of the coastline is quite disproportionate to its lateral extent — for economic reasons of course, but also in its value as a recreational resource.

The uniqueness of coastal landforms results from their origin as a product of the interaction, battle it might be termed, between land and sea. Inland lakes rarely show very distinct 'landforms' on their margins, the juxtaposition of land and water does not strike sparks. The reason is that small lakes do not have tides, do not have currents and rarely generate significant waves. By contrast the sea brims with energy, of which the tides, currents and waves are manifestations. The shape of a coastline is determined by two groups of factors. Firstly, the nature of the land, whether upland or lowland, hard rocks or soft rocks, the grain of the country parallel to or at an angle to the coast. Secondly, the energy possessed by the sea and the direction of that energy flow, for example whether waves strike the coast obliquely or at right angles; waves are much the most important of the agencies of marine attack.

> The timeless waves, bright shifting, broken glass,
> Came dazzling around, into the rocks,
> Came glinting, sifting from the Americas . . . .
> (*Lovers on Aran*, Seamus Heaney)

One important reason for the predominantly rugged eroded coastline of western Ireland is, as the poet suggests, that waves can travel in the North Atlantic for thousands of kilometres before reaching landfall in Ireland; that same ocean is a windy storm-filled place, the gales from the west, crashing great waves on to the shores of Munster, Connacht and Ulster. In addition, much of the western seaboard is mountainous, so the sea is attacking and undercutting steep slopes to produce great isolated cliffs, as at Slieve League in Donegal or Croaghaun on Achill Island. If the land is an elevated plateau then there are uniform lines of cliffs, as on the Loop Head peninsula of Co. Clare or the north coast of Co. Mayo. In parts of western Ireland, particularly in the extreme southwest, the land seems to challenge the sea, almost wilfully. Here the grain of the country is at right-angles to the coast; the long mountain ridges of ancient sandstones project seawards, separated by lowlands of limestone. The lowlands have been etched into the deep embay-ments of Dunmanus, Dingle, Bantry and Kenmare, whilst the hard ridges form long headlands, often partly fragmented into small islands. Over much of the western coastline the sea is gaining at the expense of the land but elsewhere in Ireland this is not the case.

> Did sea define the land or land the sea?
> Each drew new meaning from the waves collision.
> Sea broke on land to full identity.
> > (*Lovers on Aran*, Seamus Heaney)

Between Dundalk Bay and south Wexford the coastline is subdued, mud flats and sandy beaches alternate with low, often degraded, cliffs cut into glacial deposits. Wave energy is less on this more restricted Irish Sea coast and the wave energy is baffled somewhat by the low expanse of loose materials of which the coastal lands are formed. Thus, deposition or lateral movement of materials along the shore are more common than significant erosion. The sandspits enclosing lagoons such as Tacumshin lake in Wexford are examples, as is North Bull Island in Dublin Bay and the mudflats of Dundalk Bay. Such 'quiet' coastal environments do occur elsewhere, for example in west Galway near Roundstone and in Clew Bay where drumlins lie stranded in waters. Again, the uplands of the east commonly run parallel or at a slight angle to the coast, so projections into the sea to form headlands and cliffs are uncommon, Bray, Dalkey, Arklow and Howth Heads being among the few.

Finally, events off-stage may affect the outcome of the conflict between land and sea. In particular, sea level may rise or fall relative to the land in a particular region; this may be due to the land changing in elevation or to rises or falls in the surface of the water, or to a combination of circumstances.

On the shores of Blacksod Bay the 'cliffs', admittedly only 1-2 metres in height, are formed of peat; the peat obviously formed on dry land but has been inundated by a rise in sea level. By contrast, elsewhere in Ireland, and particularly along the coast of Ulster from Malin to Larne, are obvious cliff lines and former beaches perched several metres above the present seashore. In both instances the land-sea relationship has been made more compli-cated.

THE VENEER ON THE LAND

The results of the elemental forces of nature acting upon the solid rocks of the earth are the various landscape features. Almost everywhere in the Irish countryside, though, there is a cover of vegetation and that vegetation is

The quartzite peak of Errigal, Co. Donegal.
(photo: Bord Failte)

Glenarrif, Co. Antrim.
(photo: Hunting Aerofilms)

rooted in a layer of soil. Soil is the link between the rocks and landforms and the subject of the following chapter, animal and plant life. To most people soil is the dark dirty material of gardens or ploughlands, necessary but unexciting. In its passive function, soil blankets the land, smooths rough edges and sharp angles in the rocks beneath, and creates the long swelling slopes and broad declivities so characteristic of Irish scenery. The stark jagged landscapes of the American West or the high Alps are in part due to the absence of soil. More positively, soil is a creation of the interaction between the elements and the rocks, just as are landforms. Granite rocks yield thin, acidic, coarse soils; shales decompose to clayey, sticky, damp soils. If rainfall is high and temperatures low, soils are washed clean of their nutrients for plants; if soils develop on sandy terrain they are parched by even a few days without rain. Thus soils are a bridge between the living and non-living worlds, the most recent of creations (they must post-date the landscape on which they are developed) but also the most direct and immediate link to that most fundamental and essential of human activities, agriculture.

IRISH LANDSCAPES

In order to understand the reasons for the character of the countryside's physical landscape, it has been taken to pieces and the most important components examined in turn. It is time to reassemble the various parts and to look afresh at the landscape as an entity, perhaps with a better informed eye for the terrain. Very few landscapes are the product of, and so explicable in terms of, a single natural event or agency. A cocktail of natural forces past and present acts upon a variety of rocks and structures, the result always complex and perhaps susceptible to more than one explanation.

   The few diverse examples of Irish landscapes described below are the products of not just one, but a variety of natural agencies, shaping the geological foundations of the land.

1. Glenmalure, Co. Wicklow (page 2)

The granite rock that forms the core of the Wicklow Mountains is gashed by several trench-like valleys on its eastern side, of which Glenmalure is one. In the background is the rather featureless summit plateau, peat covered and with the broad gentle slopes characteristic of granite. The original form of Glenmalure can be seen at the extreme head of the valley, where the Avonbeg River flows in a narrow floored V-shaped declivity. The main part of the valley has been deepened and widened by a glacier flowing down-valley. Glacial and river deposits have levelled the valley floor but the craggy sides are evidence of the freshness of the glacial impact.

2. The east coast near Bray (page 39)

Ireland has 3,000 km of coastline including almost every possible variety. The section of coast in the foreground of this photograph is typical of much of the east coast south of Dundalk. Thick deposits of glacial drift are being eroded by the sea to form low cliffs and a stony-sandy beach. The glacial material offers little resistance to erosion and so the sea is encroaching rapidly on the land in this area. In the background is the northeastern extremity of the Dublin Mountains. At Bray Head (left) a band of resistant rocks, mainly quartzites, reaches the sea and so forms a prominent headland. Just inland are the elegant quartzite peaks of the Little and Great Sugarloafs, the summits of which probably protruded just above the level of the last ice sheet in the area some 15,000 years ago.

3. The plains Co. Meath (page 27)

Seen from ground level it is often difficult to distinguish the landforms, dominantly those due to material being deposited by glaciers, on the subdued terrain of the central plain. In this area south of Trim the gentle slopes are dimpled with small mounds and hollows, some of the former being of sand and gravel, hence the gravel pit in the foreground. Conspicuous in the photograph is an esker, cloaked in a scrub vegetation, winding across the countryside – the fossil cast of a stream bed beneath a glacier. All of these landforms are 'dead' in the sense that the agency that created them, ice, is no longer present. With the passing of time, slopes are becoming gentler as material moves down to accumulate at the base, hollows are becoming infilled and soils are thickening.

4. Glenariff, Co. Antrim (page 34)

The view to the southwest along Glenariff, most spectacular of the Antrim glens, extends as far as the valley of the River Bann in the distance. Between, is the bleak boggy surface of the Antrim Plateau developed on the volcanic lava flows that blanketed the region. The plateau surface at 300 metres above sea level is eaten into by the spacious valley of the Glenariff River. It developed along great vertical fracture lines in the rock strata. The valley seems many times too large for the river and this suggests that perhaps the glen was enlarged by glacier erosion. The glen itself is excavated into a geological sandwich cake. The dark steep slopes of the rim are the lava flow rock, basalt, with streams descending the cliffs in a series of waterfalls, as in the Fairy Glen. The lower slopes are in the soft lime rock, chalk. The floor of the glen consists of glacial materials and river deposits overlying sandstone rock. Farm-holdings in the area ('ladder' farms) often climb the sides of the glen, so incorporating some of each of the different soils and slopes associated with the various rock types.

SCENERY AND CONSERVATION

There can be no realistic definition of what is 'scenic', Tourist brochures list the 'sights' for visitors to see but what a person finds attractive in a landscape is very much a personal matter. It is also a matter of fashion. In the eighteenth century the mountains and moors were seen as barbarous lands to be avoided at all costs, the cultivated ordered lowlands were the 'real' countryside. Today the wild regions are usually regarded as scenic areas. In fact even if beauty is subjective, all of the Irish landscape is interesting, no two areas are the same and none are intrinsically deserving of despoilation.

Yet with increased pressure on the land, in terms of rural industrial, agricultural and tourist development, there is the danger of altering the character of the countryside and of diminishing its value as a recreational resource. As yet the alterations to the physical landscape are slight; humans can with relative ease utterly change the vegetation of the countryside, in planting crops and conifers and seeding pastures for example, but so far people cannot create or destroy landforms on any but the smallest scale. Quarrying and mining may scar the hillsides, artificial embankments may carry roads and railways, rivers may be straightened by drainage, but as yet the extent is limited. Perhaps the damage to scenery may result from the use of that resource, the erosion of coastal sand dunes by overuse for example. Alternatively the erection of power lines or a new building without sufficient regard for the environmental setting may detract from the scenery. It is considered sensible to protect certain important buildings, nature reserves, woodlands and so forth, but perhaps the protection should be extended to landscape features of particular scenic and scientific interest. Such protection might be linked with a degree of interpretation of what is to be seen in terms comprehensible to the non-specialist, as for example at the Giant's Causeway in Antrim and at Dunmore Cave in Co. Kilkenny. The national parks in the Republic, though small in number and size, are an appreciation that conservation is necessary even of the apparently unchanging rocks. The countryside is both a leisure and an economic resource for Ireland; the preservation of both aspects, appreciative and exploitative, may require delicate balances to be struck in environmental management policies.

The Burren, Co. Clare. (photo: Bord Failte)

The east coast near Bray, Co. Wicklow.
(photo: Bord Failte)

Glenariff, Co. Antrim.
(Northern Ireland Tourist Board)

Left: Muckross Gardens, Killarney National Park.
(photo: Bord Failte)

Below left: O'Sullivan's Cascade, Killarney.
(photo: Jan de Fouw)

Below: The interior of the Yew Wood at Muckross.
(photo: Roy Alexander)

Wildlife in the Countryside

ROY ALEXANDER

The frequent reference to Ireland as the Emerald Isle summarises in a simple, yet most effective, way the overriding importance of the plant cover in any visual impression of the Irish countryside. The moist and mild climate of Ireland is, of course, a key factor in the development of this prevailingly emerald landscape, but even the most casual of observers soon becomes aware that the countryside is by no means uniformly green. The interplay of climate, soils and vegetation, together with human use of the land, has yielded a subtle mixture of reds and browns with the green, these colour patterns varying greatly by locality and season. As well as colouring the landscape, the plant cover has an important influence on its surface texture. The close cropped grasslands over much of the country have a smooth powdery appearance which gives way to a wilder roughness on the coastal and mountain heaths and to billowing undulations in the wooded valleys.

Each element in this living landscape results from an integration of the physical components of the local environment with its natural and human history. The vegetation of an area develops in response to the local climate, rocks and soils, and the course of that development is influenced considerably by human use of the land. In its turn, the vegetation exercises an influence over the animal populations through its provision of both shelter and food. The end result is a community of plants and animals interacting with each other and with the various components of their environment, providing what is termed an ecosystem. The basic building blocks of the living part of the ecosystem are the species of plants and animals and each of these is adapted to living within a certain range of physical conditions, or within a certain habitat.

Due to its small size and isolation, Ireland possesses a lesser number of both plant and animal species than Britain and a much smaller number than continental Europe. These plants and animals, however, interact with the varied physical landscape to produce many ecosystems that are similar to those in Britain and Europe and also some that are unique to Ireland. In order to appreciate the diversity of the Irish living landscape it is necessary to know more about the plants and animals of which it is composed, their interactions with the physical environment and also their history.

WILDLIFE IN THE PAST

Ireland's wildlife is of relatively recent origin compared with that of some parts of the world. The prevailing cold climate and the thick ice sheets that advanced across the country during the Ice Age combined to wipe out most, if not all, of the pre-existing wildlife or at least forced it to migrate to warmer areas. As the last cold period drew towards a close some 13,000 years ago, the climate gradually became warmer and plants and animals began to return to Ireland from their refuges on the continent. This warm spell was comparatively brief, however, and a further cold snap occurred from about 10,500 to 10,000 years ago. During the warm spell much of the country was covered in grassland, heath and scrub, over which the Giant Irish Deer roamed, grazing on the abundant pastures. Although the Giant Irish Deer became extinct due to the sudden return to cold conditions, certain of the plants have remained to form part of the present vegetation.

Giant Irish Deer

Following the cold snap, the climate warmed once more and the immigration of plants and animals began in earnest. These immigrants were not simply haphazard groupings of species with good powers of dispersal. Plant and animal fossils indicate that recolonisation occurred in a series of stages as different forest trees arrived and spread across the country accompanied by other plants and animals. These waves of immigration occurred in response to the gradual improvement in climate and the formation of soils on the deposits left by the glaciers.

The earliest stage of this sequence was marked by the presence of juniper and willow together with grasses and herbs, a community similar to that of the earlier short warm phase. These plants were soon joined by birch, pine and hazel, which quickly spread across the country taking advantage of the many open sites available for colonisation. Woodlands dominated at first by birch and then by pine and hazel clothed much of the country up until about 8,000 years ago. By 9,000 years ago trees such as oak, elm, alder and ash, which are associated with the deciduous woods of today, had also arrived but these appear to have spread more slowly across the country. Eventually they overshadowed the birch and hazel and forced pine onto the more marginal soils. Shortly after 7,000 years ago, in a moist climate with temperatures slightly higher than today, the Irish forests reached their most luxuriant development. Oak dominated the forests on lowlands and many hillslopes, elm occurred on the better soils, ash in limestone areas and alder in wet sites.

Another development was occurring during this period in the midlands of Ireland. Over much of this region the uneven topography left by the receding glaciers included many enclosed basins which were frequently occupied by lakes. The open water of these lakes was soon colonised by a number of submerged plants, whilst at their margins, plants with floating leaves such as water lilies and also rushes and sedges grew in abundance. Due to the water-logged nature of their habitat, the detritus of leaves and stems produced by these plants each autumn did not decay completely but gradually accumulated over time to form a deposit of fen peat. The lakes became shallower due to deposition of marl and began to infill with fen peat around the margins, some of which were colonised by willow and birch. As the fen peats continued to accumulate and thicken, shallow-rooted plants experienced greater difficulty in obtaining adequate supplies of nutrients from the mineral-rich soil and groundwater below. Hence the peat surfaces became less rich in nutrients and were colonised by plants favouring more acidic conditions. In particular, many areas were colonised by species of bog moss or *Sphagnum* moss, which can survive on the meagre amount of nutrients contained in rainfall. As *Sphagnum* grew out to cover more of the thicker fen peat, the whole habitat became progressively wetter and more acidic, causing the thin marginal fen peats to migrate up the surrounding slopes. Ultimately, many of the lakes were infilled and the carpet of *Sphagnum*, with its marginal ring of fen peat, spread outwards and upwards, forming the raised bogs of the central lowland.

Around 5,500 years ago, two events occurred which were to alter radically the appearance of the living landscape elsewhere. First, the climate became slightly cooler and possibly slightly wetter. The second event was the advent of a primitive form of agriculture which involved clearance of the forests, albeit on a small scale at first.

In western parts of the country and on higher ground, either of these events or a combination of both appears to have led to the development of bogs. The soils became poorer, as more of the nutrients were flushed out by rainfall, and also wetter. In these conditions, rushes colonised small depressions in the land. The coarse stems of these plants broke down slowly and a thin deposit of peat began to form. This encouraged colonisation by other plants adapted to this type of habitat and the rushes were joined by sedges and *Sphagnum* moss. The peat deposits gradually thickened and spread out from their initial foci in small hollows to coalesce and mantle large areas of the landscape, forming what is termed blanket bog. There is much debate as to the role and relative importance of the climatic and human factors in the

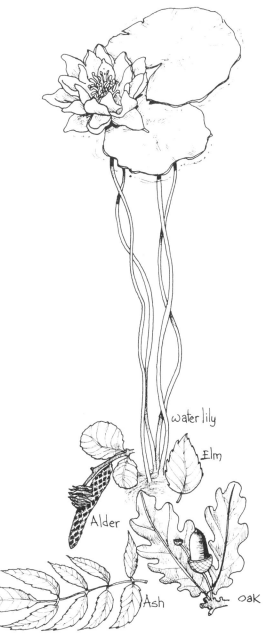

initiation of blanket bog development, but whatever its cause, these bogs appear to have grown rapidly and become the dominant plant community in certain parts of the country. As they spread, they overwhelmed many areas of forest, killing the trees and burying their remains below a thick layer of peat. The well preserved stumps of these unfortunate trees are a familiar sight at the base of peat cuttings.

Thus the changing climate and changing opportunities for individual species have brought many changes to the living landscape of Ireland in the relatively brief period since the Ice Age. The latter half of that period has, however, seen more dramatic changes that have been wrought by the human population, especially the wholesale destruction of the forests, as traced in chapter 4, with some recent planting. The result is a diversity of communities ranging from an intricate patchwork of fields and meadows to vast open expanses of heath and bog, from isolated clumps of deciduous wood to swathes of dark coniferous forest and from sheltered woody glens to open windswept mudflats and saltmarshes. Many of these communities are widespread in their distribution and occur in close proximity to one another, adding to the variety of any journey through Ireland. Others are more localised and require a specific visit in order to experience their unique features.

WILDLIFE IN THE PRESENT

The present wildlife of the Irish countryside consists of a mixture of native and introduced plants and animals which exist in a complex mosaic of communities. In order to live and thrive in any locality, each organism requires an adequate supply of food and water and a suitable range of environmental conditions; put more concisely, each requires a suitable habitat. Nowhere are the conditions ideal for every organism and each tends to occur only in one or a few suitable habitats.

Each habitat contains a network or web of feeding relationships. At the base of this network are the green plants which obtain their food by using sunlight energy to convert simple mineral substances into more complex organic compounds. Herbivorous animals get their food by eating plants and they, in turn, serve as a food supply for carnivores. The dung produced by animals is incorporated into the soil, where it is used as food by other animals, fungi and bacteria. These break down the complex organic compounds and release some of the simple nutrient materials required by the green plants, thus completing the network of feeding relationships.

Not all of a plant's requirements are met by the organic content of a soil however, and the mineral and water components are also important nutrient sources. The mineral component is derived from the underlying rocks or glacial deposits from which the soil was formed, and this parent material determines certain of the soil's characteristics. For example, soils derived from granites and sandstones tend to be acidic in nature and often contain relatively low levels of the mineral nutrients required by plants. Those derived from limestone, on the other hand, are generally less acidic and contain high levels of some nutrient elements such as calcium and magnesium. Variations of this type in the soil chemistry can have an important influence on the range of plants that are able to grow in a particular soil. Some plants are tolerant of a wide range of soil acidity but many are restricted either to acid soils, for example the heathers, or to soils rich in lime, for instance the cowslip. Similarly, plants such as gorse exhibit a preference for well drained soils, whereas sedges and rushes occur most frequently on wet or waterlogged soils. The restriction of many plants to certain types of soil implies a similar restriction on any animals which rely closely upon them for food, and hence the distribution of the major plant and animal communities displays a close linkage to geology and soils.

Climatic factors are also important in governing the living conditions within a habitat and, at a broad scale, an association can be identified between rainfall levels and the distribution of certain communities. For example, blanket bogs occur extensively in the west from sea level up into the mountains, but in the east they are restricted to the higher mountains where rainfall is in excess of 1,250mm per annum. The topography, or shape, of the land has an important influence on local climates. This can be seen in western coastal districts where, in exposed regions, trees, if they occur at all, are stunted and shaped by the wind. Here coastal heaths and grasslands dominate the scene but where landforms provide a degree of shelter from the wind, such as within deep valleys, woodland can once again develop. At a finer scale, the extremes of climate may be ameliorated within some communities by the vegetation itself. Trees serve as an effective windbreak and the interior of a woodland generally has an equable microclimate, particularly where humidity is concerned, allowing some sensitive plants and animals to find a suitable niche.

It has been seen how the plants and animals arriving in Ireland have grouped together into a range of communities that show links with the local climate and geology. To the complexities related to the varied natural factors, must be added the influence of human activities in order to appreciate the full range of diversity in the wildlife of the countryside. As the human population has increasingly made its presence felt, so the living landscape has responded. Many of the natural habitats have been reduced considerably

Left: Orchid, growing wild in Co. Wicklow.
(photo: Jan de Fouw)

Above: New bog development.
(photo: Bord na Mona).

Below: Mountain bog development, Co. Wicklow.
(photo: Jan de Fouw)

in extent through activities such as agriculture and turf extraction. The widespread clearance of deciduous trees removed also the plants and animals that relied on them for food and shelter. The living landscape is never static; human activity may have increased the speed of change and also determined its direction in many areas but change is an essential feature of all natural ecosystems. Many organisms may have been driven close to extinction but for others new opportunities have been created, as through the establishment of hedgerows. In the mountains the regeneration of trees is prevented by regular grazing and burning, but large areas have been planted with alien conifers.

In general, however, the changes wrought by human use of the land reduce the diversity of natural communities. The pace of change in the countryside has increased rapidly during the last few decades and some of the natural heritage has been lost. It is important that the reasons why these losses have occurred should be understood, so that society can appreciate better the areas of natural habitat that remain and strive to protect them from a similar fate. It is also important to view the living landscape in its entirety, to recognise any benefits that may have been derived from human-induced changes, and to appreciate the diversity that presently exists. A fuller understanding of the contemporary landscape should enable better informed judgements to be made concerning changes that are proposed in the future. To this end, the remainder of this chapter examines each of the major wildlife habitats that exist in the Irish countryside, their general features and items of specific interest.

THE BOGLANDS

Bogs cover 16 per cent of Ireland's land area and the wild open expanses of this wetland habitat leave a distinct impression in the mind of any visitor to the country. The bogs are also an inherent part of Irish culture, having formed a barrier to exploitation of the land but a natural defence against enemies, a hiding place for treasures and bodies, and a source of fuel. Most important to culture perhaps, is their role as repositories of much of Ireland's environmental history. The waterlogged acid nature of the peat has impeded the decay of plant and animal remains falling onto the bog surface, and thus the bogs are a vast storehouse of historical information neatly arranged, layer by layer, in sequential order.

The bogs are conventionally divided into the categories of raised and blanket in accordance with their respective modes of formation, as outlined earlier, with the blanket bogs being further divided into upland and lowland types. To the casual observer of their present surface features, however, it is difficult to provide precise rules for identifying a particular bog as belonging to one of these categories. Although they differ in location and altitude, the surface characteristics of the various bog types can be very similar and the plants and animals they support tend to differ in numbers and proportions rather than in kind.

All of the bogs consist of a peat-producing ecosystem that is characteristically wet and acidic, and these key features pose problems for any organism trying to live in the bogland environment. Waterlogging of the peat means that oxygen is in short supply as this vital gas is not very soluble in water. Many bogland plants get around this problem to some degree by the structural adaptation of an open cell network containing many air spaces. This makes the plant tissue very light and allows some of these plants to contribute oxygen to the rooting zone. The roots are concentrated in the upper few centimetres of peat which occasionally dry out during summer, and it is here that most of the decomposition takes place. Below this level little or no oxygen is present, giving rise to what is termed the anaerobic zone. Aerobic life, that is organisms requiring oxygen, cannot exist here and only a few varieties of very specialised bacteria are present. Their activity produces hydrogen sulphide, which smells of bad eggs, and also the gases, methane (marsh gas) and phosphine. Methane and phosphine are highly flammable, the latter so much so that it ignites spontaneously on meeting atmospheric oxygen to produce the will-o'-the-wisps that have given rise to many mysterious bog legends.

As the plants growing on the bog surface are isolated from the mineral soil beneath, it is not surprising to discover that those which thrive there have developed some remarkable methods of obtaining and conserving nutrients. Nitrogen, phosphorus and potassium are all in short supply and a number of plants have adopted a carnivorous habit in order to supplement their supplies of these nutrients. Sundews and butterworts have sticky glandular hairs on the surface of their leaves which first attract and then trap unsuspecting insects. Once trapped, the insects are doomed to death by starvation and their carcases are slowly digested and absorbed by the leaves. The pitcher plant, which grows on a number of raised bogs in the midlands, was introduced from North America in 1906. It also supplements its diet by trapping and digesting insects that fall into its funnel of pitcher-shaped leaves. The bladderworts have developed their carnivorous habit to an even finer degree, in that they are active rather than passive trappers of small animals. They live in pools on the bogs and their trap consists of a bag-like structure which can be emptied of water, only to spring open when a passing insect touches its specially sensitive hairs. The opening of the trap allows

Pitcher Plants

Common Butterwort

Sundew

water to rush in, carrying with it an insect lunch.

Other plants of the bog surface do not have such gruesome methods of subsidising their diets, but have developed other equally fascinating means of overcoming the nutrient shortages. Many concentrate their roots in the upper aerobic zone where most of the decomposition takes place, thereby ensuring that valuable nutrients are quickly recycled. Some also carry out a form of internal nutrient recycling by retaining important minerals in their tissue at the end of the growing season. In autumn, many of the plants of the bog surface change from their spring and summer green to take on shades of orange and red. This is not done simply to enhance the autumnal appearance of the countryside but indicates that the green chlorophyll in the leaves has been broken down and its constituents withdrawn to the underground parts of the plant to be reused in the following year. It is due to processes such as this that boglands make very poor winter grazing for livestock. Native herbivores are wise to this feature and concentrate their efforts on the young green shoots in spring or seek out the underground parts of these plants in winter.

The bog surface can, surprisingly, also experience a shortage of water on occasions. During winter the water may be frozen whilst in summer dry and windy weather causes high evaporation losses, posing considerable problems to plants which are used to living in a habitat that is normally very wet. Some bog plants possess adaptations to cope with this problem, such as members of the heather family which have small leaves with waxy skins that reduce water losses. Among the plants best adapted to coping with all of the vicissitudes of life in the bogland habitat are the bog mosses or *Sphagnum* mosses. The leaves of *Sphagnum* are structured like sponges to soak up large amounts of water and anyone making their first visit to a bog can scarcely fail to be impressed at the volume of water that can be squeezed from a handful of this moss. The leaves are also able to remove essential nutrients from rainwater by exchanging them for hydrogen, a process which increases the acidity of the environment. The *Sphagnum* mosses therefore play a key role in the development of a bog, helping to maintain both its acidity and its water content.

There are a number of species of *Sphagnum* moss growing on the Irish bogs and each is adapted to a precise range of conditions. The surface of any bog is never uniform but consists of hummocks and hollows of varying proportions. The hummocks grow up above the general surface level and are composed mainly of *Sphagnum imbricatum* and *S. papillosum*. Eventually the taller hummocks dry out and the *Sphagnum* mosses are replaced by plants such as ling, lichens and other species of moss. Between the hummocks are hollows which are often full of water, providing a suitable habitat for other *Sphagnum* species such as *S. cuspidatum* and also plants such as the bogbean.

In some cases the low-lying areas may be linked to form part of an internal drainage system for the bog, conveying excess water from its surface. Such areas contain flowing water which is likely to be richer in minerals and they stand out in sharp colour contrast from the rest of the bog as they are colonised by luxuriant growths of more nutrient-demanding sedge and grass species.

Where an internal drainage system is poorly developed or absent, then water may accumulate in the lower layers of the peat, causing the upper layers to float freely and giving rise to the springy feel of many bogs. As the bog grows larger, and particularly on sloping ground, a point may be reached where the living skin of peat can no longer contain the water and equilibrium may be restored through a bursting or flowing of the bog as referred to in chapter 2.

The occurrence of hummocks, hollows and channels on bogs, along with the larger scale irregularities caused by movement of the peat, combine to produce a tremendous variety of surface features. These may make the bog somewhat tiresome to traverse on foot but the varying colours and textures of the plants colonising these different microhabitats lend a great diversity of detail to any walk across a bog that, from a distance, may have appeared bleak and uniform.

Such a walk may also be relieved by a sighting of some of the animals which live in or visit the boglands. A noticeable absence of snails attests to the shortage of calcium in this environment, but other groups of animals find sufficient food or shelter to attract them to the bogs at some time during the year. In winter migratory birds roost and feed on some of the bogs, whilst in spring and summer emerging insects such as dragonflies add their dazzling metallic sheens to the pastel shades of the plants. The cry of the curlew and the rasping call of a snipe as it zig-zags its way to safety add to the rich experience of a bogland walk.

Much of the sunlight energy trapped by plants growing on the bog surface over many centuries lies stored in their partially decayed remains, the peat. This vast store of energy has long been exploited as a fuel resource but never so extensively as in recent decades when Bord na Móna has stripped many of the large red domed bogs of the midlands down almost to their base of blue clay. The pace of exploitation has also increased rapidly in areas of blanket bog, as new technological developments make the harvesting of even small areas of sloping bogland economically feasible. Whilst this use of a native energy resource is a laudable asset to the economy for the present generation, it should not go so far as to remove entirely an irreplaceable heritage asset from future generations. Only a small proportion of the total area of raised bog is required to provide for representative examples of the

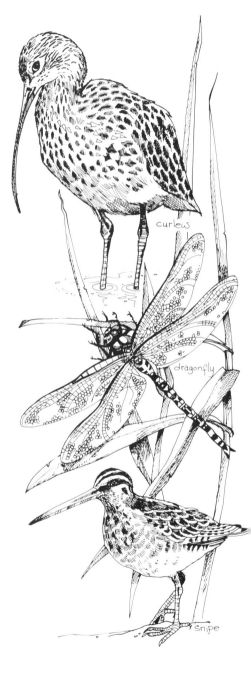

curlew

dragonfly

snipe

Left: Wild hedgerows along a country road. (photo: Jan de Fouw).

Bottom left: Wild flowers in rough summer meadow. (photo: Roy Alexander)

Below: Bog cotton in full bloom, Co. Wicklow. (photo: Jan de Fouw)

remaining diversity to be set aside for posterity. In the upland areas increased peat extraction not only affects the blanket bog ecosystem but may also have a striking impact on the whole landscape. These problems of conservation must be addressed now and they provide much food for thought during any tramp across the wild and wonderful boglands.

THE UPLANDS

Uplands may be described as being windswept treeless areas devoid of human settlement that are dominated by low-growing vegetation inter-mingled with outcrops of bare rock. This description would also apply to some lowland areas close to the west coast but over most of the country upland habitats are found above 300 metres altitude.

Plants

At the highest altitudes, where the climate can be quite extreme, soils are generally very thin and bare rock covers large areas. Here there is an open low vegetation which is dominated by mosses and lichens, together with grasses, dwarf shrubs and some herbs. The individual species of plant occurring in such areas depend very much on the characteristics of the local rocks. The hard acidic rocks of many Irish mountains generally yield only small amounts of essential plant nutrients. In the wet mountain climate, nutrients are quickly washed out of the thin acid soils by the heavy rainfall, and only a narrow range of acid-loving plants is supported. Among the prevailing dark green colours of these heather, sedge and rush communities, there appear occasional patches of a lighter brighter green denoting areas known as flushes, where mineral nutrients accumulate either from springs or freshly weathered rocks. The higher nutrient status of these areas encourages the development of a lush vegetation which is selectively grazed by sheep and deer.

Open areas of rock outcrop and scree in the high mountains represent a difficult habitat for plants. The high rainfall and strong winds experienced in these areas mean that periods of extreme wetness alternate with droughts, and few plants can survive such a harsh regime. In the most extreme conditions the rocks appear to support no life at all. Closer inspection, however, usually reveals a detailed mosaic of greys, browns and greens on the surface which is formed by the crust lichens. These plants, which are dual organisms composed of a fungus and an alga, grow closely attached to the rock surface and can tolerate extended periods of drought. They grow very slowly, providing a living skin on even the most exposed of rock surfaces.

Where crevices in the rock or between the rock fragments on a scree slope allow small amounts of mineral and organic matter to accumulate, then another hardy plant of the mountains appears. This is the moss, *Racomitrium lanuginosum*, which, in appropriate circumstances, can grow to cover extensive areas with a hoary grey-green mat, forming a vegetation type known as *Racomitrium* heath. *Racomitrium* is well adapted to a life on the mountain top; each of its leaves ends in a hair point of dead cells which in dry periods twist and overlap to protect the living cells beneath. This facility makes the plant a successful colonist of the tops of dry stone walls which present a similar habitat. Amongst established mats of *Racomitrium* more lichens can be found. These are frequently larger than the crustose forms that inhabit the bare rocks, and are composed of lobes which are raised slightly above the rock surface to form a rosette. Accompanying these rosette or foliose lichens, one often finds another type which consists largely of grey finger-like projections, one to two centimetres high, capped with a red blob of spore-producing tissue. These are members of the genus *Cladonia* and, like the foliose lichens, they can withstand periods of drought. The continued growth of these plants leads to the increased accumulation in the rock crevices of organic matter, or humus, and mineral particles, and these provide a rooting medium for other plants.

The acid rock uplands thus support a mosaic of plant communities comprising moss and lichen covered rocks and screes, together with large areas of grassland and heath growing over blocky scree and thin soils and interspersed with occasional brighter green flushes. These upland areas also contain many small lakes which support other types of plants. The handsome white flowers of the water lobelia may be seen protruding from the water surface and nodding in the light summer breezes. In the shallow margins of a few lakes in the west, the pipewort can be recognised by its stems which stand up above the water like a row of small pipes.

The grass heath community that dominates much of the uplands consists mainly of a small number of relatively common species. Heathers, ling and bilberry or fraughan dominate this community, together with a number of grasses. The predominant green-brown of this vegetation is relieved in summer by the purple flowers of the heathers and the yellow and white respectively of tormentil and heath bedstraw. Towards the west coast and at lower elevations, gorse becomes an increasingly important member of the heath community, enlivening the scene with its bright yellow flowers. In certain areas other conspicuous members of this community appear which have more restricted distribution patterns within the country. Amongst these is a heather with large purple flowers, St Dabeoc's heath, a plant from the Iberian peninsula that finds a home amongst some heathlands in

Connemara. On the higher mountains, plants with the major part of their distribution in the more northerly latitudes of Scandinavia and the Arctic find a suitable habitat. These include the bearberry, a large-leaved member of the heather family, and the clubmosses which are related to the ferns. The clubmosses belong to an ancient group of plants whose remains form the bulk of many coal deposits. The present representatives of this group are small upright plants whose branches resemble, in miniature, those of some conifers.

The minority of Irish mountains that contain bands of rock richer in mineral nutrients or are composed of limestone, support a greater diversity of plant species and have some of the rarest plants. Plants with the major part of their distribution in arctic or alpine areas, known as arctic-alpines, occur in such localities and many of these are thought to be relicts from an earlier cold period. The cliffs of the Slieve League peninsula in Co. Donegal provide a suitable habitat for such arctic-alpines as dwarf juniper, purple saxifrage and alpine meadow rue. The moss campion and least willow occur on the basalt of the Antrim plateau. The limestone of the Benbulben plateau in Co. Sligo represents another important refuge for these rare plants, though, as much of it is covered in blanket bog, they are restricted to north-facing cliffs. The very rare Irish sandwort, which grows nowhere else, is found here along with several other arctic-alpines.

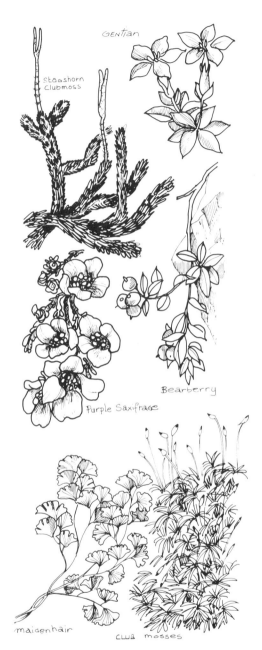

This arctic-alpine group reaches what is probably its best and most delightful expression on the comparatively low hills of the Burren in Co. Clare. Here, due to the abundance of lime-rich soils and open habitats free from the shade of trees and other tall plants, arctic-alpines occur at all altitudes from 345 metres down to sea level. The biogeographical fascination of the Burren is further enhanced by the occurrence of plants with Mediterranean affinities in close proximity to those from arctic and alpine regions. Thus in one small area of vegetation may be found growing almost side by side plants such as the greenish white flowered Mediterranean orchid and the dazzling blue alpine gentian. Close to the coast of the Burren, the pretty yellow rockrose grows on a few rock outcrops and, in some of the deep clefts, or grikes, between the limestone slabs, the delicate fronds of the Maidenhair fern may be found sheltered from the strong Atlantic winds. At higher altitudes, mountain avens cover large areas of rock with their small oak-like leaves, and provide a spectacular early summer display of white flowers. The bearberry makes a somewhat surprising appearance on the higher limestone slopes, surprising because this plant is normally associated with more acid rocks. Closer inspection usually reveals, however, that it is growing in a layer of humus that has developed on top of the limestone.

A conspicuous feature of many upland areas is the presence of large plantations of exotic coniferous trees. In the early stages of growth, they increase the structural diversity of the vegetation and provide a habitat for certain bird species, most notably the hen harrier. After a few years, however, the branches of the individual trees meet and the canopy closes, making the interior of the forests very dark. From this stage onwards the plantations support very little wildlife and their dark serried ranks are relieved only by the occasional plants of gorse, heather or foxglove which colonise the margins and rides.

Animals

In general the animal life of the mountains is less diverse than the flora but contains some interesting members. One mammal that is characteristic of the uplands is the mountain or varying hare, of which the Irish population is recognised as an endemic subspecies that is restricted to Ireland. It is very closely related to the Scottish blue hare but it has a more russet coloured summer coat and rarely develops the same full white coat in winter, retaining at least some patches of brown on its back. In lowland areas it may not change colour in winter. It is smaller than its relative, the brown hare which was introduced into several northern counties and also Co. Cork late in the nineteenth century, but which has survived only in Tyrone, Donegal and Derry, though possibly also in Down and Armagh. The piebald appearance of the mountain hare in winter blends in well with the patchy brown and white colouring of vegetation and snow in the mountains. Its presence can often be identified in the snow by its distinctive tracks, long hind leg marks slightly forward of two smaller front paw marks.

The largest mammals of the uplands are the deer, of which three species occur in Ireland. Only the largest of these, the red deer, is native to Ireland and the native stock of this species is confined to the area of Co. Kerry in and around the Killarney National Park. Part of this herd recently was introduced to the Connemara National Park in Co. Galway, an area where it was known to have occurred in the past. Red deer herds also exist in Donegal, where they were introduced from Scotland, and Wicklow, where they have hybridised or interbred with the Japanese sika deer introduced to the Powerscourt demesne in the late nineteenth century. Sika deer were introduced to Kerry also but they do not appear to have hybridised with the native red deer there. The third species of deer is the fallow which was introduced at an unknown date, possibly by the Normans. The red deer is essentially an animal of open woodland but in Ireland it has been forced onto the hills, where small herds may be seen grazing during the summer. In winter the deer move to the more sheltered lower levels and woodlands. Other mammals that may be seen in the uplands include badgers, though these occur mainly in the lowlands,

Top left: Sika deer in an upland setting.
(photo: Office of Public Works).

Above: Gannets on Saltee.
(photo: Gerrit van Gelderen)

Left: The distinctive bark of the strawberry tree,
Arbutus Undeo. (photo: Paul Cusack, Botanic
Gardens, Glasnevin)

Top left: Glendalough, Co. Wicklow. Even in this most popular of tourist sites we can find the tangible remains of silver and lead miners of byegone days.

Below left: Apart from their everyday usefulness, a myriad of signposts in rural Ireland reinforces the strong connection between place-names and historical geography.

Below right: As this scene from Co. Wicklow reminds us, the effort to enhance rural Ireland is not shared by all!

PREVIOUS PAGE: Exploitation and conservation of resources present rural Ireland with a classical dichotomy. Sands and gravels are being quarried in this esker just west of Tullamore, Co. Offaly.

The annual steam-threshing in Moynalty, Co. Meath preserves, if only for one day in the year, memories of former rural technology and more labour-intensive agricultural systems.

Eyeries, Co. Cork. The bright, even audacious use of many colours, helps to brighten dark rural winters. The rise and fall in building height reinforces the attractiveness of rural villages and towns.

and, in areas such as the Burren, herds of feral (wild) goats.

Birds are a familiar sight in the uplands, though they occur there at much lower densities than in the lowlands. On the upland heaths, the Irish red grouse, lives a life that is closely linked to the heather plants on which it depends for food, nesting sites and cover. The red grouse is now of local occurrence in Ireland and in much lower numbers than its counterpart on the Scottish moorlands. Birds of prey, or raptors, include the kestrel, the merlin and the magnificent Peregrine falcon, the latter two being less frequent. Notable amongst the crows are the raven, which occurs in many upland areas, and the chough which, although predominantly a bird of coastal cliffs, may be seen amongst the mountains of the southwest. Of the smaller birds, meadow pipits and skylarks are most common on the bogs and heaths of the uplands, and their nests are often sought out by the cuckoo in spring.

The invertebrate animals, that is those without backbones such as insects, spiders and slugs, are well represented in upland habitats and they are much more numerous than the vertebrates. A few butterflies and moths may be found, especially in the milder areas with more diverse vegetation such as the Burren. Dragonflies and mayflies are common near water, as also of course are the pestilential midges which represent perhaps one of the few unwelcome wildlife sightings, or rather feelings, of a visit to the uplands.

THE LOWLANDS

Woodland

Lowland areas comprise the bulk of the Irish countryside and one conspicuous feature is the lack of deciduous woodland. Other than Iceland, Ireland is the least wooded country in Europe and the vast bulk consists of coniferous plantations. Because of the clearance of most of the original woodland cover, the lowland landscape today is one of fields and hedgerows, bogs and fens, with only the occasional clump of woodland on a hillside, in a valley or within the grounds of an old demesne. Visitors to the countryside are not immediately aware of this lack of woodland, however, as the lowland landscape retains a wooded appearance due to the large numbers of hedgerows and hedgerow trees that fringe roads and fields alike. Although not a substitute for true woodland, the hedgerows add diversity to the lowland landscape. Most of the best examples of deciduous woodlands are now protected either as nature reserves, such as Glen of the Downs in Co. Wicklow, or as part of a national park, such as the Killarney oakwoods. Some that are not protected are under threat of clearance for timber.

Apart from conifer plantations, the woodlands that remain in Ireland are of two types. First there are the semi-natural woodlands composed mostly of native species, some of which may be remnants of the previously more extensive forests. The second type was planted on the old estates, or demesnes, by improving landlords and these often consist of a mixture of native and exotic species. Apart from the presence of exotics in the latter, there is often little difference between the general appearance of these two types of woodland today. Both are or have been managed for timber and grazed by wild and domesticated animals and this has led to similarities in their structure, but a more detailed examination usually reveals a greater diversity of species in the semi-natural type.

Lesser Celandine

Structurally, the deciduous woodlands consist of three layers. First there is the canopy layer, formed by the taller tree species. The dominant tree of most Irish woods is the oak, which grows to a magnificent size in good sites but is often stunted on poor soils and steep slopes. The oak is often accompanied by ash, which can itself dominate small patches of wood in limestone areas. In planted woods, beech, which was introduced to Ireland in the eighteenth century, is often an important constituent of the canopy layer. Birch may also form part of the canopy, especially in wetter areas and at higher altitudes, but it is more generally an important component of the middle layer of tall shrubs. Other species of the shrub layer include hazel, rowan, the evergreen holly and the introduced sycamore which is a vigorous invader of many woodlands.

Wood Anemome

Many Irish woods have a relatively open structure and this feature, combined with the deciduous habit of the major canopy formers, means that the woodland floor receives plenty of sunlight especially in spring, encouraging the lush development of the bottom, or ground, layer. In contrast to the relative uniformity of the two upper layers, the ground layer vegetation shows much variation between different woodland sites. The plants growing at this level are more sensitive to variations in local microclimate, soil character and rock type. In the more sheltered woodland sites and on rich soils, a profuse development of herbaceous plants frequently carpets the forest floor with a garland of flowers in spring. Amongst these is found that delightful harbinger of spring, the lesser celandine, and others which appear slightly later, such as wood anemone, wood sorrel and bluebell. In disturbed sites and on poorer soils, the ground layer may be dominated by the bracken fern and brambles along with ivy. In wetter areas, grasses, mosses and rushes such as the great woodrush become more conspicuous. On the poorest, most acid soils, the ground layer takes on a heathy appearance, being dominated by plants such as heather and bilberry.

Wood-Sorrel

The climatic trend of increasing rainfall and humidity westwards across Ireland is reflected in the woodlands by a larger proportion of ferns and mosses occupying the ground layer and an increasing luxuriance in what is called the epiphyte flora of the western woods. Epiphytes are plants which grow on other plants rather than in the soil. They are not parasitic but simply use the branches of trees and shrubs as a convenient ledge on which to grow. The more humid climate of the wetter western woods provides ideal conditions for epiphytes and many of the trees are quite literally festooned with mosses and lichens. In extreme cases ferns and even heather and other shrubs may adopt this habit also.

Two other features of the woodlands in the Killarney region merit special mention. On the limestone part of the Muckross peninsula within the Killarney National Park is a small area of woodland composed almost entirely of yew. Yew is a native tree which is difficult to classify. It is not strictly a conifer but its small evergreen strap-shaped leaves resemble the conifers more than the broad-leaved deciduous trees. The yew wood at Muckross has a relatively open structure but the interior remains quite dimly lit throughout the year due to the evergreen habit. Grazing by deer has removed most of the shrub layer and the ground layer consists almost entirely of springy cushions of moss.

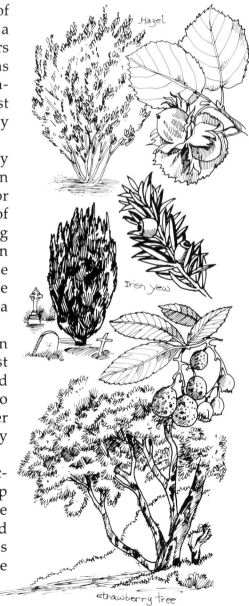

Further along the peninsula and in many other parts of the Killarney woods there occurs a rather unusual tall shrub which hails from the western Mediterranean. This is the strawberry tree or *Arbutus* which, typically for Mediterranean shrubs, has leathery evergreen leaves. It produces clusters of small creamy white flowers in the autumn from which, the following autumn, small red berries develop. These berries resemble strawberries in appearance, though not in taste, giving the plant its common name. The strawberry tree is one of a small group of plants and animals which have the major part of their distribution in the western Mediterranean but with a northerly outpost in western Ireland.

One other plant community that almost qualifies as woodland occurs in parts of the Burren in Co. Clare. This is a dense scrub composed almost entirely of hazel which has spread to cover large areas of abandoned farmland in recent decades. This hazel thicket varies in height from two to about five metres and can be quite difficult to penetrate. The ground layer consists predominantly of tall growing mosses but also contains many flowering plants.

The remaining deciduous woodlands have survived either due to protection by landowners or by virtue of their location in sites which were too steep or isolated to be of any practical use for agriculture. A striking example of the latter type of site is provided by some of the myriad small islands that stud the Irish lakes. These can present something of an enigma in areas such as Connemara where, amidst a sweeping expanse of blanket bog, a small lake island only tens of metres from the shore may be densely clothed in woodland. The isolation of these islands has protected them from cultivation and often from grazing also. The woodlands there are characteristically asymmetrical in shape, being severely wind-trimmed on their exposed western sides but taller and better developed on the sheltered lee side. Their margins frequently consist of a dense thicket of willows, making them somewhat impenetrable. Amongst the taller trees of the interior there is a profuse growth of saplings and shrubs, providing what is perhaps the closest contemporary example of how many of the primeval Irish woods may have appeared.

Deciduous woodlands support a wide range of animal life. The oak alone provides a home for more than 200 species of insect, a figure which is in stark contrast to the mere 37 supported by the Sitka spruce of the conifer plantations. Such an abundance of insects provides ample food for many other animals and the woodland contains a complex web of life. The treecreeper, songthrush, jay and woodcock are woodland residents as is the woodmouse. As woodland has declined in extent, so many of these animals have been forced to seek a home elsewhere.

Hedgerows

Hedgerows contain a variety of tree and shrub species and they are normally flanked, at least on one side, by a verge of grasses and herbs. Thus they provide a similar habitat to the woodland edge and they represent an important refuge for wildlife. Hedgerows vary in structure and composition in different parts of the country and each type provides a suitable habitat for certain animals and birds. In hilly districts and towards the western coast, hedgerows often consist of little more than a broken line of gorse bushes on an earthen bank with occasional clumps of fuchsia near to habitations. In the midlands and east, however, they are frequently more substantial and stockproof, consisting of hawthorn and ash, often with some taller oaks or sycamores at the corners. On better-drained richer soils, elm may also be an important constituent, though numbers of this tree declined markedly due to Dutch elm disease. Shrubs such as spindle and elder appear occasionally as do the climbers, honeysuckle or woodbine and old man's beard or traveller's joy.

Hedgerows provide an important habitat for a number of common bird species and an early morning walk along a well-hedged country lane in spring provides an ideal opportunity to see and, more especially, to hear many of these. The most common hedgerow birds are the dunnock or hedge sparrow, wren, robin, blackbird and chaffinch, and these may account for up to three-quarters of the bird population of a hedgerow. Many of the hedgerows were planted during the land enclosure of the eighteenth and early nineteenth centuries but some consist of the remnants of cleared woodland and these usually possess a greater diversity of plant species and a more varied structure. In this type of hedgerow occur some of the less common Irish birds which have more specific habitat requirements. These include the blackcap, which is found in hedgerows containing some tall trees together with plenty of undergrowth, the whitethroat and the spotted flycatcher.

The presence of butterflies, wasps, ants, aphids, beetles and flies turn the hedgerows into hives of industry during the summer months as they busily flit from flower to flower in search of food. These insects form an abundant food source for other hedgerow residents such as hedgehogs and pygmy shrews. The brown rat is a general scavenger in hedgerows, especially near to farms, whilst wood mice and rabbits feed on the seeds and herbage of the hedgerow plants. These, and other small animals, provide a food source for carnivores such as stoats, foxes and badgers, many of which use the linear hedgerows as preferred routeways to avoid crossing open ground.

Badgers are relatively common in the Irish lowlands, though being nocturnal creatures they are rarely seen. They live in setts which are tunnelled into slopes or small cliffs, usually in forested areas which border fields. They are fastidious animals which pay much attention to cleanliness, regularly bringing their bedding of hay and bracken to the entrance of the sett to air. Studies in the northeast of Ireland have shown that their diet consists largely of earthworms, but there is some evidence that they also eat some insect pests and rodents and may thus be beneficial to agriculture. Many farmers, however, believe that they are carriers of cattle diseases and for this reason badgers are frequently gassed and their setts destroyed. Whether badgers represent an asset or a threat to farmers is a question that requires further study.

As part of the continuing development of agriculture, some hedgerows are being removed or replaced by wire fences, especially in tillage districts. This, combined with the increased use of artificial fertilisers and pesticides, leads to a reduction in the wildlife of such areas. Arable land generally supports less wildlife than pasture but some weeds of cultivation are very hardy and continue to thrive in and around even the most intensively managed fields. Birds such as the lapwing, woodpigeon, rook and pheasant also coexist with farming, finding opportunity to feed or nest in arable areas.

Whilst many would, justifiably, decry loss of wildlife habitats, it is important to recognise that change is an essential feature of an agricultural landscape, and wildlife will, as in the past, adapt to changing conditions. However, it must also be stressed that there is ample opportunity for

compromise between the interests of conservation and farming and that unwise or unnecessary destruction of habitats should be avoided. Such benefits of hedgerows as the shelter and firewood that they supply would argue for the retention of at least a proportion of them, and the needs of wildlife can frequently be met in part by planting trees and shrubs in the corners of the fields which are inaccessible to machinery and on other small patches of less productive land.

Grassland

The larger part of the Irish lowland countryside consists not of tillage but grassland. The term grassland includes a wide variety of pasture types and these also have experienced many changes in their form of management in recent years. Land that has been under grass for a considerable time, so called 'permanent pasture', may originally have been sown with a mixture of grass species. Over the years, these were joined by many wildflowers to give the herb-rich hay meadows that are still common in some western areas. In spring and early summer these meadows are a riot of colour, as the yellows of cowslips and yellow rattle merge with the purple of vetch and red of ragged robin. Where such pastures are still mown in the traditional manner, the grating call of the shy corncrake, once a familiar sound in much of the Irish countryside, may still be heard. Sadly, from the wildlife viewpoint, such meadows have decreased because of reseeding with a few improved grasses, application of commercial fertilisers and spraying with herbicides, affecting also the field margins. This reduces not only the wildlife diversity of the countryside but also the variety of colour that such a diversity produces.

   In many parts of the lowlands, pastures are poorly drained and frequently waterlogged. These provide suitable habitats for rushes and the delicate cream flowered meadowsweet, and feeding ground for moorhens and wildfowl. Although drainage has reduced the abundance of this type of meadow, there remain many areas of the country where wet pastures merge imperceptibly into marshes, fens and lakes.

FRESH WATER

Due to its maritime location, Ireland experiences high levels of rainfall so that water is a characteristic feature of the landscape and represents an important habitat to many plants and animals. Rivers, lakes, marshes and fens abound in the countryside and each supports a characteristic range of wildlife.
   The type of wildlife that any water body contains depends on the charac-

teristics of the water, in particular its chemistry, fertility and oxygen content. Many mountain streams flow over acid rocks or peat, so are themselves acidic in nature and of relatively low fertility. Their fast and broken flow ensures good aeration and a high oxygen content but poses problems to wildlife in that there is a tendency for everything that is not securely anchored to be washed downstream. The relatively small number of organisms inhabiting these upland streams have developed some fascinating strategies to overcome this problem.

Dipper

The plant life is commonly restricted to algae and mosses which stay in place by growing tightly attached to the rocks of the stream bed. In amongst these rocks the flow is slower and a number of small animals take advantage of this fact. The freshwater shrimp is found in this quieter water, as are the larvae of midges which live amongst the moss leaves. The larvae of stoneflies and mayflies cling to the underside of rocks and stones, attaching their flattened bodies by the tail, whilst those of the caddis fly surround themselves with small stones to give added ballast. These small animals feed on the plant life and other smaller organisms and they in turn form a food source for larger predators such as fish and birds. Among these groups the diversity is also low and the brown trout and eel are the only common fish. The birds are represented by the grey wagtail and the dipper which is a delight to watch as it skims along a stream and suddenly slips below the surface to seek insects and small fish.

In their lower reaches the rivers become wider and their flow is frequently more sluggish. In many areas they flow over limestone or lime-rich glacial deposits which neutralise the acidity and increase the nutrient status. The bed of the river also changes and is more likely at this stage to be composed of mud or fine sand than of rocks and stones. These changes are accompanied by changes in the wildlife. Submerged plants such as the water crowfoot can colonise the bottom sediments and at the edge of the channel, where the flow is slower, large emergent plants such as rushes and reeds appear. The more tranquil flow of the lowland rivers frequently means that less oxygen is present and the animals now need larger gills to extract it or, alternatively, have to spend part of their time on the surface.

Boatman Insect

The animal life is generally more abundant in these lower reaches, with a number of crawling, swimming and burrowing invertebrates being present. Mayfly larvae again occur but here their bodies are more cylindrical in shape. Water boatmen and water beetles are amongst the few adult insects and they have to make regular forays to the surface to obtain a supply of air. The rich invertebrate life provides a plentiful food supply for fish which achieve a greater diversity here, though most, if not all, of the 'coarse fish' are not native but have been introduced into Ireland in historical times. In the past

mayfly Larvea

salmon, trout, eel, stickleback and lamprey were the only fish in Irish rivers. These have since been joined by many others, including pike, perch, bream and rudd which are frequent or dominant in many lowland river systems.

The kingfisher is quite a common sight along slow lowland streams and canals where the water is relatively clear. Moorhens and swans are also common and the majestic heron frequents many of the lowland rivers. Frogs are conspicuous along riverbanks and in other wetland habitats and several mammals are associated with rivers including the shy otter which, despite trapping and shooting, remains quite common. Another river mammal, the bank vole, was first discovered in 1964 and occurs only in parts of the south-west. There is no water rat but brown rats are often seen in stretches of river near farms and other habitation.

Lakes are the other major fresh water habitat in Ireland and there is a great number of these due to the low-lying nature of much of the countryside and the influence of the glaciers in creating many depressions with impeded drainage. Those in western areas on acid rocks and blanket peat are, like the rivers, low in nutrients. The small amount of wildlife they support consists largely of a marginal fringe of bog plants, together with animals such as midges and dragonflies. The fish are restricted to slow-growing trout and char, an arctic species that has remained in Ireland since the Ice Age.

Where lakes receive a greater input of nutrients from their surrounding slopes and inflowing streams, there is a richer variety of wildlife. Here there is a fringing marsh of sedges and rushes which give way to horsetails, bullrushes and willowherb in the shallow water at the lake's edge. Further out, the spikes of reeds and clubrushes, and floating plants such as water lilies and pondweeds indicate deeper water. This profuse growth of vegetation provides food and, more importantly, shelter and nesting sites for a number of birds. Coot, grebe, water rail and sedge warblers make use of this habitat and duck such as mallard and teal are common close to the open water.

The source of food on which many lake dwelling organisms depend, directly or indirectly, is represented by the algae. These plants live either as colonies attached to the lake bottom, or as microscopic cells and threads floating freely in the water. Under certain conditions, these plants may reproduce rapidly to form an 'algal bloom' which can result in the death of invertebrates and fish due to toxins produced by the algae or because of oxygen starvation. The algae produce oxygen during the day but they also require it themselves for respiration, as do the bacteria which decompose these short-lived plants, leading to oxygen deficiencies. The process by which an algal bloom comes about is known as eutrophication and is a natural phenomenon, but in some Irish lakes it has been exacerbated in recent times by pollution from indust-

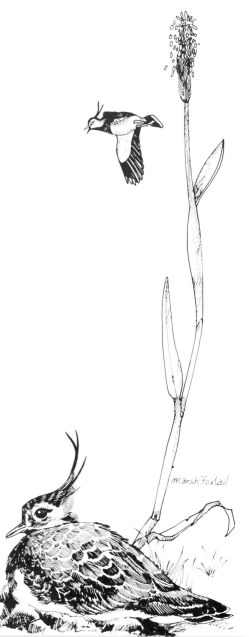

marsh Foxtail

Lapwing

Black-headed gulls and flock of
swans near Oxford Island,
National Nature Reserve.
(photos: Craigavon Borough
Council)

rial and agricultural wastes and fertiliser run-off, all of which represent a rich nutrient source for algae. Eutrophication can result in severe oxygen depletion within a few days and, in extreme instances, may cause lakes to become totally devoid of fish life.

One aquatic habitat that is peculiarly Irish is the turlough or 'dry lake'. These are grassy depressions in limestone areas that fill with water in winter and dry out in summer. This alternation of wet and dry periods makes a difficult habitat but a number of plant and animal species are able to cope. The flora consists largely of species typical of fens or wet grasslands, for example marsh foxtail, white clover and water mint, but it also contains some specialities such as the fen violet and water germander. Particularly characteristic of the deeper parts of the turlough which are regularly flooded each winter is a dark green-black moss, *Cinclidotus fontinaloides*. This moss, which grows on rocks and walls, thrives in the lime-rich waters in winter but is able to withstand long periods of drought. Its presence can be used to distinguish turloughs from other grassy depressions during summer. The animal life of turloughs is quite restricted and may consist only of a few opportunists, such as snails and water lice which survive the dry period by burrowing into damper soils or by laying eggs which hatch only when the water level rises again. During summer the turloughs are grazed by cattle but in winter they provide food for a number of birds, including white fronted geese, widgeon, curlew and lapwing.

Other wetland habitats include fens and marshes. The former are relatively restricted in Ireland today as many have formed the basis of raised bogs as described earlier. Some remain however, as at Pollardstown in Co. Kildare, and they support a rich vegetation of sedges and rushes together with meadowsweet and ragged robin. They also have a rich insect and mollusc fauna and are visited by snipe and water rails. Marshes are common in many parts of the country, especially around lakes and beside rivers. On some of the larger rivers, such as the Shannon, distinctive areas of marshy grassland, known as callows, occur. Like the turloughs, these callows are regularly flooded in winter and they represent important feeding sites for migrating wildfowl and waders.

Marram Grass

THE COAST

The larger rivers ultimately flow into the sea through broad estuaries, where the mixing of fresh and salt water and the deposition of much of the fine mud they have carried, give rise to new habitat conditions. Between the estuaries, the land meets the sea either as low ground with broad sandy beaches and dunes, or as hills which have been cut into steep rocky cliffs. Each of these coastal landscapes provides a different set of habitats which are occupied by a specialised array of plants and animals.

On reaching an estuary, the flow of a river is arrested and this causes it to deposit much of its load of fine sands and muds, carried down from the higher reaches, to form mud flats. Mud flats are a very rich habitat, as each high tide brings in a fresh supply of nutrients and flushes out waste products, and consequently they are utilised by a number of plants and animals. The lowest areas of mud are colonised by eel grass and the strange looking herb, glasswort, which has been used in salads because of its tangy salty taste. The presence of these plants reduces the speed of the water locally, causing more mud to be deposited around them and, as the mud level rises, they are replaced by plants adapted to slightly shorter periods of inundation. In some areas the cord grass has been introduced to stabilise mud flats and prevent erosion. This plant is a very efficient accumulator of mud and can quickly raise the level of mud flats to produce dry ground.

The accumulation of muds and other sediments by the plants produces a very gently sloping shoreline known as a salt marsh. The salt marsh is divided into a series of zones, each of which is inundated to differing extents by the incoming tide depending on its height above sea level. It is dissected by a series of narrow channels through which the falling tide runs back to the sea. Different plants colonise the different salt marsh zones and the sequence may be repeated, in miniature, on the edge of some of the larger drainage channels. Above the cord grass zone a range of plants occurs, including the common salt-marsh grass and, at higher levels, sea aster, sea lavender and other grasses and rushes.

Due to the constant flushing by the tides, mud flats and salt marshes are a rich habitat for invertebrate animals, especially worms and molluscs. These in their turn serve as a plentiful food source for birds, and the estuaries and marshes around the Irish coast are very important wintering grounds for many migratory birds. Amongst the ducks, widgeon is the most numerous, with mallard, teal, shoveller and pintail also being common. Wading birds are very numerous on the mud or in the shallows, probing with their long bills for the buried animals. Oystercatchers, dunlin and redshank all maintain small breeding populations in Ireland but their numbers are augmented by a vast influx of winter visitors to the estuarine mud flats and salt marshes. Swans and geese rely on these habitats also, with brent geese numbering up to 15,000 at Strangford Lough in Co. Down, where they gather each year in November before dispersing to other localities. Bewick's swans make use of several coastal sites, including the reclaimed sloblands in Wexford, which are probably better known as being the sites where up to half the world population of the Greenland white fronted goose gathers each winter.

In some of the estuaries and along many of the low lying coasts, large deposits of sand have accumulated and these often form sand dunes. The growth of sand dunes is a fascinating process which relies not only on the wind, to carry the sand, but also on plants, to trap and stabilise it. Where conditions of wind direction and sand supply are suitable, the sand may accumulate into ridges or small dunes in the area just above the strand line, allowing an important plant of the sand dunes to establish itself and the dune building process to begin. This plant is marram grass, which is very well adapted to cope with the difficulties of this extreme habitat, such as a shortage of water due to the freely draining sand and strong drying winds. Marram can develop roots up to 12 metres long which penetrate the deeper sands in search of fresh water. It spreads by means of underground stems, or rhizomes, and the combination of stems and roots forms a type of underground scaffold which binds the sand tightly to stabilise the growing dune. Marram can also roll up its leaves when the humidity of the air is low, in order to prevent an excessive loss of water from the leaf pores. The upright stems of this plant act as a windbreak, increasing local sand deposition and if it becomes buried by fresh deposits, it simply grows upwards more quickly to keep on top of the growing dune.

As soon as the marram is well established the sand is held firmly and other plants are able to colonise. A characteristic dune vegetation develops, with the dog lichen, sea spurge, birds foot trefoil, rest harrow and sand pansy prominent in the early stages of development, and creeping willow later on. This vegetation is grazed by rabbits and hares and, amongst the birds, pied wagtail, ringed plover and meadow pipit are present all year, with the wheatear being a summer visitor to some areas. The ringed plover and also the oystercatcher nest on shingle beaches, as does the little tern in southeastern counties.

Around much of the country, but especially in the north and west, rocky shores and cliffs dominate the coastal scene, though sandy beaches are still frequent in sheltered bays between the headlands. The rocky shore is a delightful area to explore, especially the small rock pools which are left behind as each tide recedes. These are like miniature water gardens or aquaria, with a profuse range of colours among the numerous plants and animals they contain. Small fish and shrimps may often be seen scuttlling between the fronds of brown, green and red seaweed that fringe the barnacle and limpet encrusted rock.

Viewing the seashore from a greater distance, a similar range of colours is again seen but this time they are organised in a definite sequence from low to high watermark and above. At the lower level is a brown zone where large seaweeds cling to the rocks by means of specialised structures called holdfasts, allowing their fronds to float on the water surface, often supported by air bladders. Within this zone and above it, comes a strip of white barnacles clinging tightly to the rock exposed at low tide. Next there is usually a black zone which has the appearance of tar smeared on the rock. This is not tar but a lichen called *Verrucaria* which clothes the open rock surfaces from well below the high tide mark. Above the *Verrucaria* comes an orange zone composed of several species of yellow and orange coloured lichens, and above this, the rock is coloured green-grey by the upright tufts of yet another lichen, *Ramalina siliquosa*. At about this point and above, the simple colour sequence breaks down and the rocks take on, in summer, a more varied colour pattern as a number of herbs come into flower. Amongst the greens of the various grasses and the sea beet are mingled the pink flowers of thrift and the white of the sea campion.

The distinct zonation of differently coloured organisms on the rocky shore comes about in a way similar to the zonation on salt marshes and is related to the varying conditions on different parts of the shoreline gradient. The lower parts of the shore are exposed only for a short time between the tides

Sand dune erosion on the Antrim Coast. (photo: William Carter, University of Ulster, Coleraine)

but this exposure period increases in length higher up the shore. Above the high tide mark, inundation by salt water occurs only rarely during violent storms and exceptionally high spring tides. Salt water droplets are constantly present, however, in the form of sea spray carried on the wind. Gradually even this diminishes as one moves further inland from the high water mark. Each of the organisms in this sequence is adapted to a certain range of conditions of inundation, exposure to drying winds and sunshine, or salt spray, and hence the sequence develops, painting the rocky shores with their own brand of rainbow.

The character of the rocky shore and nearby cliffs is completed by other sights and, especially, sounds. These are the ever present seabirds which provide one of the most spectacular sights of Irish wildlife. Common among the resident nesting seabirds are the herring gull, great black-backed gull, shag and cormorant. That most accomplished of diving birds, the gannet, is also resident but has a more restricted distribution. It maintains a population of 20,000 pairs on the Little Skellig, Co. Kerry, and two smaller populations off the coasts of Cork and Wexford. Kittiwake, razorbill and guillemot are commonest among the true seabirds which come ashore only to nest. Less frequent members of this group are the fulmar and black guillemot and, more locally, the puffin, shearwater and storm petrel may be seen, adding yet more colour and diversity to rich coastal landscapes.

Thus there is a great variety of wildlife even within the narrow coastal zone, which itself is only one component in the diversity of wildlife in the Irish countryside – a diversity which must be conserved.

Above: Prehistoric standing stones, alignments and enclosures exposed by bog clearance, Beaghmore, Co. Tyrone. (photo: Department of Environment, Northern Ireland)

Right: Motte and nearby circular religious enclosure partially preserved, Co. Louth. Crop marks show the extent of the original enclosure. (photo: Cambridge University Collection of air photographs)

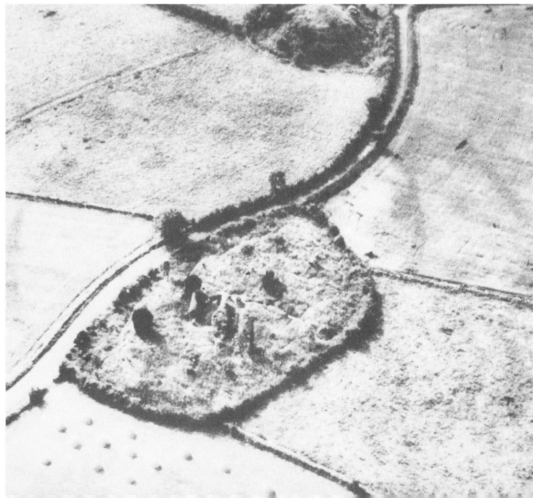

Imprint of the Past

FREDERICK AALEN

In a long and widely settled area such as Ireland, the human imprint on the countryside is particularly strong and the landscape is not the product of contemporary activities alone but of people's work over lengthy periods of pre-historic and historic time and in long-compounded patterns. The great regional variety of landscapes, which is such a striking feature of the Irish countryside, is owing not only to contrasts of natural environment but also to varied patterns of historical development. In any region the rural landscape is not just an immense aesthetic resource but a major cultural and historical legacy, a tangible expression of the region's past or, more precisely, of the unique historical interaction between the inhabitants and their natural environment.

Past phases of human activity have influenced the present landscape in two main ways. First, the appearance of the landscape has changed substantially through time, reflecting economic and social developments and population fluctuations, but as new landscape patterns emerge they are influenced, either directly or subtly, by earlier arrangements. This is apparent even after phases of major abrupt rural reorganisation, such as follow conquest and large-scale immigrations of culturally distinct people or agrarian reforms under powerful landowners or government bodies. Thus, the present landscape is the end product of a long process of development in which, to varying degrees, each successive phase has conditioned the next. The course of this long-term development can be revealed only by detailed analysis and study.

Second, although the artefactual or cultural landscape is subject to continual reworking by successive societies and most evidence of earlier land use thereby disturbed or obliterated, a limited number of human features survives relatively intact from earlier periods. These fossilised remnants of former rural landscapes are often difficult to interpret in isolation from the economic and social systems which produced them. Features have survived for a variety of reasons. Sometimes, like the prehistoric stone tombs whose members often weigh many tons, they are highly durable and too bulky to remove. Some were located in places undisturbed by later change, for example the fragments of ancient obsolete field systems preserved in hill areas or buried under bogs. Certain features, such as raths and standing stones, came to be regarded with superstitious awe by country people and were consequently unmolested for many centuries. Official protection of antiquities by the state is recent and, it seems, not as effective as the ancient taboos.

LANDSCAPE STUDY

The study of landscape development in the prehistoric period is concerned with two main things. First, the clearance of the natural vegetation cover of forest and, second, the character of the human landscape that increasingly replaced it. It is a study to which the historical geographer, palaeobotanist and archaeologist have made important contributions. The relatively new approaches of landscape archaeology, emphasising the study of the total landscape of prehistoric communities rather than isolated sites, should considerably enhance understanding of landscape history. Analysis of fossil pollen, preserved in datable layers of ancient peat bogs and other recent geological deposits, has been a major source of evidence for prehistoric environmental history, demonstrating broad regional trends in the amount, composition of, and human interference with, the vegetation. Combined with the archaeological record, this evidence permits important insights into, but by no means complete understanding of, the origins of the cultural landscape, of the changes that took place in time and space and people's changing adaptations to their habitat. In the historical periods, documentary sources are available to the landscape historian and archaeological evidence is relatively limited. Not until the eighteenth and nineteenth centuries were maps prepared showing landscape features with any accuracy or detail.

Ireland is a rewarding country for the study of landscape history, combining varied ecological conditions with a long eventful history of human settlement and a plentiful and relatively well preserved archaeological record from most major periods. The potential of pollen analysis is exceptional owing to the widespread distribution of old bogs both in uplands and lowlands, and ancient earthworks survive in abundance undamaged by ploughing in a countryside with deep-rooted pastoral traditions. Furthermore, the conservative nature of Irish society and the survival of ancient lifestyles down almost to the present day allow useful ethnological perspectives on the prehistoric data.

EARLIEST HUMAN IMPACT

The first human immigrants, reaching Ireland around 8000 BC, settled in a well-forested environment. However, the early communities appear to have been small in number and dependent on a simple hunting and gathering economy, exploiting in particular sea and river resources. Over the several thousand years of their occupation there were apparently no major changes in the vegetation cover. Significant change began with the development of a farming economy around 3500 BC, when clearances were made to provide open areas for cereal cultivation and livestock grazing. The forest cover was thereafter gradually depleted and farmed land expanded. However, the process was lengthy and uneven, mainly achieved in the prehistoric period but extending down to early historic times, with several major phases of forest clearance and regeneration before extensive clearances became permanent.

Although cereal cultivation continued, Irish conditions, especially the mild and moist climate, were best suited to livestock, particularly cattle, which soon became of major importance in the rural economy and the evolution of the rural landscape. As forests disappeared they were replaced by permanent grassland on the better lowland soils and by moorland, suitable only for rough grazing, on the uplands. The two major forms of vegetation cover, grassland and moorland, are thus largely the products of farming activity, and much of the land if untended would revert to its natural condition of deciduous woodland. Bogs too, however wild and natural in appearance, are in part the outcome of human activity and disturbance of the forest ecosystems, as discussed in chapter 3.

PREHISTORIC FARM LANDSCAPES

Knowledge of settlement and farm economy during the Neolithic (3500-1800 BC) and Bronze Ages (1800-500 BC), when the forests were first being cleared, is limited. Some prehistorians have concluded from the scarcity of archaeological evidence of settlements that a nomadic way of life prevailed and durable solid houses and villages were not required. The pollen records also reveal a complex pattern of vegetation change, suggesting phases of farming settlement and woodland restoration. However, this is hard to reconcile with the existence of over 1,200 massive stone tombs or megaliths, mostly dating from the Neolithic period. Their substantial nature suggests sedentary farming communities already deeply rooted in particular localities, as does the existence of fossil field boundaries. Stone walls, buried

Above: Excavations of prehistoric fields, cultivation ridges and house in Co. Mayo. (photo: S. Caulfield, University College, Dublin)

Below and right: (a) Proleek Dolmen, Co. Louth; Megalithlic tombs – (b) Caherphuca wedge gallery grave, Co. Clare; (c) Carrowkeel Passage Grave, Co. Sligo; (d) Creerykeel Court Cairn, Co. Sligo. (photos: Office of Public Works)

thousands of years ago beneath spreading peat bogs, have frequently been revealed in modern times where peat has been cut for domestic fuel. The pre-bog remains vary from fragments to extensive field systems. Since bog growth started at widely different periods, it is sometimes difficult to know to which period the prehistoric fields belong. Often, however, they are associated with megaliths and other features of known age and thus can be dated with reasonable confidence. A network of fences argues for a fixed sedentary pattern of farming. However, the full extent of prehistoric fields is not clear. Survivals occur under bogs but in other localities the walls, especially if they were made of earth, sods or other perishable materials, might have been obliterated by continuous land use. Thus, available evidence is insufficient to show whether the earliest Irish farmland was everywhere divided into fixed fields much as at present. Moreover, it cannot be demonstrated that there has been any significant continuity of fieldscape from the prehistoric to the present. Any similarity between old and present field systems may not illustrate absolute continuity but rather a case of history repeating itself, of similar needs in different periods producing similar results.

The megaliths are burial chambers constructed with massive undressed stones. Normally each tomb was covered with a mound of stone or clay but this has often been eroded away and only the large stones of the chamber survive. Megaliths are found widely in western Europe but are exceptionally numerous in Ireland. Irish megaliths fall into four broad categories distinguished by shape and size. Moreover, there is a tendency for certain styles to be concentrated in particular regions, perhaps reflecting the existence of diverse cultural strains among the early farming populations. Court tombs are the most common type and located mainly in Ulster. They consist of a curved forecourt flanked by standing stones, giving access to a segmented burial chamber originally under a long straight-sided cairn. The distribution of portal tombs overlaps with that of court tombs, although numerous examples occur in south-eastern Ireland too. Typically they consist of two tall portal stones and are covered by an enormous capstone sloping down to the rear of the burial chamber. Like the court tombs, they are associated with long cairns. The passage tombs are the most impressive category and are found mainly in clusters or cemeteries, often sited on hilltops. Their burial chambers are approached by passages and the monument covered by a substantial circular cairn. The stones of these tombs are often inscribed with mysterious geometrical motifs. Wedge tombs consist of a rectangular chamber of stone slabs often narrowing and declining in height towards the rear. The cairns can be round, oval or D-shaped. Wedge tombs are more widely distributed than the other forms, with many occurring in Munster where other types are rare.

On the not unreasonable assumption that tombs and settlements were adjacent, the distribution of megaliths may serve as an indication of general population distribution in the Neolithic period. Many megaliths lie on upland flanks around the limits of present day cultivation and early farmers indeed may have selected these localities because the soils were well-drained and thin enough to be worked by primitive techniques. However, an elevated location was not invariable and some massive tombs, such as Newgrange and Knowth in the Boyne valley, were established on lowlands. The correlation appears to be with relatively light soils rather than altitude *per se* and tombs occur right down to sea level on well-drained soils.

While upland soils would generally have been more easily worked than most lowland soils by early farmers, they would also have been more readily degraded. After deforestation, deterioration of the acid soils could have led eventually to the growth of blanket bog in the Bronze Age which sometimes submerged earlier settlement and field systems. Tools and ornaments from the Bronze Age and early Iron Age (500 BC to Birth of Christ) are numerous and have a wide distribution but archaeological evidence of settlements is conspicuously limited. Compared with the Neolithic, the Bronze Age has few striking monuments; modest stone circles, probably used for ritual purposes, exist in a few localities as well as numerous standing stones, set singly or in groups, of uncertain purpose. Burial sites marked by earthen tumuli or stone cairns were sometimes sited on hill tops and still form conspicuous landmarks. The majority of burials, however, were in inconspicuous cist graves, frequently located on well-drained sandy soils associated with lowland esker and kame deposits.

FIRST MILLENNIUM AD

Abundant remains of settlement survive in the Irish countryside from the first millennium AD, which includes the second half of the Iron Age (Birth of Christ – AD 500) and the Early Christian period (AD 500-1000). The problematic term 'Celtic' is conventionally applied to remains from this period. Certainly a recognisably Celtic way of life and language was fully established in Ireland by the Early Christian period but when celticisation commenced is uncertain. Archaeology does not suggest any large scale incursion of people at the beginning of or during the Iron Age, and the Celts or their predecessors may have entered much earlier.

Whereas Celtic society in Britain and on the continent was overwhelmed and substantially modified by Roman imperial expansion, in Ireland, where the Romans never penetrated, Celtic tradition evolved without serious disruption down to the middle ages. Hence, the numerous sites from the first millennium provide an exceptional opportunity to reconstruct Celtic social organisation and settlement patterns.

In contrast to earlier periods, first millennium settlement sites are plentiful and burial places few. Most numerous are the raths or ringforts, circular spaces defined by earthen or stone banks, which in most instances were the sites not of fortresses but of mere single farmsteads. Raths are undoubtedly the commonest archaeological sites in the Irish countryside, their present number being estimated between 30,000 and 40,000. However, many have been destroyed in recent centuries and the surviving sites are under serious threat from land reclamation. While the bulk of raths have an internal diameter of approximately 20 to 60 metres, large examples can be found over 100 metres in diameter. A single bank and outer ditch is the most common form of enclosure, the material from the ditch actually forming the bank, but double and triple banked enclosures are to be found. It is likely that each rath originally contained a farmhouse and other farm buildings; the foundations of these sometimes survive but generally there is no surface trace of any building. Some raths, however, possess subterranean stone-lined passages called souterrains, probably used for storage and perhaps refuge too. In stony areas in the west of Ireland, the earth banks are replaced by stone walls and the sites described as cashels. A few of the cashels possess substantial dry stone fortifications and may have been occupied by warrior chieftains.

Broadly contemporary with raths and cashels, comparable in size, and again roughly circular in shape, were the crannogs or lake dwellings. They were sited on semi-artificial islands for security and made with timber, sods and stones. Crannogs are still conspicuous in lake-strewn areas such as Fermanagh, as neat, round and scrub-covered islets. Promontory forts, whose purposes were clearly defensive, are numerous around the coasts. They lack any trace of substantial buildings and consist only of small areas on cliffed promontories, with ramparts and ditches on the landward side. The great hill forts, such as Moghane, Co. Clare and Rathgall, Co. Wicklow, where walls and ditches surround one or two hectares of a hill top, are the largest enclosures in prehistoric pagan Ireland. Like promontory forts, they lack any traces of substantial buildings and may have served as tribal meeting places and cult centres rather than permanent residences.

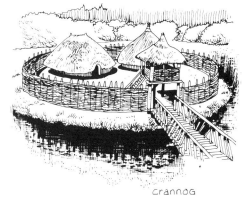

crannog

While raths and cashels vary considerably in size and the elaboration of their defenses, presumably according to the social status of the occupants, most were probably the settlements of relatively well-to-do farmers rather than overlords. The sites show a preference for the better soils of lowland areas and defensive considerations do not seem to have been of great impor-

Prehistoric field walls in the Burren.
(photo: Frederic Aalen)

Rath at Toor, Co. Wicklow.
(photo: Frederic Aalen)

tance. In some areas raths lie close to existing farms and almost equal them in number. Small irregular fields can sometimes be faintly discerned around the raths and cashels, preserved best in hill areas and stony terrain where later agriculture has had little impact. A few upland enclosures contain numerous hut sites and may represent transhumant or temporary summer quarters. Many early earthworks have been much modified and sometimes almost obliterated by erosion, overgrowth, re-use or deliberate destruction. Sometimes, for example, the banks have been incorporated in later field systems or the enclosures used as sheep pens. Close scrutiny of a piece of countryside almost invariably reveals one or more ancient earthworks hitherto unrecorded.

Judging by the great number and widespread distribution of raths, cashels and related settlement forms, the Irish landscape in the first millennium was well settled. The broad distribution of much of the rural settlement was comparable to the present, with noteworthy concentrations in the eastern and central lowlands, around the Shannon estuary and in the broad valleys of Munster. These lowland areas, owing to their forest cover and poor drainage, were initially harder to colonise than the free-draining hill flanks but, once settled and developed, remained among the most populous and productive parts of Ireland. It is tempting therefore to think that this early pattern of dispersed rath forms and associated enclosures, through piecemeal change and expansion, has evolved directly into the modern rural pattern of scattered farms and enclosed fields. However, it is striking that so many of the raths have been abandoned and that their fragmentary field systems underlie the present day fields which are on the whole larger in area, more rectangular and even-shaped; the contrast suggesting superimposition rather than evolution. The modern settlement pattern too has developed through several distinct phases. Rather than perpetuating Iron Age and Early Christian traditions, the modern scatter of farms has often developed in recent centuries from nucleated settlements whose precise historical antecedents are unclear.

The major components of the Irish landscape are not therefore 'Celtic' in any strict sense. Some landscape features survive from the Celtic period but they are fossils, such as the abandoned raths. It is true that the Irish language of modern times and some social traditions have developed directly from the ancient Celts. Many landscape features have Irish names but this does not mean that they are necessarily of great antiquity.

Clonmacnoise

Christianity and the landscape, AD 500 to AD 1100
Raths and cashels were occupied throughout the first millennium, and in some instances even as late as the seventeenth century. However, the advent

of Christianity in the fifth century AD introduced new features into the landscape and it is clear that the church came to play a major role in Irish society. Scattered over the countryside is a large number of abandoned sites which originally served diverse but imperfectly understood religious functions. Most common is a burial ground or a church with a burial ground within some form of enclosure, usually but not invariably circular. The enclosures, built either of earth or stone, vary greatly in size; some are little larger than the average rath but bigger examples enclose several acres. A holy well, stone cross, standing stone, souterrains and bullaun stones (cup-marked stones) may often be found either in or close to the enclosure. In the past most sites have been loosely interpreted as Early Christian monasteries. Recent research suggests that some sites were indubitably monastic but others simply the sites of small local churches either tribal or private, hermit-ages, or graveyards.

It is likely that burial grounds were the oldest forms, to which in many but not all instances churches and other buildings were later added. By around the eighth or ninth century AD some sites had evolved into monasteries. These characteristically contained a loose concentration of small churches, dry-stone domed huts, or clochans, in which the monks lived, a burial ground and high crosses. The whole invariably was surrounded by a rath-like enclosure or cashel and frequently a larger outer enclosure can be recog-nised. In the ninth century tall round towers were built to serve as refuges and campaniles. Ancient documentary sources, much of them ambiguous, suggest that major monasteries may have served as commercial as well as religious centres, with satellite settlements lying around them. However, only the cores of the monasteries, containing sacred buildings, have survived. Remains at the large famous centres, such as Clonmacnoise, Co. Offaly and Glendalough, Co. Wicklow, are substantial, lying within large enclosures some 10 hectares in extent.

Most of the monasteries were abandoned at an early stage and the sites largely ignored by the monasteries of continental orders established from the twelfth century onwards. Only the stump of a round tower and church foundations remain and the much reduced enclosing earthworks. The outer enclosures are often traceable only on aerial photographs, surviving merely as a degraded bank or ditch, a modern field boundary or a laneway.

Recent research has shown that enclosed ecclesiastical sites are much more numerous than earlier supposed, especially in the central lowlands. Most sites were abandoned early and the enclosures survive fossilised in field systems as small curves and bulges in the otherwise straight field bound-aries. In some places the sites are observable only as crop marks or shadows on aerial photographs. A number of sites developed into full-scale monas-

Celtic Cross and Round Tower, Clonmacnoise Monastic Site , Co. Offaly.
(photo: Bord Failte)

Well-preserved tower house and bawn constructed 1643, Derryhivenny, Co. Galway.
(photo: Frederic Aalen)

teries as previously described, while others continued as church sites through the middle ages and even into the modern period. Others continued to develop, and now either form the cores of villages and towns or are in close proximity to them. A number of abandoned sites were re-used as burial grounds (killeens or calluraghs) in recent centuries, often for unbaptised infants.

Clearly the early Christian church played a very important role in Ireland and its organisation may be the key to the development of many long-standing features of the settlement pattern and landscape generally. However, it is uncertain how far the early church played a pioneering role in the establishment of settlements or merely attached itself to pre-existing foci and gave them a new significance. There is certainly a likelihood that numerous pagan sites were taken over by the church during its remarkably energetic and widespread early growth.

MEDIEVAL AND EARLY MODERN LANDSCAPE, AD 1100 TO AD 1600

In the twelfth century Ireland was invaded and partially colonised by Anglo-Normans, many of whom originated in neighbouring Wales. The newcomers established themselves most firmly on the productive agricultural lowlands of the south and east of the country, where their castles, fortified towns, monasteries and churches survive in plenty. Elsewhere in Ireland the extent of Anglo-Norman colonisation was patchy; in the north and west in particular little headway was made and native life continued relatively undisturbed. Thus, both Gaelic and Norman areas were fragmented and the colony could neither be adequately protected nor culturally insulated. Both communities adopted cultural traits from each other to produce eventually a hybrid culture. It is wrong therefore to envisage any sustained division of medieval Ireland into two self-contained cultural provinces, Gaelic and Anglo-Norman. Descendants of the more important Norman families retained some distinctiveness for many centuries but the colonists were not, as conventionally thought, solely urban or aristocratic. Indeed there is evidence of rural colonisation by considerable bodies of Welsh and English peasantry and artisans, who settled in villages on manorial estates. Much of the Anglo-Norman rural settlement pattern, however, was later abandoned, swept away or much modified. The features which have survived best are the major fortified sites and the towns, but these give a misleading impression of the overall character of settlement in the colony.

As colonists, the Anglo-Normans required strongholds to secure subdued territories. During the early phase of conquest and settlement the most common form of stronghold was the motte-and-bailey earthwork. Around 400 of these impressive features survive in the present landscape, sometimes overgrown or much reduced by quarrying. The motte is an artificial mound, occasionally sited on a natural elevation, with a fosse around the base. A wooden tower and palisade were erected on the flat-topped summit but have long since vanished. Attached to the motte is a bailey or courtyard. Many of these strongholds now lie isolated in the countryside but originally they may have been associated with some form of settlement. Often indeed the mottes may have been erected on the sites of Irish chieftains' strongholds and some were built at ancient ecclesiastical sites where semi-urban settlements may have already developed.

After 1200 AD or thereabouts the motte-and-bailey earthworks were succeeded by more substantial stone castles, fewer in number but superior in strength. Many mottes may have continued to serve as minor strongholds and indeed to have been built until the thirteenth century but the castles, frequently located on top of mottes, became the key defensive elements. Under their protection new forms of settlement, particularly the villages and towns, were able to flourish.

The distribution pattern of mottes corresponds closely to other features of Anglo-Norman settlement, with the greatest concentration in the east and diminishing westwards. Only a few outliers occur in Connacht. However, curious gaps occur in the eastern distribution pattern, especially in Munster where the Anglo-Normans are known to have settled widely. There may therefore have been other methods of protecting early castles, perhaps with ringworks or earthen banks rather than raised, defensive platforms. Such circular defences were common in medieval South Wales where the Norman lords originated. In a number of instances the indigenous raths may have been re-used as a basis for ringworks and also for mottes.

Perhaps the most important contribution made by the Anglo-Normans was the network of fortified urban centres built to protect their lands or serve as commercial centres. In most, castles had a dominant position. This was the case at Kilkenny, Trim, Maynooth, Nenagh and Galway, for example. Some of these settlements grew into major towns, but others remained small and some failed to survive. The viability of the settlements seems to have depended on the density of the surrounding colonial population and the existence of settled secure conditions for commerce and agriculture. Most towns possessed their own common fields outside the walls, as well as extensive communal grazing territories. Indeed the smaller towns were essentially agricultural and, in most respects, little different from villages.

The Normans divided the land into large estates or manors and organised the countryside into parishes; indeed there was a close correspondence

Motte and Bailey, Castletown Geoghan, Co. Westmeath. The circular steep-sized mound with a flat top is the motte; the lower mound alongside is the bailey. Both features are surrounded by a ditch. The motte is the main strongpoint and would originally have been fortified by a tower and palisades. A ditch separates the motte from the bailey and connection between the two parts was probably by a drawbridge. To the north is a cluster of farms and cottages around an ancient circular churchyard. (photo: Leo Swan)

between manorial and parochial boundaries. In the south and east of the country compact villages with parish churches were established on the manors, associated with open-fields and scattered strip holdings worked communally on a two- or three-field system. Village organisation was thus broadly comparable to that operating in lowland England and other parts of Europe. It seems that villages declined widely in the late medieval period and few surviving examples can be found except in the hinterland of Dublin. Vestiges of the old strip-fields lingered on in a number of places almost to the present day, although the open-field system went into decline many centuries ago.

New monasteries and friaries organised on the lines of continental orders were introduced into Ireland from the twelfth century, many of them located in or close to towns but also in the countryside. The compact communal nature of the buildings of the new orders contrasted with the more informal dispersed Celtic arrangements. Most enterprising were the Cistercians who settled in more than 35 places, usually in isolated rural settings. Typical Cistercian sites with impressive ranges of buildings include Mellifont and Bective in Co. Meath, Jerpoint in Co. Kilkenny and Holy Cross in Co. Tipperary. Cistercian estates were substantial and carefully organised into a number of granges or outlying farms. No grange buildings, however, seem to have survived. Dominican and Franciscan friaries also spread far outside the Norman colony and were often located in the countryside, where their ruins are evocative and picturesque elements of the rural landscape.

In Ireland, as in many west European countries, the late medieval period was one of general unrest and population decline; settlement desertion occurred, waste and woodland expanded, and there was probably a swing from arable to a more pastoral type of farming. Eventually, the authority of the English crown, apart from in walled towns, was limited to 'the Pale', comprising roughly the counties of Dublin, Meath, Louth and Kildare. Ditches were dug to mark the boundary, fragments of which survive, but the limits of the Pale were not stable or well defined and there was often unrest within it. Deteriorating climate may have been responsible for some of the troubles, especially in economic life, but the Bruce Invasion (1315) and the Black Death later in the century were contributory factors.

The troubled late medieval period was marked by the appearance of two characteristic defensive settlement forms. Tower houses became a familiar feature of the landscape in both Anglo-Norman and Gaelic areas in the fourteenth century, remaining so until the seventeenth century. The towers were small stone castles or keeps, normally three or four storeys high, providing secure residences for the landowning aristocracy and larger free tenants. Animals lived on the ground floor and the family above. Walled enclosures were linked to the towers. Many thousands of tower houses, abandoned and decaying, are scattered over the countryside, especially in the south-west and west. They occur also in medieval towns and villages, such as Carrickfergus, Co. Antrim, Carlingford, Co. Louth and Newcastle Co. Dublin, but the bulk are dispersed rural settlements. Indeed the ability of the rural upper classes to build so many substantial towers suggests an underlying economic vitality and wealth, perhaps difficult to reconcile with so many other symptoms of unrest and decline.

Also defensive but less widely distributed than tower houses are moated farmsteads. The typical site is a low rectangular platform, averaging 30 x 50 metres, surrounded by a ditch and ramparts. Over 700 moated sites have been recorded; farms survive in a few but the majority are now empty. They occur mainly in lowlands in the south-east of the country and were probably defended residences built in Anglo-Norman territories under pressure from the resurgent Irish. Analogous and roughly contemporary sites occur in lowland England and elsewhere. Unfortunately many of the Irish sites, perhaps as much as a half, have been removed by recent land reclamation and 'improvement'.

It is difficult to assess how much of the landscape of the Celtic period survived the Norman settlement. In the east much of the older order withered away; rath settlements disappeared and a new settlement network emerged. Towns and villages eclipsed the old Irish monasteries as focal points in the landscape but sometimes grew on earlier religious sites and inherited some of their features, such as the church and its circular enclosure. Outside the south and east there was more direct continuity. In the areas subjugated but not intensively settled by colonists, many of the raths and cashels continued to be occupied and the widely dispersed new towns, such as Sligo, Galway and Dingle, had little impact on the countryside. Manors and parishes were formed here but village organisation was not introduced. In the unconquered areas, such as west Ulster and south-west Cork, the essential pattern of Irish life survived intact, although even here Anglo-Norman settlement features were borrowed, including motte-and-bailey earthworks and stone castles. The Anglo-Norman colony thus had an indirect influence on the landscape of even the most Irish territories.

THE MAKING OF THE MODERN LANDSCAPE, POST 1600

Introduction
The protracted wars of the late sixteenth and seventeenth centuries saw the final reduction of all Ireland to English authority, the creation for the first

time of effective centralised government and the foundation of a new economic and social order. Ownership of land was progressively transferred to new immigrant landowners, mainly of English origin. In some regions state-organised schemes of large-scale colonisation by British settlers took place but with varying degrees of longterm success. Everywhere, however, even in Ulster where the plantation policy was most effective, the native Irish survived in substantial numbers. Planter elements were conspicuously few in the west of the country and there the traditional life of the Irish peasantry continued undisturbed. In the relative peace and stability of the following centuries there were important economic and social developments which created the essentials of the present landscape, although various features were inherited from earlier times.

A brief review of these formative developments is required before the modern landscape can be adequately interpreted and understood. There was, first, a long period of economic, and especially agricultural, expansion accompanied by marked population growth. In the eighteenth century the Irish population probably doubled and by the 1840s exceeded eight millions. Population growth was strongly stimulated by the agricultural boom during the Napoleonic wars and the temporary shift in farming emphasis from the traditional livestock interests to intensive crop production. This expansionary phase was followed after the early nineteenth century by sustained depopulation and relatively stagnant economic conditions. The Great Famine of 1845-7 was a major setback but only the worst of a succession of famines which highlighted the acute pressure of rapid population growth upon the island's resources. Massive emigration and population decline in the nineteenth century seems to reflect not only the famine but a fundamental failure of the Irish economy to industrialise and urbanise on a scale sufficient to provide employment for its rapidly expanding labour force. There was, save in the north-east, no major transformation of the economy; not only was the industrial revolution abortive but the established small-scale manufacturing enterprises, many of them in rural areas, withered away. The rural economy was thus deprived of the stimulus of a growing and prosperous home market.

Economic Expansion and Landscape Development, AD 1600 to AD 1840
The rural landscape went through its most formative evolutionary phase in the earlier period of economic and population growth, and, owing to the subsequent decline, landscape features survived relatively unchanged down to present times. During the expansionary phase, agriculture in Ireland, as throughout most parts of Western Europe, changed considerably, becoming more commercialised and scientifically based than hitherto. Irish landlords,

interested in their large compact estates as sources of income, were often major instruments of change, attempting to introduce new methods of land management and patterns of landholding. Along with farmers, they improved the land and reclaimed new tracts by clearance and drainage. There was considerable variation in the energy devoted to these enterprises and some landowners and their tenants appeared indifferent to progress. While agricultural improvement was the main basis of economic growth, expansion of the old urban centres, such as Dublin, Cork, Limerick and Waterford, also served as a stimulus to development in their broad rural hinterlands.

A clear indication of the growth of rural population and prosperity was the emergence of a network of new service centres and routeways in the countryside between the old and widely separated medieval towns. Major landlords frequently built small well-planned towns and villages to serve as the commercial foci of their estates. Some of these were on the sites of decayed medieval centres but more often they were entirely new settlements completely owned by the landlord. Estate settlements did not contain farms but accommodated estate workers and tradesmen providing services for the surrounding countryside. Encouraged by the landlords, a network of roads and canals grew up to link together the new centres. Moreover, many small settlements sprang up spontaneously at crossroads and nodal points in the ramifying road system, further to provide the elementary services demanded by a rural community growing in size and living well above mere subsistence level. Such spontaneous growths lack the planned, ordered appearance of estate settlements, consisting usually only of a few houses, shops and a Roman Catholic church. Both planned and spontaneous settlements however, although essentially urban in their functions, are integral parts of the countryside and usually village-like in their scale and somnolent life.

One of the most important changes in the landscape since the seventeenth century has been the spread of field enclosures, a lengthy process gathering momentum in the eighteenth and early nineteenth centuries but not completed in some remote parts of the country until the twentieth century. In contrast with earlier open landscapes, the present farmed land is almost everywhere divided into rectilinear fields separated by permanent divisions or enclosures, most commonly formed by banks of stone and sod or, less frequently, dry stone walls. Where hedges exist they usually grow on the banks. Spreading with remarkable uniformity over all the cultivated land, enclosed fields are the dominant features of the cultural or human landscape, distinguishing the Irish countryside from many rural areas of Europe where the farmed land is open and undivided. Formed during a period of much higher rural population density and to meet the needs of small-scale

Farm landscape enclosed by hedgerows and banks – West Wicklow/Kildare borders. (photo: Frederic Aalen)

Westport House, Co. Mayo. (photo: Bord Failte)

unmechanised agriculture, Irish fields are often unsuited to modern farming methods, particularly where topographical controls or various historical factors have distorted them into irregular inconvenient shapes.

Some field banks and walls are doubtless ancient and their purpose obscure but the new field network was mainly formed to facilitate mixed arable and livestock production, crop rotations and individual management of consolidated holdings. The new regular subdivisions often replaced older systems of open-field organisation with intermixed holdings, the narrowness and curved boundaries of the enclosed fields sometimes reflecting the earlier patterns of strip holdings. The most regular enclosures occur on newly reclaimed hillsides and bogs. Erection of field boundaries and the ditching and draining of the land were often complementary operations.

Lazy-beds

The evolution of rural settlement patterns was closely linked to that of fields. Old nucleated villages of the Pale and the traditional farm clusters of the Irish areas, both of which had been the foci of open-field systems, lost their basic purpose and were either abandoned or at best survived in a reduced form. Rural settlement became increasingly dispersed, a trend encouraged not only by land consolidation and enclosure but also through piecemeal colonisation of wasteland, the building of new road networks and a generally increased sense of security. Different forces thus combined to produce the present typical rural settlement pattern of single dispersed farms connected by a lengthy network of roads and lanes. Ancient farm clusters now survive only in scattered localities bypassed by the forces of improvement, although sometimes where clusters were small, land consolidation could be achieved without much farm dispersal.

Rural depopulation since the famine period has considerably reduced the number of small farms and labourers' cabins but the medium and large farms were relatively little affected. Thus, most of the landscape retained its earlier pattern of farms and fields. Successive Land Acts, passed from the 1880s to the 1920s, transferred farm ownership from landlords to tenants and this new fixity of ownership has further contributed to the continuity of landscape features.

There is considerable local and regional variety in the development of fields and farms. In the richer lowlands of the east, the enclosures and dispersed farms appear to be older on the whole than in the west. Piecemeal enclosure appears to have commenced in the middle ages but it was generally confined to the arable areas around villages. Eastern farms also tend to be larger and their fields more extensive in area and regular in outline. In the west of Ireland, farms were smaller, major landlords fewer, and towns fewer and smaller in size. Modernisation of the western landscape was commenced by the landlords, but from the end of the nineteenth century government agencies played a major role. The Congested Districts Board, for example, between 1891 and 1923 undertook numerous agrarian reorganisation schemes, generally along the lines pioneered by landlords. Old farm clusters with intermixed holdings were much reduced. On the lowlands reorganised holdings were normally laid out in blocks and an even spread of farms produced. On hillsides holdings tended to be rearranged in narrow parallel strips running down the slopes, and so termed ladder farms, with farmsteads conveniently relocated in a linear manner along new roads and tracks. The experience of northeastern Ireland was broadly comparable to that of the west. At the end of the eighteenth century only the richer lowlands such as the Lagan valley, had been influenced by enclosure. In the first half of the nineteenth century far-reaching changes occurred, usually under the auspices of landlords; farms were dispersed from the old farm clusters and the landscape enclosed in small fields surrounded by hedged banks. Farm clusters and vestigial open-field organisation have survived only in a few remote localities.

Land reclamation and settlement expansion
Post-plantation economic and population growth and increasing interest in the improvement of farming methods led to reclamation and settlement of waste land, forest and bog. At the end of the middle ages Ireland was, relative to England, well wooded. The fertile eastern part of the country had been largely deforested but wild woodland still occurred in the north-east, south and west of the country. The commonest type of woodland was described as 'shrubby'. Particularly widespread on the rocky limestone areas, such as east Galway and east Clare, it was probably a survival of prehistoric hazel woods.

By the beginning of the eighteenth century the countryside had been virtually cleared of woods, and the treeless landscape was frequently commented on by visitors to the country. Cleared land was usually used as rough grazing for the expanding livestock industry but initial clearance and felling was undertaken for a variety of reasons. Woods provided refuges for outlaws and rebels and thus were sometimes cleared for security and military reasons. The provision of timber for building, for barrel staves and for iron smelting, which used charcoal as a fuel, led to rapid clearance in many hill areas. Much of Slieve Bloom in Laois-Offaly, for example, was wooded until late in the seventeenth and early eighteenth century but eventually cleared to supply fuel for local ironworks. The great oak forests of south Wicklow, which still flourished in the late sixteenth century, were plundered for timber and industrial fuel. Considerable inroads were also made into the Killarney woods for charcoal burning. In Ulster, plantation and colonisation greatly accelerated the pace of forest removal for timber and farmed land.

Irish woods were often clear-felled and there seems to have been little effort to manage woodland as a renewable resource. As the forest resources dwindled, the timber and iron industries declined and, eventually, died. The widespread availability of peat for domestic fuel may have encouraged thoughtless and complete clearance of woodland. Some ancient woods may have been incorporated in seventeenth and eighteenth century demesne plantations but they have not been identified. Sites of woods eventually became ordinary farmland and left few traces of their former presence, not even old trees surviving along the field boundaries.

Not only the natural vegetation cover had to be cleared to create new farm land but also the boulders and large stones frequently found in the soils. Stony material was laboriously built into the field boundaries, where it is now usually concealed by sods and vegetation. Sometimes, however, it was piled up in mounds or clearance cairns, which provided a ready source of material for later walling and building. Many of these clearance features survive, especially on the margins of improved land. Some cairns are ancient features, however, perhaps related to prehistoric reclamation, while large cairns in prominent positions beyond the limits of worked land are in most cases prehistoric burial mounds or territorial markers.

Population growth and the need for more farmland led, especially in the west of Ireland, to piecemeal encroachment by landless people onto rough hillsides, commons, boglands and offshore islands. The old upland pastures, or booleys, for example, traditionally used in summer months by transhumant herders, were frequently settled on a permanent basis. From the seventeenth century onwards the potato became a major element in the diet of the poorer elements of rural society, whose numbers were multiplying rapidly. Able to thrive in thin acid soils, the plant played a crucial role in the process of population growth and settlement expansion. Impoverished communities grew up living off the land at bare subsistence level and heavily dependent on potatoes for their food. During the nineteenth century such marginal communities were severely affected by emigration and the existence of many is now marked only by ruined cottages and overgrown fields containing old spade-formed potato ridges, or 'lazy beds', often well above the present limits of cultivation.

Not only was the area of farmed land expanded, its productive capacity was much enhanced by a variety of new methods. Drainage projects accompanied the most impressive landlord improvements of the eighteenth and nineteenth centuries and were important in the eastern areas, where they tended to reinforce the natural superiority of the soils. Early drainage enterprises were undertaken by private landowners, but arterial drainage schemes were given public support from the 1840s and widely carried out as relief schemes during the aftermath of the Great Famine. New materials and fertilisers were used by farmers to alter and improve the soils. The wide distribution of eighteenth and nineteenth century limekilns is evidence of the application of lime to counteract soil acidity. Most of the kilns are substantial circular stone structures which sometimes continued in use until the introduction of modern chemical fertilisers. Sand and seaweed have long been applied to the soils of coastal areas. Coastal reclamation was not carried out on any large scale but in scattered locations, such as the Wexford slobs and the shores of Lough Foyle, salt marshes and tidal mudflats were converted to farmland by embanking and drainage, mainly in the nineteenth century.

Demesne landscapes

In the eighteenth and nineteenth centuries a system of large landed estates embraced the whole country. Although the system has been almost completely dissolved, major elements of the rural scene are residual from the time when it flourished. In many areas the quality and character of the countryside is largely owing to landlord enterprises, including the pattern of the fields and the planned location of farms, routes, deciduous woods and lines of trees. The old demesnes, which were the cores of the estates, remain, even in their decay, some of the most distinctive and picturesque elements of the landscape. Often defined by high walls, their characteristic components are great houses with extensive outbuildings set in parkland with ornamental trees, gardens and lakes. No longer distorted by defensive considerations, the architecture of the upper classes flourished and many elegant demesne houses were built, mainly in Georgian style. The ornamental hardwoods planted in the demesnes were the first steps in the reafforestation of the Irish landscape. A fringe of substantial farms was often associated with a large demesne. Some wealthy estate owners developed small villages and towns close to the demesne, indeed often at the gates. The short period during which these settlements were built and the assured, uniform architectural standards of the time help to explain the similarities in their appearance. The typical arrangement is a single main street lined with two- or three-storied buildings in a demure Georgian style, a market square and market hall, and a Protestant church. Some of the larger settlements, however, such as Birr, Co. Offaly, Westport, Co. Mayo and Mitchelstown, Co. Cork, have a more elaborate layout and architecture. A standard range of landscape features thus give the demesne localities a distinctive character which is in considerable contrast to the surrounding areas dominated by modest farms.

The influence of estate organisation is ubiquitous but uneven in its distribution. It is most evident in Ulster and north Leinster with important concentrations in Kilkenny, Laois-Offaly, the Wicklow-Wexford borders and the great river valleys of Munster. The slopes of major river valleys such as the Boyne, Liffey and Blackwater provided vistas and were particularly favoured locations for demesne houses. Lake and lough shores were also favoured. In Ulster, for example, gentry houses are numerous on Lough Erne, Lough Neagh, the Clogher valley, and the shores of Loughs Swilly and Foyle. In the west of Ireland estates were often extensive but there were fewer of them and the small farms of the native Irish dominated the landscape. Demesnes, however, were numerous in east Galway and on the Limerick lowlands.

The closer framework of estates in the east of the country contributed to the more orderly nature of the rural landscape, which even strong population growth was unable seriously to disrupt. Although agricultural labourers were increasing in number, some could be absorbed on the large farms or move to employment in the relatively numerous towns. Smallholdings and cabins proliferated on the roadsides and hill margins but the orderly framework of the improved landscape remained intact. In the west demographic pressures were stronger and had more marked impact on the landscape. Population increase led to uncontrolled subdivision of the already small farms and increasing fragmentation of the intermixed holdings. Settlement spread into poor inhospitable territories, such as Connemara and offshore islands, usually in a piecemeal unplanned manner. Landlord rural reorganisation in the west came relatively late; it was often abrupt and radical but did not extend to all areas, so that reform of the farm structure was often carried out belatedly by state bodies such as the Congested Districts Board and the Irish Land Commission.

Landlordism was weakened by the Great Famine and, following the widespread agrarian unrest of 1879-1882, legislation was introduced to transfer the holdings to tenants, a process which took several decades to complete. The great houses were increasingly abandoned by their owners and the demesnes have suffered general neglect and sometimes destruction.

Mining and Quarrying

A variety of minerals have been worked in Ireland at many stages in history but they proved of small significance for modern industrial growth. Ironworks were numerous in the seventeenth century but most of them closed in the course of the eighteenth century, owing mainly to the exhaustion of forest reserves and British competition. In the nineteenth century copper and lead were the major interest but mining experienced a general decline in the 1880s, owing to foreign competition and exhaustion of easily worked deposits. Copper mining prospered for a short period in the mid nineteenth century. It was worked extensively in association with iron in the Vale of Avoca in Co. Wicklow, where a variety of mineral workings have had considerable impact on the landscape. The coastal areas of Waterford, and south-west Cork and Kerry also possessed significant copper resources and mines. Lead is widely distributed but the Wicklow Mountains were the major source area and the remote mountain glens contain numerous traces of past lead mining. Small-scale intermittent mining of the country's scattered coal resources has taken place since the seventeenth century, with a noteworthy expansion in the nineteenth century. The Castlecomer plateau in Kilkenny was the major coal mining area, with minor centres in the Ballycastle area, Co. Antrim and Coalisland, Co. Tyrone. Sporadic abandoned workings and tips occur but nowhere is the landscape dominated by coal workings and colliery settlements.

Domestic Industry

There was considerable growth of rural industry in the eighteenth and early nineteenth century, much of it small-scale domestic enterprise. Landlords often encouraged manufacturing, not only in the estate towns but in the countryside because of the high dependence on water power. The dense rural population provided cheap labour and a market but much produce was exported. Domestic spinning and weaving of linen, mainly by women, spread in the late eighteenth century, most widely among the small farmers of south Ulster and north Connacht. It was a supplement to the main business of farming and provided a major source of off-farm income, allowing diminution in the size of holdings and even heavier densities of rural population. Farmers grew their own flax and the yarn was woven by the women and also bleached at home. Linen production was later attracted to the towns and by the 1840s had become largely a factory industry. Today the main relics of the cottage industry are clumps of wild flax and abandoned weavers' cottages attached to bleach greens. Domestic woollen manufacturing was also widespread and a number of woollen mills operated in Munster in the eighteenth century. Pottery, glass and leather manufacturing occurred too on a small scale.

A variety of agricultural industries grew up including corn milling. The largest enterprises were in major towns but many hundreds of small cornmills and corn-kilns were scattered over the countryside, mainly along rural rivers and streams. Distilling, much of it illicit, flourished in the countryside. Small breweries were numerous too, but only the larger successful ones in the towns continued to work after Father Mathew's temperance campaign of the 1830s and 1840s and the Great Famine.

This early phase of manufacturing ended with the general rural decline of the nineteenth century and the growth of urban factory production. Few of the early enterprises survived into the twentieth century and their major legacy is a scatter of ruined installations in the countryside, such as water-wheels, windmills, kilns and mills. On the other hand, the new settlements established by landlords to invigorate commercial life on their estates had an enduring influence as markets and service centres for the surrounding farming communities. The nineteenth century industrial revolution had a modest outcome in Ireland; it had little impact on the countryside and was confined largely to the north-east and a few major urban centres. However, significant developments occurred in communications which influenced the rural landscape.

Communications
The close and complex communication network is an important element of the rural landscape, especially in the lowlands. In the seventeenth century Irish roads were few and neglected but in the eighteenth and nineteenth centuries road patterns were revolutionised and an elaborate system grew up to link old and new settlements and to serve the diffuse patterns of settlement and a population much larger than at present. There was a rapid development of turnpike trusts in the 1730s and 1740s and later in the century the Grand Juries (bodies of landowners providing local government within the baronies) undertook road building on a considerable scale. Often following remarkably straight courses, Grand Jury roads are clearly the product of planning, and contrast with the older evolved road network which is a maze of winding roads closely adjusted to local topography.

Road building continued in the nineteenth century, some of it famine relief work. Ambitious road projects were carried out in mountainous areas. Some were for military purposes, as in the Wicklow Mountains after the 1798 rebellion. Others were connected with landlord schemes to provide access to upland bog resources and permit the transport of lime for reclamation projects.

New road systems had important effects on rural settlement patterns. Farms and cottages were increasingly located along the new roads, reducing the significance of the traditional nucleated rural settlements. Moreover, old settlements through which roads passed were often re-orientated to become street-like in plan.

Encouraged by the low relief of central Ireland, canal building was energetically pursued in the eighteenth and early nineteenth centuries. The primary objective was to link Dublin with the Shannon and the Atlantic.

This was achieved by the construction of the Royal Canal, 1789-1817, and the Grand Canal, 1756-1804. In Ulster, Lough Neagh became the focus of the new waterways. Irish canals were unable to compete with the later railway network and fell into disuse. Moreover, they did not stimulate settlement growth to any great extent. The substantial canal bridges, locks and harbours, however, have survived, as well as the derelict canal hotels, and the lock cottages, many of which are still inhabited.

A network of railways developed from the 1830s onwards, serving the whole island but closer in the more populated and urbanised north and tending to avoid poorer western districts. The railways were expected to break the isolation of remote towns in rural areas and facilitate new industrial growth, but their main effect was to centralise economic life in major cities, especially Dublin and Belfast, and to extinguish the canals. At the end of the nineteenth century state-subsidised light railways were extended into remote western areas. They were short-lived, being unable to compete with improved roads and motor traffic. Among other things, however, they conveyed tourists to the picturesque Atlantic seaboard and the hotels built at their terminals were the germs of the modern tourism industry in western Ireland. Many of the remaining railways were abandoned in the twentieth century and their only traces are old cuttings and embankments and derelict stations.

Rural buildings: farms, cottages and cabins, churches, schools, creameries
Ordinary farmhouses before 1700 were insubstantial and built with perishable materials, and few if any have survived. In the eighteenth and most of the nineteenth century, the farming population dwelt mainly in humble single-storey thatched houses with rectangular plans, characteristically one-room in width and divided laterally into two or three rooms. Local building materials were used, mud and stone for the walls and straw and reeds for thatching. Whitewashing of walls spread in the late nineteenth century, mainly for hygienic purposes.

There were regional variations in house style. In Leinster and east Munster hip-ended thatched roofs were characteristic, with a two-roomed ground plan and centrally located hearth and door. Mud was a common building material. On larger farms there were more substantial two-storey houses, sometimes based on the central-hearth model. These were frequently replaced, especially in the nineteenth century, by Georgian style houses with two or three storeys and slated hip-ended roofs. In western Ireland the basic dwelling house type was the byre-dwelling, or 'long-house'. It was stone built and gable-ended, with humans and animals living at opposite ends of an undivided chamber, which had opposite doors. The hearth was located

Irish cottages.
(photo: Frederic Aalen)
(b) (photo: RTE)

(a) Farm labourer's cabin,
Wicklow Hills; (b) Thatched,
gable-ended farmhouses,
West Donegal; (c) Thatched,
hip-ended farmhouse, Co.
Meath; (d) Labourer's cottage,
Wicklow Co. Council; (e)
Labourer's cottage, Meath Co.
Council; (f) Modern
bungalow-type residence,
Co. Mayo.

(a)

(b)

(c)

(d)

(e)

(f)

Typical rural national school in Co. Mayo. (photo: Frederic Aalen)

Church of Ireland church, Dromahair, Co. Leitrim. (photo: Desmond Gillmor)

Post-emancipation Roman Catholic church, Hollywood, Co. Wicklow. (photo: Frederic Aalen)

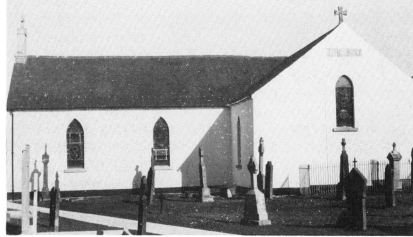

towards the gable end. Many of these primitive structures were improved at the end of the nineteenth century; cattle were moved to outbuildings and the houses were divided into different rooms, with the former byre converted to a bedroom. Ulster contained houses of both western and eastern type. In the lowlands the standard house type was of two rooms with a central chimney, but numerous comfortable two-storey houses were built by better-off farmers. In the hill areas single-storey unicellular dwellings with gable hearths were common, often accommodating people and livestock as in the west of Ireland.

Farms usually possess a range of outbuildings grouped in a variety of ways. Usually they are unimpressive structures, although some of the largest farms have elaborate barns, stables, granaries and cartsheds arranged around courtyards. In south-eastern Ireland the house and farm buildings, even on holdings of modest size, are often grouped around a yard but many old farms exhibit no regular layout of buildings. In the north and west of the country older farmyards typically form a long range of buildings, with house, stable and byre joined together, an arrangement which has evolved directly from the long-house. Agricultural modernisation has introduced larger buildings and barns, new building materials often including metal, and farmsteads everywhere are tending to assume a loose, often linear arrangement to facilitate the use of tractors and bulky machinery.

Small cottiers and landless rural labourers were very numerous in the early nineteenth century. Save where landlords had provided improved and sometimes picturesque cottages for their workers, the labourers lived in primitive, one- or two-roomed 'cabins', many even lacking doors and windows. Massive emigration of the rural poor led to abandonment of most of the cabins by the end of the nineteenth century. In some places no trace of the cabins remains but often their foundations survive in remarkable profusion. Occasionally old cabins in out-of-the-way places survived as residences until the 1960s but today they are almost extinct. From the 1880s onwards, legislation enabled the local authorities to demolish cabins and rehouse many of the labourers in new solid 'cottages' of brick or stone with slate roofs, scattered along the roadsides on small holdings of 0.2 hectares. This, the first major public housing enterprise in the British Isles, had most effect in Leinster and east Munster where by 1921 40,000 cottages had been built. Simultaneously in western Ireland the Congested Districts Board provided new houses for the impoverished small farmers and encouraged the improvement of many unhygienic byre-dwellings. The widespread distribution of early public housing is one of the distinguishing features of the Irish countryside. After 1921 the local authorities and the Land Commission continued to build small houses for rural labourers and smallholders.

Left: The Water Carriers. (photo: Bord Failt)

Below: Milk cart, Co. Mayo.
(photo: Bord Failte)

The house is the element of the Irish landscape which has perhaps changed most since the famine period; certainly in most areas the framework of fields and the settlement patterns have altered little. Considerable improvement and rebuilding of thatched houses took place during the relatively prosperous decades of the 1850s and 1860s when the cattle trade flourished. Second storeys and slated roofs were often added to houses. The Land Acts and peasant proprietorship at the end of the nineteenth century unfortunately coincided with deep agricultural recession, so that large-scale housing improvements were restrained. Throughout the twentieth century traditional thatched dwellings have been steadily replaced. In recent decades many rural families have built new houses, chiefly bungalows, in urban styles. Older houses, where they survive, are frequently relegated to use as storehouses or byres. Among country dwellers there is little evidence of concern or enthusiasm for the modernisation and preservation of old houses.

Although farms are the most numerous rural settlement features, the churches are the most prominent buildings and, with the exception of estate houses and buildings, the most substantial. Churches are often associated with denominational schools, graveyards, church halls and the residences of the incumbents, either a Church of Ireland rectory or a Roman Catholic parochial house. Most medieval churches are now ruinous and often isolated from modern settlements. A few, however, have continued in use as places of worship by the Church of Ireland which became the established church after the Reformation. A major wave of building by the Church of Ireland took place in the early nineteenth century supported by government grants. The motives were political as well as religious, an attempt to equip, and assert the presence of, the Protestant minority who made up only a tenth of the total population. Many of the older parish churches were abandoned and replaced by new 'toy-like Gothic churches' of the 'tower and hall' variety and very similar throughout the country. A further wave of church building occurred after the disestablishment of the Church of Ireland in 1870. Rapid decline of the rural Protestant population in the Republic of Ireland since Independence has led to reorganisation of Church of Ireland parishes and disuse of many churches. Presbyterians and Methodists, while rare in the countryside of southern Ireland, are common in the north where both denominations use mainly hall churches of undemonstrative Classical style.

Catholic church building in the sixteenth and seventeenth centuries was very limited but towards the end of the eighteenth century, as the Penal Laws were relaxed, building activity quickened. At first the churches were few, modest and simple, but in the nineteenth century, especially after Catholic Emancipation, foundations were more numerous, the buildings larger and styles more ostentatious. The Gothic Revival style was most popular. Early churches were long halls, with the altar on one of the longer sides, sometimes converted to a T-shape by the addition of a new nave. Later, the fashion changed to a more elaborate Gothic, with the altar at the end of the long nave, although sometimes Classical styles were used. In the twentieth century there has been experimentation with a variety of styles.

Schools are numerous in the countryside, since rural education has traditionally been organised on a parochial basis with separate Catholic and Protestant schools, usually located near their respective churches. Primary schools, which are the most numerous, are usually domestic in scale, single-storey rectangular buildings built to simple standard styles which varied only slightly over many years. With declining rural populations and improved transportation, many small schools were closed, some converted to dwellings and others abandoned. In recent decades selected schools have been appreciably modernised and enlarged or replaced by new schools as part of the rationalisation of educational facilities.

Creameries were widely distributed in rural areas, notably in the Munster lowlands and the north. They were organised on a co-operative basis and were the earliest major form of modern rural industry. They originated in the Golden Vale of Tipperary in the 1880s and many more were established before the end of the century. Invariably the creameries were elementary rectangular buildings of little architectural attraction. Most of the small units were closed as milk processing became concentrated into large expanded plants.

Ogham Stone

PLACENAMES

Placenames are some of the most durable elements of the countryside and properly studied can make a useful contribution to understanding of the earlier condition of the landscape and changes in it. However, the study of placenames is fraught with difficulty and requires expert handling. Most official placenames, it seems, have at least medieval or early modern origins. Some names may well be very much older, especially those applied to rivers, lakes and mountains, which could be corruptions of pre Celtic names. The majority of rural placenames are of Gaelic origin but have been anglicised and their meaning often obscured. Even the great upheavals of the seventeenth century plantations generally led to anglicisation of extant Gaelic names, although some new ones were added. Many placenames were standardised and sometimes distorted in English when the Ordnance Survey carried out detailed official mapping of the whole country in the nineteenth century.

Above: But for the last ice-age, this scene in the Burren, Co. Clare, could be typical of much of rural Ireland. The limestone rock-base has been greatly enriched by the layer of glacial drift deposited over much of Ireland.

Right: A young schoolgirl comes to terms with the clints and grikes of the limestone pavement of the Burren, Co. Clare.

Above and opposite: Studies of colour and detail from the Mt. Usher Gardens, Co. Wicklow. *Below:* The soft Irish rain, so fabled in conversation and writing, merges easily with a cobweb on a demesne wall near Kenmare, Co. Kerry.

The 'Giant's Rocks' are part of our glacial history. East of Kenmare, Co. Kerry. *Above*: A huge erratic (a rock carried out of its natural location by ice) of limestone resting on a sandstone ridge. *Below*: A capstone of sandstone sitting on a pedestal of limestone.

The most common placename elements are *raith* or *baile*, anglicised as rath and bally, respectively. Originally *raith* may have been applied only to Celtic earthen forts and *baile* to small clusters of farms, but by the seventeenth century the terms were virtually interchangeable and referred to holdings and settlements in general. Intrusive names are recognisable. Anglo-Norman settlements, for example, often possess the suffix 'town', signifying not an urban settlement but simply a farm or holding. Placenames with a town element are concentrated in the east of the country where the Anglo-Normans were most numerous. Elsewhere, placenames which indicate settlements have elements almost exclusively of Gaelic origin, such as rath, lis, dun and cahir. There are, however, no clearcut territorial distributions and it is known that the town suffix was often replaced by baile in the period of Irish recovery in the fourteenth century. The so-called 'New English' who settled in Ireland during the seventeenth century plantations tended to respect pre-existing territorial divisions and use their old names, albeit in anglicised form. This indeed is a characteristic practice of immigrant communities in their new country. Diagnostic new placename elements of the period include demesne, mount, court, park, ville, close, brook and lawn, revealing the interest of the new settlers in prestige residences and attractive living environments.

Many rural placenames obviously refer to the physical characteristics of the locality, for example Knockbeg (little hill), Slievecorragh (rocky mountain), Dromore (big ridge) and Glenlahan (wide glen). Often, however, names describe features long since disappeared. Numerous townland names, for example, begin with derry (*doire*, oak wood), implying the former existence of an oakwood, or with ros (*ros*, wood). Such names are useful evidence in the reconstruction of landscape history. A substantial group of placenames refers to settlements, both secular and ecclesiastical, ranging from churches and monasteries to raths and farm clusters. The early church in particular left a rich legacy of placenames. Many include the elements kil (*ceall*, small church), disert (*diseart*, hermitage), and temple (*teampall*, church), usually followed by an adjective (Kilmore, the big church) or the name of a saint (Kilcolman, the church of St. Colman). Early land use may also be hinted at. The element boley (*buaile*) usually implies the former existence of a summer transhumant settlement, cloghan (*clochan*) a dry-masonry hut, cappagh (*ceapach*) a tillage plot, gort (*gort*) a tillage field, and clon (*cluain*) a meadow. Almost every field was given an individual name by local farmers but the names do not appear on official maps and seem to be mainly of eighteenth or nineteenth century origin, consistent with the recency of enclosure in many areas.

THREATS TO THE HISTORICAL HERITAGE

In the Irish countryside there is perhaps the densest concentration of surviving field monuments of any country in Europe. On the first Ordnance Survey maps, published in the 1840s, a total of about 100,000 ancient monuments and sites was shown. These included about 40,000 raths and cashels, approximately 3,000 ancient ecclesiastical sites (churches, monasteries, graveyards etc.) and a roughly equal number of castles and tower houses. The remaining sites included megalithic tombs, standing stones and cairns. However, the total number of field monuments has never been clearly established. The Ordnance Survey certainly was not exhaustive and it is likely that the national archaeological and architectural heritage from the prehistoric, early Christian and medieval periods comprised between 150,000 and 200,000 monuments.

Destruction rates prior to the 1840s are hard to assess because of the absence of reliable records, but modern field surveys show that many sites recorded on the first Ordnance Survey maps have been destroyed and at an accelerating rate in recent decades. Agricultural intensification has been the main cause but also peat production, forestry, urban expansion, quarrying and road construction. One of the consequences of agricultural change has been the removal of field enclosures and modification of field patterns, some of deep historical significance. For example, around the old villages in the hinterland of Dublin the long narrow fields which are relics of medieval open-field systems frequently have been built over, and in the Burren in Co. Clare prehistoric field boundaries have been obliterated in land clearance operations. It is estimated that about 15 per cent of field boundaries have been removed in recent decades and the losses are higher in certain areas. Most of the recent damage, however, has been to ancient earthworks, primarily the raths and moated enclosures, which often have been swept away in land improvement schemes by heavy mechanical earth-moving equipment. Yet all categories of archaeological sites have suffered, with overall rates of destruction in most counties varying from a third to half of the total number of sites. At present rates of destruction, the rich heritage of the Irish countryside will have been reduced by the end of the century to a pitiful remnant.

In a country whose rural life and traditions have been so central to the search for national identity, it is remarkable that the rural landscape, which enshrines so much of the island's history, seems to be so poorly understood, generally undervalued and persistently abused by private and public activities. The study and protection of historical landscape features have been undertaken more seriously in Northern Ireland, but destruction there has been substantial nevertheless, owing to the higher levels of population density, urbanisation and intensive land use. In the Republic of Ireland only a small proportion of historic sites are legally protected and even they are molested with impunity. Although many archaeological monuments, especially the raths, had been preserved because of the superstitious reverence of rural folk, this form of protection is rapidly waning and must be promptly replaced by strong legal and official safeguards backed up by educated public opinion. A new perception of the landscape must be encouraged as a major cultural and historical legacy expressing and shaping national and regional identity. Not only young people but all those involved in farm improvement and rural development work must be made aware of the richness and diversity of the monuments and sites of archaeological and historical significance in the countryside and of the urgent need to preserve them.

It cannot be overemphasised that conservation makes commercial sense. Abundant evidence shows that the traditional countryside is a substantial economic asset because of its visual and historical attraction for tourists and its importance as a setting for educational activities. Fuller recording of historic landscape features, more effective protection and better presentation to the public through improved signposting, access, and on-site interpretation facilities would permit wider and more profitable use of landscape resources. It is essential that conservation concerns are not confined to individual sites and buildings but broadened to embrace the totality of the rural landscape.

Jerpoint Abbey

Top left: Ulster Folk Museum: A forge from Lisrase, Co. Tyrone; a bleachgreen watch-hut from Tullytish and a Weaver's House from Ballyduggan, both in Co. Down. (photo: Ulster Folk Museum)

Above: St. Kieran, on the road side near Killybegs. (photo: Jan de Fouw)

Left: Traditional cottage, modern living, Co. Galway. (photo: Jan de Fouw)

Folklife and Folk Traditions

olklife is the study of life and culture but primarily it examines cultures which are still alive, relating elements of them to past and forgotten practices, observing how new elements are either accepted or rejected and how culture changes through the years. Folklife is a Scandinavian concept which in its application to the study of the intimate and domestic history of Irish rural areas has contributed much to understanding the people in the countryside.

History is a continuum and in recent decades Irish rural society has witnessed dramatic and unprecedented changes. Older people with good memories and active minds are still the most valuable source of information about folktales and songs, old customs and traditions, knowledge of crafts and agricultural machinery, and other aspects of life in the past. They deserve the utmost attention, for, once buried in the soil, their knowledge of an undocumented way of life can never be dug up again. Not all things in everyday use by ordinary people had great antiquity. Many items of household furniture, including chairs, beds and domestic items such as forks, kettles and pans, were introduced at various stages throughout the centuries. The patterns used in the now world-famous Aran style knitting are less than a century old. Traditional forms of rural vernacular architecture have only a tenuous continuity from earlier times in that they formed shelter and homes. The great advantage of the folklife approach and the aspect of the study which gives it its widest scope, involves going for evidence to the living community. Not only does this enable information and objects to be acquired but the ways in which certain items are made can be seen and recorded on film. It is an approach which also clearly illustrates that folklife is not concerned solely with the past and that it is in the acceptance of new ideas that continuity is maintained.

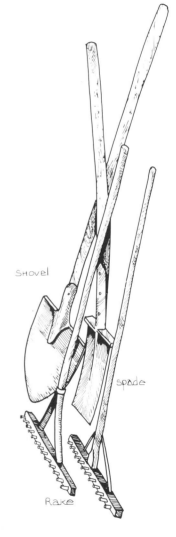

SHovel

SpAde

Rake

FARMING PRACTICES

Agricultural innovations
A remarkable feature in the development of Irish agriculture during the past

Left: Kieran Darcy and his son Kieran, ploughing in Clonascra, Clonfinlough, Co. Offaly in 1981. (photo: National Museum of Ireland - Dublin)

Below: A view of the 'meitheal' after the threshing with a horse threshing machine at Clonascra, Clonfinlough, Co. Offaly in 1965. (photo: National Museum of Ireland - Dublin)

two hundred years has been the introduction and slow diffusion of new implements, machinery and ideas alongside the retention, improvement and adaptation of older implements and methods which have been practised for centuries. When the agriculture of a country is in an undeveloped and backward state, and when the majority of those working on the land consists of very small landholders, small tenant farmers and landless labourers, a very limited range of implements of simple and basic construction is used. This was true of Irish farming at the beginning of the twentieth century and it was not until the widespread diffusion of the tractor on Irish farms after the second world war that farming was gradually modernised.

In every aspect of farming practices, from the beginning of the agricultural year in the spring to the harvesting of crops in the autumn and early winter, it is possible to see how improvements were accepted, or rejected, and how farming techniques developed. It was a slow business which began to take effect in the eighteenth century, especially with the establishment of the Royal Dublin Society in 1731, through which ideas and information were gathered and disseminated among landowners and farmers. From the 1770s, machinery from Irish foundries and imported improved products began to appear. Pierce of Wexford was in production in the 1830s. By the mid nineteenth century, both Sheridan and Paul and Vincent of Dublin, Ritchie of Ardee, Co. Louth, Grey of Belfast and Hanson of Antrim were manufacturing a wide variety of agricultural machinery. This included ploughs, harrows, rollers, seed drills, turnip sowers, winnowers, threshers and potato diggers. Mowing machines, reapers and, by the 1880s, binders were imported.

Cultivation
Except in areas where winter wheat was grown, the farmer's year began in the springtime with the preparation of the land for sowing crops. The main implements necessary for the principal cultivation work on small farms involved just three, a spade, a rake and a shovel. On those farms which were large enough to employ horse power, the essential tillage implements included plough, harrow and roller. On lands worked by improving landlords in the nineteenth century and gradually as farming became more modernised in the twentieth century, further implements and machines were added as circumstances allowed.

Of the implements still in use on Irish farms, the plough is one of the oldest and the modifications made to it mirror the development of Irish agriculture during the past two hundred years. Ploughs have been in use in Ireland for several centuries but little is known about the early types. No complete plough from a period earlier than the eighteenth century has come to light but it is known, from the evidence of numerous plough socs and coulters in museum collections, that at least one version of the common old Irish plough was a heavy and unwieldy implement. It was claimed to be inefficient and required not only the ploughman but also a man to lead the horses and another who, with the aid of a forked stick, kept the plough in the ground. Improved plough designs came from America and Britain but by the early twentieth century the Scottish swing plough was the most popular. Its easily adjustable draught, operated by the plough handles, suited both hilly and uneven surfaces. Later a great variety of plough types was produced.

Despite the many improvements to plough design, there was great resistance to change from the old cumbersome plough. The new implements not only required more skill to manufacture and use but also they reduced the number of people needed to operate them. Ploughing teams involving three or four workers had existed among some families for generations. There is evidence that neighbours and family members joined together for ploughing operations from at least the seventh century and that co-tenants co-operated with each other for mutual assistance. The word used to describe this partnership was *comhar* and it referred in general to a match or a union but more particularly to a joint ploughing agreement. Not only did the different members of the plough team have different tasks to perform but also they had to contribute different parts of the ploughing apparatus. Such a system was still prevalent in many parts of Ireland in recent decades when *comhar* agreements existed between two farmers, especially for ploughing and general farm work. The introduction of improved ploughs implied an immediate change in an important facet of social organisation which had existed in rural Ireland for centuries. It is no wonder that the change was only slowly accepted.

Ploughs, the basic function of which is to expose a fresh surface of soil to atmospheric influences, were used from earliest times alongside the spade which has remained the universal digging implement to the present day. There is a greater variety of spades than any other agricultural implement, many examples of which exist in museum collections. In the north of Ireland spade and shovel manufacture was gradually taken over by water powered mills from the mid eighteenth century but, before this time and until well into the nineteenth century elsewhere in the country, spades were made to suit the local soil conditions and the stature of the worker. Despite the great variety of spades used in Ireland, there are clear regional differences in design. For convenience they can be divided into two broad groups, one-sided spades which were used mainly in the south and west and two-sided spades which were more popular in the north and east.

Once the ground was ploughed or dug, it was then prepared for seed

Above: Two men threshing corn by beating it on stones, Aran Islands, *c.* 1890. (photo: National Museum of Ireland - Dublin)

Right: A man winnowing corn with a flat wickerwork basket. The man standing beside him is holding a straw besom or broom. Each of the men is wearing a pair of pampooties. (photo: National Museum of Ireland - Dublin)

Below: A man reaping. (photo: National Museum of Ireland - Dublin)

sowing. Hand tools and labour intensive devices were still very popular at the beginning of the century and labour saving innovations were adopted only slowly. Harrows, for instance, which break the soil in preparation for the seed, have been used in Ireland for at least a thousand years. Early examples consisted of no more than a block of wood to which a set of wooden teeth were attached. Eighteenth and nineteenth century improvements concentrated on making heavier and stronger implements which broke up the soil effectively. A wide range of harrows was developed from the common harrow to the rhomboidal shaped, which consisted of two parts hinged at two points and covering a width of three metres at a time. Drill harrows were employed in the after cultivation of root crops, helping to loosen the ground between rows of plants, and saddle harrows were run over the ground in which potatoes were sown to facilitate growth. In many soils the sod turned over by the plough was only with difficulty loosened with the harrow. To overcome this, the ground was pounded with wooden mallets and iron *grafáins*, a tedious job, the back breaking nature of which was considerably lessened when the horse-drawn grubber or cultivator was introduced.

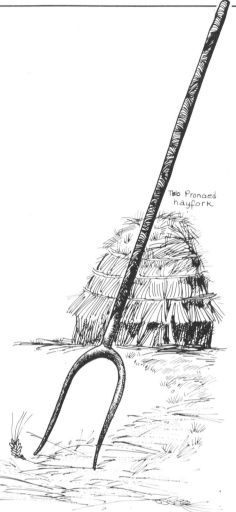

Two Pronged hayfork

On most small farms up to well within living memory, seed was sown broadcast by hand from sheets, goggaring bags and baskets. Seed sowing machines were devised in the early nineteenth century, the first ones being designed for sowing turnips. Improvements concentrated on refining the sowing so that the seed was dropped into drills or rows, making the job of weeding and hoeing much easier.

Harvesting

The harvesting of crops was the most urgent of all farm tasks, to ensure the safe housing of the produce before the onslaught of inclement weather. The first successful reaping machine, developed by Patrick Bell in 1829, was not improved or modified until the 1850s, by the American firm of McCormick. Sickles, reaping hooks and scythes, however, remained the main implements for the harvesting of corn crops until the end of the nineteenth century and each implement had particular advantages. The corn was said to have been left in the best state for binding after it had been cut with a hook or sickle. The scythe was more advantageous from an economic viewpoint because of the greater speed of reaping. The hook was more beneficial when the crop had been damaged and flattened by heavy rain and wind and also on headlands where the worker did not have space in which to swing the scythe.

On small holdings, machines were both impractical and expensive, while the larger farmers still found it more economical to hire temporary labourers

An Aran woman carrying a load of hay on back, *c.* 1900.
(photo: National Museum of Ireland - Dublin)

A man on horseback showing wicker cleeves for transporting seaweed and manure, Coomeenoble, Co. Kerry.
(photo: National Museum of Ireland - Dublin)

Above: A meitheal' of haymakers. (photo: National Museum of Ireland - Dublin)

Right: A haycock lifter swinging cocks onto a cart.
(photo: National Museum of Ireland - Dublin)

with their sickles and reaping hooks until well into the nineteenth century. Reaping hooks have an ancient history, examples having been recovered from Bronze Age sites, while the toothed sickle was introduced in late medieval times. Only when emigration led so many former labourers to seek more lucrative employment abroad from the 1870s onwards, did the farmers begin to re-examine the situation. The scarcity of workers initially led to an improvement in the labourers' wages and conditions. These advantages were shortlived, however, and the continued spiralling of wages prompted many farmers to purchase machines, despite heavy and often violent resistance by labourers, who saw the machines taking away their livelihoods.

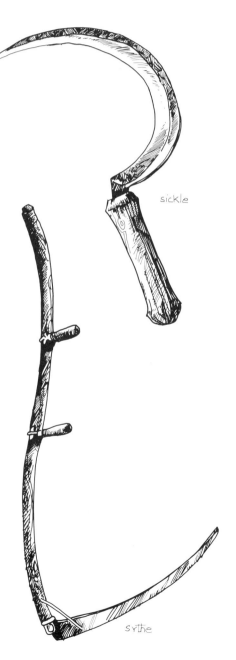

sickle

sythe

Meadows also were mown with smooth-edged hooks. The scythe may have been introduced to Ireland in the twelfth century but it was adapted universally as a popular agricultural implement only in the nineteenth century. Ironically, it was the mower, known in Ireland as the *spealadóir*, who was afforded every respect and became an important member of the farming community. He stood next only to the ploughman as a worker who was attributed with extraordinary skills and stamina, paid the highest wages and given the best food to eat. As it was necessary for a good ploughman to understand the interrelationship of the different parts of the plough, so also was it necessary for a good *spealadóir* to know how to use his implement effectively and to maintain it. The greatest gift which a *spealadóir* had was that of sharpening the scythe blade, or putting up edge, and many stories are told of this aspect of the mower's craft. Some mowers were believed to have special powers by which they never had to sharpen their scythes, while others were believed to be working with supernatural help, usually that of the devil who might appear in the handle of the scythe in the form of an insect.

Haysaving began to be mechanised on the larger farms, especially after the 1860s when mowing machines diffused throughout the country. Turning hay, an operation formerly done with the hands or two-pronged forks, was soon to be superseded by the use of horse-drawn hay tedders. Wooden and horse-drawn hay gatherers or sweeps, commonly called hay paddies, were introduced from America and became popular very quickly, being much cheaper than the iron equivalent from Britain.

Threshing and winnowing operations, that is separating the grain from the straw and the chaff from the grain, were tasks which did not require the same degree of urgency as harvesting, as they could be undertaken in the shelter of barns and outhouses during the winter months. For hundreds of years, the flail was the universal method by which threshing was done. Early prototypes of threshing machines were developed in the eighteenth century but they were cumbersome and costly. Small horse-powered threshing machines were developed in the second half of the nineteenth century and the remains of many can still be seen on Irish farms.

The majority of Irish farmers depended on threshing contractors who travelled around from farm to farm with horse and steam-powered machines which both threshed and winnowed the corn. These men made a good living and were treated well by their clients. The daily charge to the farmer for the use of a machine at the turn of the century was £3, together with payment for the engine driver and his helper and supply of the coal for the engine. There was also the potential cost of paying the other workers who were necessary for the threshing, people to pitch the sheaves on to the platform of the thresher, to untie them, to feed them into the machine and to remove the straw and the sacks of corn and chaff. Fortunately farmers rarely had to meet this latter payment because of the system of co-operative labour which worked so well in rural areas.

flail

sheaves of corn

In addition to the long-established *comhar* agreements amongst farmers for ploughing, a great variety of other co-operative arrangements was practised for both work on the land and other miscellaneous tasks from house building to scutching flax and spinning. *Meitheal* groups of from three to thirty workers convened in most areas of the country to help each other in activities such as cutting turf, saving hay and threshing. Other terms for the co-operation were confined to local areas or specific types of work done. For example, in the Malin area of Co. Donegal, a 'banville' gathered to help the blacksmith to dig his potatoes or bring home his turf. 'Boons' were found only in Ulster, being conspicuously absent further south than Cavan, and they included shearers, flax pullers, threshers and harvesters. In Connemara a group known as a *feidheal* worked at turf cutting. The 'match' in Monaghan and Tyrone referred both to a group of spinners and also to a number of people who had gathered to plough for a needy neighbour.

Supplementary activities

Smallholders and landless labourers were continually on the lookout for alternative employment to supplement their meagre incomes. Some became part-time fishermen, especially those living near the coast. Although fish was an article of trade in Ireland as early as the thirteenth century, both sea and river fishing remained primarily part-time activities until recent decades. The south and west coasts developed an important fishing industry during the late medieval period but this had virtually ceased by the nineteenth century, due to badly maintained ports, inadequate boats and primitive equipment. Herrings were especially abundant in the nineteenth century and there were fish-curing stations at many places along the coast, particularly in the west. The women from the Donegal islands especially were renowned herring gutters and curing station workers who travelled from station to station during the season. Many even went to work in stations along the British coast.

Other men and women supplemented farm incomes by working on the land in areas away from home, as migratory labourers either elsewhere in Ireland or with farmers in Great Britain. Women worked in the tattie fields of Scotland from the 1860s right through until the 1950s, while their menfolk had been making annual work migrations to England since at least the fourteenth century. Seasonal and temporary movements of agricultural workers from Ireland to Britain were undoubtedly well established by the eighteenth century. Then and in the early nineteenth century there was substantial growth as transport facilities and the availability of information about opportunities increased. Equally important had been an internal movement which was predominantly from western areas of Ireland to counties in the east. References to it appear first in the late seventeenth century and, unlike the official documentation of the migration to Great Britain, the evidence survives in the poetry of the time. This internal movement had probably passed its peak by the 1830s, when the higher remuneration expected in Britain far outweighed the advantages of working nearer home.

In one way, annual work migrations can be seen to have aggravated the stagnation of districts in which it remained popular, as the earnings were not invested in improvements but went almost exclusively towards maintaining the subsistence economy. On the other hand, leaving the home area to work elsewhere did have certain advantages. Having the money to pay the rent and the bills was, of course, the basic and fundamental advantage. Links were never broken with the home area, as they would have been through emigration, and the migrants returned with certain innovative attitudes and with new ideas, customs and occasional novel objects acquired on their journeys.

THE BUSINESS LIFE OF THE COUNTRYSIDE

Fairs and markets

As early as the ninth century, the business and social life of the countryside was conducted at assemblies known as *aireacht* and *oenach*. The *aireacht* was convened almost exclusively to settle the business matters of the province in which it was held. The *oenach*, which the head of every tribe was bound to convene, dealt with law suits, the exchange of goods and a plethora of social activities, including horse racing, games and competitions.

The modern Irish word for a fair is *aonach* and suggests some continuity from the ancient *oenach* to the modern fairs. The essential difference between them, however, is that while the ancient *oenach* was a regional gathering, the modern *aonach* depended on an economy which included the movements of livestock and produce into and out of a region. Fairs were the most important event throughout rural Ireland until the 1950s, since which they have been largely replaced by livestock auction marts. The modern fairs probably originated in those introduced by the Anglo-Normans in the twelfth and thirteenth centuries. By that time western Europe was growing in commercial importance and the right to hold a fair was granted by a charter from the king. Many charters continued to be granted in Ireland in the following centuries. The plantation of Ulster in the early seventeenth century brought the incorporation of towns and the subsequent establishment of fairs throughout that province. As a means of social intercourse, fairs became the focal points of the year and, with the postfamine dominance of the cattle trade, the importance and number of fairs increased. By the early twentieth century most towns had several fairs during the year, each with its own special date.

Markets were held for the sale of the ordinary produce of the farms and patents were usually granted for them at the same time as for fairs. They were held more frequently than fairs and many towns had weekly markets which attracted tradesmen, such as coopers and turners selling their wares, and dealers in household crockery and agricultural implements. Market houses were built in some towns and villages. Fields were designated as fairgreens, although these were often left unused owing to the muddy conditions which developed after hours of trampling by humans and livestock. Many towns have squares and diamonds in which the fairs and markets were held but otherwise the streets accommodated both livestock and stallholders.

Some fairs achieved notoriety and the most famous of all was the Donnybrook fair near Dublin which lasted from 1204 to 1855. The Puck fair in Killorglin, Co. Kerry, the horse fair in Ballinasloe, Co. Galway, and the Ballycastle fair in Co. Antrim are still popular events in the social calendar. The May and November fairs are remembered as the important fairs of the year and their prominence in former times was attributed to the fact that, in the absence of feeding stuffs, the farmer was anxious to dispose of his stock before the onset of winter. The spring fairs in February and March were popular, especially for dealing in horses, and sheep and wool were sold at the Lammas fairs in July and August.

The commerce of the countryside flowed through the markets and fairs and by mid nineteenth century some towns had begun to specialise in certain produce and commodities. In Aughrim, Co. Galway there was an October turkey fair, Dromore, Co. Down had an important flax market and a

Above: Carrying currachs to the sea, Inishmaan.
(photo: Bord Failte)

Top right: Galtering Help, Aran Islands.
(photo: Bord Failte)

Donegal fishermen. (photo: Bord Failte)

Right: A fair at Maam Cross, Connemara, Co. Galway. (photo: National Museum of Ireland - Dublin)

Bottom: A market day, the Market Square, Dungannon, Co. Tyrone. (photo: National Museum of Ireland - Dublin)

Opposite top: A view of the market in Tubbercurry, Co. Sligo in 1955. (photo: National Museum of Ireland - Dublin)

Opposite bottom: A market day in Galway City. (photo: National Museum of Ireland – Dublin)

Left: A group of men and women gathered at the market scales, Oughterard, Co. Galway. The women's shawls are particularly clear. The donkey in the background right is wearing a straw mat under the wooden straddle. (photo: National Museum of Ireland - Dublin)

Below: A horse fair in Galway City, *c.* 1940. (photo: National Museum of Ireland – Dublin)

very large linen market was held regularly in Ballymena, Co. Antrim. Limerick city was the main market centre for surrounding counties, with markets for hay, straw, wheat, butter and potatoes, in addition to having four livestock fairs per annum. The principal trade of Cork city was in agricultural produce and its butter market was especially famous.

Many towns, particularly in the northern counties, were the centres of two or more hiring fairs each year, usually held in May and November. Both young and older people who were looking for employment gathered on the fair day of the month in a certain part of the town. They showed by their general demeanour and appearance, by wearing of an emblem such as a straw or by carrying a peeled stick or the tools of their trade, spades and reaping hooks, that they were waiting for someone to hire them. The more important of the northern hiring fairs were Newry in Co. Armagh, Letter-kenny in Co. Donegal, Strabane in Co. Tyrone and Derry city. The usual hiring term was for six months, while servant boys and girls hired elsewhere in the country were more often engaged for an eleven month term. Hiring markets were especially popular in Munster and there were several centres where seasonal workers, the *spailpíní* and the *cabóga*, found farmers to give them work for a few days or weeks.

Industries and trades

Irish industry had begun as various crafts based in the homes and in small workshops and some traditional crafts are still to be found in activities such as handknitting, weaving tweeds and a limited amount of forge, saddlery and tailoring work. As people rose above subsistence level and standards of living improved, the demand for manufactured goods increased and factory items began to replace those formerly made at home. Clothes, food, house-hold furnishings and agricultural implements were all replaced with shop goods. While this led to the growing prosperity of grocery, hardware and other shops and the expansion of industries which supplied them during the first four decades of the twentieth century, many of the home-based small industries and local tradesmen began to lose custom because of their inabil-ity to compete.

A large number of shops already existed in rural Ireland in prefamine times. The 1831 census recorded almost 7,000 male shopkeepers. In the early years of their spread, especially in the countryside, there was a limited amount of goods for sale in shops. High on the list of purchases were seed potatoes and meal and also cloth, soap, tobacco, candles and salt. Tea was bought by all but was considered a luxury item by smallholders and labour-ers. In the two postfamine decades, because of the introduction of maize meal to the diet, there was a steady and growing reliance on shops which multiplied rapidly, especially in the west and north-west.

Before the spread and acceptance of factory and shop goods, a whole range of tradesmen and craftsmen supplied the needs of the people, from millers, spinners and weavers to masons, carpenters, coach and cart makers, blacksmiths, nailers and tinsmiths. For centuries the blacksmith's trade had been considered as the most important of all. His services were required by nearly every member of the community in which he worked, whether it was for shoeing a horse, making a gate, making and effecting repairs to farm implements, or producing a variety of domestic items including rushlight holders, oatcake toasters, fire tongs and cranes. Many blacksmiths owned a plot of land for their own supply of vegetables. No blacksmith had difficulty in gathering a group of neighbours to till his garden and woe betide anyone who refused to help when asked, thereby taking the smith away from his more important work in the forge. The blacksmith was both a respected and a feared member of the community. There was a cure for warts and other skin ailments in the water of his trough and some were believed to have the power to mete revenge by turning the anvil while cursing the person who had done the wrong.

Stone was used to form field boundaries from Neolithic times. Stonemasons, cutters and carvers have worked throughout the centuries, building walls, houses and churches, and decorating stone monuments including crosses and grave slabs. There were never great numbers of men skilled to work with stone and they naturally tended to congregate in areas where there were good quarries. On the contrary, the woodworkers were the most numerous and universal of all the tradesmen. They included coopers and furniture makers, currach and boat builders, wheelwrights and cartmakers, and makers of spinning wheels, looms, hurleys and musical instruments. Turners helped the wheelwrights by turning the hub of the wheel, but also made a whole range of essential items from chair legs and spade handles to functional domestic objects such as bowls, cups and plates which often displayed great beauty of form.

Coopering flourished in Ireland in the eighteenth and nineteenth centuries, when coopers were producing a variety of casks, tubs, churns and miscellaneous containers. From the end of the nineteenth century trade began to decline for a variety of reasons, including the establishment of creameries which led to a gradual decrease in home buttermaking, the use of materials alternative to wood for making containers and the introduction of refrigeration which dispensed with the need to store food in casks. Today some coopers produce ornamental and novelty pieces from miniature wine and sherry casks to garden seats.

Other trades have also managed to survive because of their ability to adapt

and produce marketable goods. Blacksmiths who survived installed welding equipment and began specialising in wrought iron work. Others set up in the motor repair industry. Tradesmen such as stonemasons and carvers, signwriters and some harness makers and wheelwrights still have a certain demand for their services. The last surviving old time tailors and shoemakers are in business solely on the reputations which they built for themselves and the appreciation which their customers have for the quality of the product. Some trades had died out completely before they were reintroduced in recent times in the sphere of fine art crafts. The making of coarse pottery and woodturning are examples. Pottery for everyday use was produced in Ireland for at least six thousand years and although small country potteries produced many household items from milk crocks, jugs and pitchers to basins and flower pots in the eighteenth and nineteenth centuries, very few competed successfully to survive into the twentieth century. Yet today there are more craft potters working in Ireland that at any other craft.

The craft of woodturning was practised in Ireland during prehistoric times and many examples of woodturned bowls, cups and dishes are included in museum collections. Cheap china, tin and plastic gradually replaced the objects made by the woodturner, who began to lose his customers and standing at the beginning of the twentieth century. There were only a few old time woodturners still working in the 1930s. Woodturning was introduced later as a fine art craft in Ireland and several woodturners have achieved international recognition for their work.

SOCIAL LIFE

Storytelling, singing and dancing
The Irish have long had a reputation for friendliness and sociability, freely visiting each others' houses for céilís and *airneáin*. At such events people spread local news, listened to and told stories and legends, danced and sang, and sat silently while one member of the group read the national and international news from the newspaper. This was all before the age of modern entertainment and telecommunications, especially radio and later television which, since the 1960s, has done more than anything else to change rural social habits that had existed for centuries.

The art of storytelling is as old as humanity. There are folktales of all different ages, some being thousands of years old while others were composed in medieval times and in recent centuries. The function of a folktale was to entertain a group which had gathered together, and events in the tale, while commonly known to be fictional, were sometimes believed. The number of active storytellers in any community was always limited. Many people might have known the stories but only a few related them and passed them on. Depending on the abilities of the storyteller, one tale could take hours and occasionally days to relate. Stories were told in many settings: by the fire in the house, at fairs, markets, weddings and wakes, while walking along the road, by workers on the roads and in the fields, or by people out fishing. They were spread easily from one place to another in this way and also by beggars, migratory workers and travelling tradesmen and pedlars who were welcomed into houses in the expectation of them having news and stories to tell. The more gifted of the active tradition bearers had only to hear a story once to be able to retell it word perfect.

Hundreds of international folktale types have been recorded in Ireland, primarily due to the untiring efforts of the staff of the Irish Folklore Commission, the present Department of Irish Folklore at University College Dublin. They tracked down and recorded many precious gems from the *scéalaí*, those (usually men) who could relate the longer international tales, the *seanscéal* or *märchen*. The *seanchaí* (men and women) were able to tell stories and legends relating to the local area and had inestimable knowledge of family and local histories. Relatively few storytellers lived to be visited by folklore collectors, but a common trait of those who did was that they knew the importance of their stories, that their craft was dying and that there was an urgency for as much as possible of their repertoires to be collected.

As with folktales, although some may have great antiquity, it is impossible to assign a date to many Irish tunes and songs. A tune is only as old as the written source in which it is found, a manuscript or a printed book, and the earliest Irish example dates from the sixteenth century. A few have also been noted in seventeenth century works but collecting and noting music really began with the great collectors of the following two centuries. Edward Bunting published his first volume of Irish melodies in 1796 and Henry Hudson, George Petrie, James Goodman and Patrick Weston Joyce continued collecting and publishing throughout the nineteenth and early twentieth centuries. The work which they started has been carried on since then by numerous individuals and musicians and by the staff of the Irish Folk Music Section of the Department of Irish Folklore.

Most of the older folksongs, especially those written in Irish, were songs about love, lullabies, religious songs and songs sung about the different work done in and outside the home. Ploughing and spinning songs seem to have been especially popular. Many English folksongs also made their way into the repertoires of singers by contacts with English speakers and settlers and those returned from seasonal and temporary work in Britain. In the early nineteenth century folksongs composed in English became increasingly popular when Irish as a spoken language began to decline. Many of these were reproduced on broadsheets sold at fairs and markets and they were based on themes current to events of the time, such as emigrant songs and those about insurrections. There has been a modern revival of interest in Irish traditional music, with the work of Comhaltas Ceoltóirí Éireann playing a prominent part.

While dancing is undoubtedly as old as storytelling and singing, it is curious that there are no references to the pastime earlier than the fifteenth and sixteenth centuries. At that time dances known as the Irish Hay, the Withy Dance (*Rinnce an Ghadairigh*), the Long Dance (*Rinnce Fada*) and the Sword Dance (*Rinnce an Chlaidhimh*) were known. By the seventeenth and eighteenth centuries dancing had become a universal pastime and many new dances were introduced. The first mention of the jig in Ireland was in 1674. Arthur Young, who toured Ireland in the 1770s, saw jigs, minuets and cotillons being enjoyed and practised. It seems that the reel was introduced from Scotland and the hornpipe from England at the end of the eighteenth century. Dancing masters too appeared at this time and they travelled around the country with a piper or a fiddler, spreading the new steps and teaching deportment to children. Throughout the nineteenth century quadrilles were modified and adapted to numerous local sets, until by the end of the century they had become more important than the jigs and reels. The modern Irish *céilí*, a night of Irish dancing with sets and waltzes danced to Irish music, was introduced in the 1890s in an effort to foster interest in the pastime. The Irish Dance Commission (*An Coimisiún le Rincí Gaelacha*) was established in the 1930s to continue the fosterage and also preservation and promotion of Irish dancing by means of competitions which helped to retain many of the old steps and introduce new developments.

Patterns and pilgrimages
Social life outside the home and immediate group of neighbours included many activities, from attending fairs and markets to visiting holy wells and travelling to many pattern and pilgrimage sites all over the country. In the recent past and certainly within the memory of many elderly people, it was the practice in every parish to pay special devotion to the local patron saint on his or her feast day. There are thousands of holy wells in Ireland and the custom of visiting them is undoubtedly pre-Christian in origin. They attained special importance in the early years of Christianity, when they became associated with various saints and were thus tolerated by the Christian church and allowed to survive. Some of the pagan elements of the visits were retained until recently when people tied rags on bushes and trees in the vicinity of the well and believed that the so-called cursing and swearing

stones had powers to elicit truth and do good or evil. The veneration of these stones formed part of holy well visits in many areas and they are still to be found at some sites where they are now believed to have the power to cure minor ailments and diseases.

The festivities on the pattern day began with religious devotions to the saint's shrine. In most parishes there was a holy well dedicated to the saint, while elsewhere the congregation visited a special place associated with the saint, a ruined church, an island or a monastery. The religious element of the pattern consisted of making 'rounds' and praying. In years gone by, once the religious devotions were over, the rest of the day was spent playing music and drinking, often to excess.

A holy well still visited every year in early June is that of *Tobar na mBan Naomh* in Teelin, Co. Donegal. The shrine consists of an altar and holy well set on the side of a hill overlooking the small fishing village of Teelin. The rounds at this shrine involve walking from the well to the altar a few metres away a set number of times while reciting decades of the rosary. When the praying is over, the devotees drink water from the well and leave a small token such as a coin or a holy medal. The stones at the altar are said to hold a cure for sores and ailments. Formerly, activities at patterns were often more involved. The pattern of Kilbride in Callan, Co. Kilkenny, for example, was well attended until the beginning of the nineteenth century. The people who visited it on 1 February had come from many kilometres around and those who could afford it brought baskets of bread and butter to distribute to the poor. The graves near the well were decorated with evergreens such as box and laurel. The keeners, or *mná-chaointe*, uttered their weird chant. A branch of a tree which was decorated with white ribbons and flowers, and known as a *craobh maighdionais*, was placed on the grave of a recently deceased young girl.

Some saints had several holy wells named after them scattered throughout the country and patterns to these occurred on different dates. St. Patrick and St. Brigid were obviously especially popular and so also was St. Gobnait, particularly in the south of Ireland. On her feast day, 11 February, there is a large pattern to her holy well in Dunquin, Co. Kerry and another at the well dedicated to her in Ballyvourney, Co. Cork. The month of June and midsummer were popular dates for visiting holy wells. Despite attempts to discourage them by ecclesiastical authorities and secular legislation, patterns continued to play an important part in the social life of the countryside until well into the nineteenth century. Some survived and have been revived and strengthened in recent years. Our Lady's well in Mulhuddart, Co. Dublin is visited each year on 8 September and the wells dedicated to St. Mullins in Carlow and St. Brigid in Brideswell, Co. Roscommon still attract large

Above: Workers at the granite quarry of John Brady, Ballyknockan, Co. Wicklow, 1953. (photo: National Museum of Ireland - Dublin)

Left: Liam O'Neill woodturner, Co. Clare, turning a large elm bowl in 1986. (photo: National Museum of Ireland - Dublin)

OPPOSITE PAGE
Top left: Two young girls carrying a *Brídeog*, Co. Galway, *c.* 1945. (photo: National Museum of Ireland - Dublin)

Top centre: A rag branch from the wart well at Dungiven Abbey, Co. Derry. (photo: National Museum of Ireland - Dublin)

Top right: St. Brigid's Well, near Mullingar, Co. Westmeath. (photo: Bord Failte)

Bottom: Pilgrimage to St. McDara's Island 1943. (photo: Bord Failte)

numbers of devotees.

Pilgrimage sites were not as numerous as pattern sites but they were as popular. Some centres became particularly important as places of both pattern and pilgrimage, for example, Mount Brandon, Co. Kerry, Glendalough, Co. Wicklow, and Glencolmcille, Co. Donegal which still attracts thousands of visitors each year. As June was a popular month for patterns, so August and the festival of *Lúnasa* especially, became associated with pilgrimages. The pilgrimage to Lough Derg, Co. Donegal is attended by thousands of penitents each summer. It is still an austere and difficult pilgrimage, with all-night vigils and fasting, and many of the devotions are performed in bare feet. Pilgrims also visited mountain sites such as Corleck Hill, Knockbride, Co. Cavan, Kinard on the Dingle Peninsula in Kerry and, the most famous one of all, Croagh Patrick, Co. Mayo. Popularly known as The Reek, Croagh Patrick is still an important place of pilgrimage and is climbed by thousands each year on the Sunday nearest the *Lúnasa* feast, 1 August. Although many pilgrimage sites have been abandoned as places of popular worship, that is not to say that Irish people, young and old, do not still attend pilgrimages. Knock Shrine in Co. Mayo ranks as one of the most important pilgrimage sites in Europe.

Calendar customs
The social customs connected with calendar customs reveal a wide panorama of folk tradition. They reflect many aspects of the lives of the people, from their religious practices to what they ate to their belief in divination and healing. They also include features of amusement and entertainment. As with other facets of folk custom and tradition, some calendar customs are of great antiquity. Some may have pre-Christian or pre-Celtic origins and others are Christianised pagan feasts. Some were introduced in medieval times and later by groups of outsiders and settlers who influenced tradition during the centuries.

Certain days marked the time by which farmwork should have been commenced or concluded. St. Brigid's Day, 1 February, was traditionally the first day of spring, when it was hoped that the weather would improve so that the farmer could think about ploughing and sowing crops. The parades, processions and celebrations on St. Patrick's Day are of relatively recent origin. Farmers liked to have some crops planted by that day and most farmers and gardeners nowadays make an effort to have the potatoes in the ground by 17 March. The first crops should have been ready for harvesting by *Lúnasa*, the harvest feast which is still remembered on the last Sunday in July or the first Sunday in August. It was a good sign if the reaping of crops could begin on the Autumn Lady Day, 15 August, and the farmer aimed to have all work done by the end of October.

Calendar custom also imposed work restrictions and prohibitions. Fisher-men would not go to sea on the spring Lady Day, 29 March, or on the feast of Michael the Archangel, 29 September. No nail could be driven or wood burned on Good Friday and no work at all was to be done on May Day. In parishes dedicated to St. Brigid, the inhabitants would not do any work which involved the turning of a wheel, in honour of the saint, and no miller would work on St. Martin's Day, 11 November.

Other calendar custom activities included the lighting of bonfires on St. John's eve, 23 June, on the feasts of SS. Peter and Paul, 29 June, and at Hallowe'en. Candles were set lighting in the windows of houses on other days, such as Christmas and New Year's eve, and houses and bushes were decorated with flowers on May Day. Special food also formed part of the celebrations and festivities. St. Brigid is the patroness of the dairy and of cattle so that, along with sowens, apple cake and colcannon, it was impera-tive that butter formed part of the meal on 1 February. There was a feast of meat and eggs on Shrove Tuesday in preparation for the austerities of Lent. The Lenten restrictions, however, were set aside on St. Patrick's Day, which was traditionally a day of feasting and drinking when meat should be eaten at the main meal. At Easter time there was an abundance of eggs after the Lenten fast and these were eaten in great quantities, painted and given as presents. A goose or sheep was ceremoniously killed on the feast of St. Michael, and at Hallowe'en colcannon, nuts and fruit were always plentiful.

Wearing emblems and masks and carrying effigies also formed part of calendar custom. Straw, rush and wooden crosses of a variety of shapes and sizes are still made and hung in houses, barns, schools and offices on St. Brigid's Day. Crosses were also made on St. Patrick's Day and simple badges and sprigs of shamrock are pinned to lapels and hats. A far more widely practised custom in former years was the wearing of straw costume at Hallowe'en, at Christmas time, on St. Brigid's Day, on May Day and also at weddings and wakes. The costumes were relatively easy to make and consisted of simple plaited or woven straw.

Dressing up at Hallowe'en is still an exciting pastime for groups of children, though especially in urban centres. Nowadays, the disguises worn vary greatly and include mainly mass-produced masks and costumes. They originally consisted of straw hats and skirts, with straw ropes tied around the arms and legs. Groups so disguised and made up travelled from one house to the next playing music and dancing. They received gifts of food and money in return. The amusement was not always quite so harmless and good-spirited. Often the licence given for mischief-making on the night resulted in animals being whitewashed, gates and doors being removed from their hinges and crops destroyed.

After Hallowe'en, Christmas was the next holiday period and another occasion for the wearing of straw costume. There were, and still are to a large extent, two separate customs when costume was worn at this time of the year. In all Ulster, parts of Leitrim, north Louth, north Dublin and south Wexford, the mummers and Christmas rhymers act out their plays in a centuries-old tradition, with characters such as the Captain, Prince George, the Turkey Champion, the Doctor, St. Patrick and Jack Straw to name but a few.

In an almost complementary distribution, the custom of the wren boys doing their rounds has been recorded from all parts of the country except large areas of Ulster. Both the origin and purpose of the wren boys' tradition remain enigmatic and unexplained. In many parts of the country groups of them still call to houses on St. Stephen's Day, dressed up and looking for money. The tradition is very strong, especially in and around Dingle, Co. Kerry. In nearly every county in which the custom was observed, the wren boys carried a wren which was placed in a box or coffin or attached to a furze or whins bush. Arriving at a house, a rhyme like this one which was heard in Dublin in 1947, was chanted:

> The wren, the wren, the king of all birds,
> St. Stephen's day he was caught in the furze,
> Although he was little his family was great,
> Get up young lady and give use a trate.
> Up with the kettle and down with the pan,
> A penny or twopence to bury the wren.

On three of the four quarter days, that is the days which divided the year into four seasons, effigies were carried by groups of adults and children from one house to another in the district. On St. Brigid's Day the members of the group were known as 'biddies' or *brídeóga*. On reaching a house they introduced the effigy as St. Brigid and asked in rhyme for some small token to help with their celebrations.

Only a few of the communal activities formerly practised on May Day survived to the twentieth century. Visiting houses with the May queen or May baby was a weak tradition in Ireland and it is known to have existed in just a few places in Louth, Meath and Monaghan. In the early part of the nineteenth century in Co. Louth, childless couples attended exhibitions at which the May baby was paraded, accompanied by a man and woman dressed entirely in straw. By their attendance it was believed that the couple would become fertile and have children of their own. In scattered areas around the country the May bush is still decorated outside the house and school children especially erect an altar to Our Lady and decorate it with flowers. One strong survival of the May baby custom exists in parts of Ulster. Groups of children dress up in costumes, elect one girl as the queen and call to houses in the locality looking for money. Somersaulting over a brush shaft held by two members of the group and singing a song as they go along, form part of the entertainment.

HOME LIFE

The house

As the centre of all the daily activity of the household and of much of the social activity as well, the dwelling house acquired a collection of beliefs and practices. The house site was carefully chosen, either to avoid bad luck or to bring good luck, and in its choosing the advice of the old people was always sought and accepted. Even today people are careful to avoid interfering with a rath or ringfort and any unpleasant happenings either to the inhabitants or the house itself are attributed to the fact that not enough care has been taken in choosing the site. When it was established that the house was safe, further actions were carried out to ensure its luck. In some places a coin or medal was put in the foundation. Elsewhere a bird or a small animal was killed and buried under the floor. A custom which seems to have been popular throughout the country was the burying of horse skulls near the hearth.

While there were professional carpenters, masons and thatchers in nearly all communities, most men were good handymen and, with the help of neighbours who gathered a *meitheal* for the job, the task of building a house was undertaken with ease. As all the cooking for the family and livestock was done over the open fire, a good draught was naturally essential and most attention was paid to the construction of the hearth and chimney. To bring further luck to the house, it was customary to take some live coals from the old home to light the first fire and every effort was made to keep that fire lighting and not allow it to quench. It was unlucky to give away a live coal from the fire unless one or two sods were left in its place.

Fuel

Turf was the most common fuel but in places where there were no bogs, or turf suitable for burning, alternatives had to be found. Mud-turf was made on dry peaty bogs where the turf was less fibrous and consequently less cohesive and too crumbly to cut with a slane or turf spade. The peaty soil was well mixed with water, spread thickly on the bank or edge of the bog and

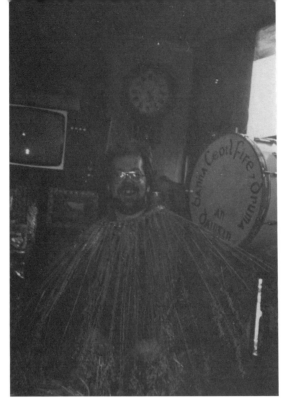

Right and below: Dingle, 1989. (photos: E. Healy)

Top right: Wren boys.

Right: Wren boys, Naas Road, St. Stephen's Day, 1933. (photos: National Museum of Ireland - Dublin)

worked into sods. The sods were turned several times and then won in much the same way as ordinary turf: four or five sods were set leaning against each other in what were known as 'footings', after a week or more they were 're-footed' in bigger heaps and eventually formed into large clamps before being carted home.

A form of charcoal was also made from turf and it had particular advantages for blacksmiths in that it gave good heat but with very little flame. The dry turf was placed in a large heap in a hole, kindled and then covered either with wet sacking or bog mud. The covering excluded the air from the smouldering turf, which in a matter of hours had formed into black hard lumps, resembling coal. In areas near coalmines, especially around Castlecomer, Co. Kilkenny, a fuel known as culm was prepared from a mixture of crushed anthracite and clay, mixed together and formed into small ovoid shapes. Culm crushers, the large stones which crushed the anthracite to a powder, are still to be seen in Carlow and Kilkenny.

On the Aran Islands a certain amount of turf was delivered by the hooker boats from Connemara but a common fuel there, as elsewhere, was dried cow manure. Furze was used as a fuel throughout the country. In many places it was favoured for baking bread either in the pot oven or on the griddle and, as the withered tops especially gave rapid heat, it was universally utilised to boil water quickly. In that area of the south from Cork to Wexford where there was an absence of turf, furze was extensively used as a fuel for all cooking and heating needs.

Food and drink

The area around the hearth was the woman's work space and when she was not cooking a meal for her family, she was preparing food for livestock. Before the potato was introduced and became the mainstay of the diet of the majority of the population from the closing decades of the seventeenth century, popular foods were corn, comprising oats, barley, wheat and rye eaten as both bread and porridge, and also milk products. Meat eating was not predominant and only pork and bacon were consumed in any quantities. Vegetables included both wild and cultivated varieties such as watercress, nettles, wild garlic, carrot and beet. Fish was never an element of popular diet but varieties of seaweed were eaten. The main food for most humans and animals throughout the nineteenth century was potatoes, which were boiled together in a large pot suspended from a fire crane over the open fire. When cooked, the small potatoes for the livestock were put into a tub in the yard and mixed with maize, commonly known as yellow meal, and some oatmeal. The larger potatoes were taken out and placed in a round basket to dry off for the family's meal. Condiment was provided by sparing use of salt and butter or the gravy from grilled salted herrings. In later years potatoes might have been eaten with bacon and cabbage or turnips. Poaching, especially for salmon and trout with spears, was common at all times. Trapping and snaring of animals were practised as both pastimes and through necessity. Many simple but effective devices were invented for catching birds, mainly blackbirds, thrushes, snipe and wild geese and ducks, and rabbits and hares.

Bread baking formed part of the daily routine of the woman's work. While barley and also peameal and branmeal were used, bread was made principally from two bread grains, oats and wheat. Throughout the historic period, owing to climatic conditions, oats was the chief grain crop sown throughout the country. It is probable that oaten bread was, therefore, the more popular, with wheaten bread being considered a greater delicacy. In more recent times oaten bread became the main bread type of the north and west of the country, while wheaten bread predominated in the south and east. Nowadays, homemade bread is made from bleached wheaten flour, to form white or soda bread, or whole wheatmeal, to make brown bread. The making of oaten bread is confined to northern areas.

Not all grain grown, however, was used to make bread, as various forms of porridge formed the next basic element of the popular diet throughout the nineteenth century. It was made in various consistencies and was served sometimes in a piggin from which it might be drunk, or in a noggin from which it was eaten with a spoon. While the broad term porridge was known throughout the country, the dish was also known as stirabout or gruel in many areas and Irish terms include *brochán*, *leite*, *praiseach* and *menadach*. This latter might also at times refer to another preparation of oatmeal used as a sustaining food from at least the eighth century. Its popularity owed much to the fact that it was so easy to prepare, consisting solely of meal mixed with butter. A similar dish which was a mixture of oatmeal and milk or cream, was known as *práipín* in parts of Leinster and south Munster, and *cubhrán* in Connacht.

Milk was popular as a drink and also as food in the form of curds and whey. The first milk from a cow immediately after she had calved was considered a great delicacy. The beastings, as it was called, was put into a can and heated gently on live coals. It soon turned to the consistency of custard and was eaten with relish. While the cow was in calf, there was a certain shortage of milk for household use. In some areas kind neighbours provided small quantities from their own supplies and they were subsequently rewarded with a can of beastings. A milk substitute, sowens, was also made from the inner seed or hull of oats which was available for the asking at most corn mills. The seeds were steeped in a crock of boiling water for a number of days to produce an opaque liquid.

Other than milk and sowens, ale was a common beverage from early times and domestic brewing was widespread until the eighteenth century. The spread and acceptance of tea was a very slow process and only accelerated during the mid nineteenth century. It was regarded as an inferior drink by many observers who considered the laziness of workers to be due to the fact that they drank too much tea. Its increasing popularity could be attributed to migratory labourers returning from work in Britain and not only spreading the idea of tea as a drink but also expecting it with their midday meal when working nearer home.

Built-in ovens were common only in areas of the southeast but elsewhere all cooking and baking were done over the open fire. Cooking utensils were few and basic including, for the most part, cast iron kettles, skillets, pot ovens and griddles. Local blacksmiths forged fenders, oatcake toasters and meat forks.

oatcake toasters

Furnishings
Furniture, too, was sparse and practical and seems to have developed from furniture which was originally hung on the walls or hinged to them. The hanging dresser developed into the freestanding version which was to be seen in every household, complete with an array of jugs, plates and mugs. It was set against the wall, as were the table, chairs and meal bin, leaving the centre of the kitchen free for easy movement. Bedrooms were also simply furnished. Some might have had wooden washstands with pitchers and basins, in addition to beds with low wooden ends and *súgán* or rope bases. Local carpenters also made box beds and four poster beds, and beds with iron or brass ends became popular in the nineteenth century. Settlebeds formed part of the kitchen furniture. These were practical items of furniture which were used as seats by day and, when opened up and supplied with a tick mattress, became comfortable beds by night.

rush and candle holder

In parts of the north and west, houses built in the vernacular tradition often had an outshot set into one of the walls to the side of the hearth. The dimensions of the outshot varied but averaged 2 x 1 metres. The outshot was known as the *cailleach*, a corruption of the Irish *cúilteach*, and also as the 'pristy' in parts of Roscommon and Mayo. It is known that these outshots have formed part of the vernacular housebuilding tradition for centuries and may originally have been used for food storage. They are still to be seen in many older houses and, when furnished with mattress and blankets, were until recently used as beds.

Home crafts
Apart from the daily routine of cooking and cleaning, industry in the house

also included spinning and weaving, and making and mending clothes and footwear. Home crafts were promoted from the 1890s by the Congested Districts Board, through the organisation of courses on lacemaking, weaving and dyeing throughout the western counties. It also encouraged the homespun industry through loans for the purchase of looms and spinning wheels.

While most of the work around the house was done by the women, men also had indoor jobs. They busied themselves in the evenings and on wet days making baskets for use in the home and on the farm and constructing a variety of practical everyday objects from natural materials such as straw, hay and rushes. In Ireland there were as many different types of basket or wickerwork container as varieties of material which went into their making. Although people were generally able to make baskets for their own needs, basketmaking was also a specialised craft and much fine wickerwork was produced. In the nineteenth century the industry was especially centred in two areas, the shores of Lough Neagh in the north and in the Suir Valley in Co. Tipperary.

The greatest variety of baskets was in the group in use around the house, the commonest of which was a round flat-bottomed basket with shallow sides. Commonly known as a skib, from the Irish *sciob*, it was also called a *bascáid geal* in Donegal and a *ciseóg* in Galway. Its main function was as a potato teemer or strainer and, when provided with handles, it was used for bringing washing to and from the clothes line. Other general purpose baskets were oval or rectangular in plan and served a variety of functions, from containers for seed and harvested potatoes to receptacles for turf and other fuels. Household baskets were also made from straw.

Baskets in use around the farm included wickerwork containers made to fit into wheeled vehicles, such as the wheeling basket which was placed on a turf barrow and was useful when spreading turf, or the very large kish made in parts of the midlands to carry goods in the four-laced car. The very popular donkey creels were used in all parts for transporting such essentials as turf, manure and seaweed. They were generally made of sally rods and were used in conjunction with a plaited straw mat on the donkey's back, and over which was placed a straddle of wood provided with pegs from which the creels hung.

Natural local materials were widely used before the adoption of mass-produced items and the spread of modern methods of transport. Simple devices for carrying large loads were developed, such as the burden rope which was in use from medieval times. Head rings of straw were adopted especially by women who commonly carried heavy loads on their heads, a practice known to have occurred from Sligo to Cork. Pack saddles of thick hay and straw rope were placed on the backs of beasts of burden for carrying varied loads. Entire sets of harness, including collars, saddles, bridles and straddles, were made from natural fibres. Plaited straw mats acted as a cushion on a donkey's back when working as a draught animal and they served many other purposes throughout the country.

Ropes were made from many different materials, including hay, straw, grass, bog wood, horse hair, rushes, sally and heather, and they were put to many uses. On houses along the windy western seaboard they kept the thatch securely in place. Soaked in mud and twisted between a wooden frame, they formed a canopy over the hearth. They were used as seating for chairs and belts for clothing. It was customary for the man of the house to prepare a good supply of ropes during the winter months for all uses and they were in steady demand as tethers and spancels for livestock. Sheep, cows, goats, horses and donkeys especially were restricted in their movements in this way and it was also formerly common to see hens and geese so restrained.

MUSEUMS

There are more than 150 museums in Ireland, the majority of which include some folklife objects in their collections. They range in size from the National Museum in Dublin, which has a sizeable and comprehensive folklife section, and the Ulster Folk and Transport Museum at Holywood, Co. Down, in which aspects of life at the turn of the century are represented, to the many small local museums scattered throughout the country. There is little funding from government sources for museums and most are run on a voluntary basis or by small grants from local authorities. The displays depend very much on the interests of those in charge; the vast majority include miscellaneous gatherings of what might be known as 'bygones', emphasising especially work on the farm and in the home. Bunratty Folk Park in Co. Clare, Muckross House in Co. Kerry and Glencolmkille Folk Museum in Donegal attempt to recreate life at different periods of the nineteenth and early twentieth centuries. Each is well worth a visit, as are the county museums such as those in Clonmel, Co. Tipperary, Monaghan town, Enniskillen, Co. Fermanagh and Enniscorthy, Co. Wexford. The agricultural museum at Johnstown Castle, Wexford, is also interesting, the main exhibits including farm machinery manufactured in the Wexford foundries and reconstructions of house and dairy interiors. The Ulster-American Folk Park near Omagh, Co. Tyrone illustrates eighteenth and nineteenth century emigration from Ulster to North America in a series of reconstructed buildings centred around the birthplace of Thomas Mellon.

Turf boat. (photo: Bord Failte)

While it is true that on a national scale museums have not received the interest or finance necessary to bring them into line with standards in other European countries, the interest and commitment of local groups and societies throughout the country merit great pride. In the larger museums, especially the Ulster Folk and Transport Museum and Bunratty Folk Park, efforts are being made to introduce various craft and farming activities as educational aids in their programmes of events. Through their untiring efforts, at least some aspects of the recent past have been preserved for the future.

Top left: Errigal, Co. Donegal. (photo: Bord Failte). *Above*: A view of the Water Mill at Leitra, Co. Galway, 1914. (photo: National Museum of Ireland - Dublin). *Left*: A thatched farmhouse and sheds at Tuam, Co. Galway, 1914. (photo: National Museum of Ireland - Dublin). *Below*: A straw hen's nest from Knocknakilla, Inagh, Ennis, Co. Clare. (photo: National Museum of Ireland - Dublin)

Above: John Kelly Mor, Ballyarha, Bullaun, Loughrea, Co. Galway, his wife Brigid McInerney. Kelly Mor who is wearing a white frilled cap, *c*. 1900. *Top right*: A group of men and a young boy, Aran Islands, *c*. 1908. *Centre right*: Grandmother and grandchildren, Inishmaan. (photo: Bord Failte). *Bottom right*: A group of women and children on the Aran Islands, *c*. 1900. *Below*: Weaving on a handloom at Ardara, Co. Donegal in 1898. Finishing the web. (photos: National Museum of Ireland - Dublin)

Land, Work and Recreation

DESMOND GILLMOR

and is the basic natural resource of the countryside. No longer do the vast majority of rural dwellers live close to the land in the sense that they did in the past but yet land remains vital to the physical character and human existence of the countryside. Most of the Irish countryside is a working landscape, in that its surface is dominated by features fashioned and used by people in pursuit of making a livelihood. Much of this work is based directly on using the resources of the land and water in the primary industries of agriculture, forestry, fishing and mining. Alternatively, people may be employed in rural manufacturing and service industries but many of these are dependent in various ways on the primary activities or their locations may result from the attractions of the countryside. Employment of whatever form is necessary for the maintenance of the rural community. In addition to work, increasingly, leisure is making an impact on the countryside. The use of leisure time in recreation and tourism may be based on the land resource in a sense similar to the way farming is based on the soil.

LAND USE

The type of land use and the nature of the land cover comprise the most widespread feature of the Irish countryside. It forms an intricate mosaic, as may be seen from a prominent viewpoint or from the air. This pattern results from the diversity of land type, the varied historical evolution of land use and the complexity of modern life. The variety adds greatly to the interest of the countryside.

The pattern of land use in Ireland is represented in Figure 6.1. It is clearly dominated by farmers, with over four-fifths of the area serving agricultural purposes. Part of this is rough grazing for sheep and cattle, mainly in the uplands. The remainder comprises crops and pasture, or 'improved agricultural land', and it corresponds approximately with the area enclosed in fields. This improved land occupies two-thirds of Ireland but its distribution varies regionally (Figure 6.2). In some areas it comprises almost the entire countryside. The gaps in the pattern of fields corresponds mainly with the uplands and peat bogs and are most pronounced in the west.

Figure 6.2 conveys also a general impression of the quality of the land. Not only is the unimproved land of poor quality for agriculture but also where it forms a high proportion of an area, the improved land there tends to be of lower quality than elsewhere, generally being adjacent to hills and bog. The nature of the land affects the range of choice available to land users. The use of upland soils may be limited to forestry and rough grazing, whereas on the most favoured lowlands the wide use range includes forestry, pasture and a variety of arable crops. The proportion of land classified as having a wide use range is 88 per cent in Meath but only 3 per cent in Leitrim. The land use range is most limited in the west but local variations in soil suitability occur in all parts of the country. Also, the land uses differ somewhat in their land suitability requirements. Thus heavy wet soils may be highly suited to forestry but very unfavourable to agriculture.

The most fundamental distinction in how farmers use their improved agricultural land is that between tilling it for arable crops and having it under grass. This is the distinction also which is most evident in the appearance of the landscape. The grass is for grazing livestock or it is mown in summer for fodder in the form of silage or hay. The proverbial greenness of the Irish countryside noted by many visitors is attributable mainly to the extent of grassland and its luxuriance in response to the moist and mild conditions. In addition to being favoured by climatic and soil conditions, the emphasis on grass is related to the strong pastoral tradition in Irish rural society and to the market outlets for livestock and their products. Only one-tenth of the improved land is tilled but there are striking regional differences in the extent of arable cropping (Figure 6.3). Tillage tends to be most common where the climate is driest and sunniest, where soils are well drained, where farms are larger and where the external historical influence of landlords and tenant farmers was greatest.

The distinction between improved land and rough grazing is not always clear and even more so than between rough grazing and 'other land', as there is often a gradation between them. The other land includes peat bog, mountain heath, bare rock and water but also buildings and roads. Some mountain land serves several purposes, which may be grazing for sheep, water catchment for urban supply, recreational space for hillwalkers and as a scenic amenity. Use of land for two or more purposes constitutes 'multiple

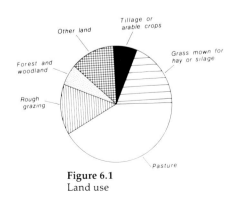

Figure 6.1
Land use

land use'. Its success depends upon the levels and compatibility of the uses. Conflict arises where there are incompatible land uses, as has occurred between military use and walking at the Glen of Imaal in Co. Wicklow. Similarly, there is incompatibility between angling and water skiing on a reservoir at the same time and between arable cropping and recreational use of land. Good resource management aims at maximising the benefits of multiple land use while minimising the conflicts.

Competition between uses for the finite land resource results in changes in land use. Historically, the major land use trend in Ireland was the spread of farmland at the expense of the natural forest cover. The bringing of land into agricultural use was a fluctuating process, however, with retreats as well as advancement. Evidence of this may be seen in the prehistoric fields beneath peat bogs, in medieval deserted villages and in former tillage ridges on abandoned hillsides. The area of improved land reached its peak, not under the population pressure of prefamine times, but in the late nineteenth century before an agricultural recession initiated decline. Extension and contraction may occur at the same time, as in recent decades the total area of improved land has expanded through the reclamation of hill land by many farmers, while in some places there has been abandonment and reversion to the wild state, particularly in the west.

The largest change in Irish land use in recent times has been the reversal of the trend in the forest area. It occupied less than 1 per cent of the land in the early decades of the twentieth century and has expanded to over 5 per cent through afforestation. This has occurred mainly at the expense of rough grazing but also on some of the other land and improved land.

Much less extensive than afforestation has been the conversion of farmland to building and road construction, though the quality of the land involved has been much higher. Adequate information on this and other land use trends is lacking but urban land is probably only about 3 per cent of the country. This low proportion has contributed to the absence of the controversies about the loss of agricultural land to urban development which have occurred in other countries, despite the rapid growth of urbanisation. Encroachment upon the country's major area of market gardening in north Co. Dublin might prompt concern and minimisation of the loss of good agricultural land should be a general consideration. Urban expansion has effects on rural land use extending beyond the edge of the built-up area. As the value of the land for building development increases, the incentive to invest in it, maintain it and use it intensively for agriculture diminishes. Also farmers in urban fringe areas may experience problems relating to trespass, gates being left open, broken glass and litter, damage to property and pilferage, and worrying of livestock by dogs.

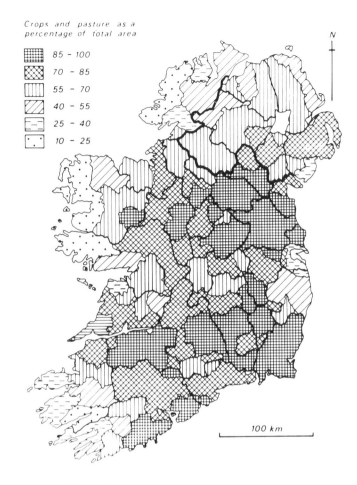

Crops and pasture as a
percentage of total area

▦	85 – 100
▨	70 – 85
▥	55 – 70
▧	40 – 55
▭	25 – 40
⦂	10 – 25

N

100 km

Figure 6.3
Arable cropland

(photo: Jan de Fouw)

(photo: Jan de Fouw)

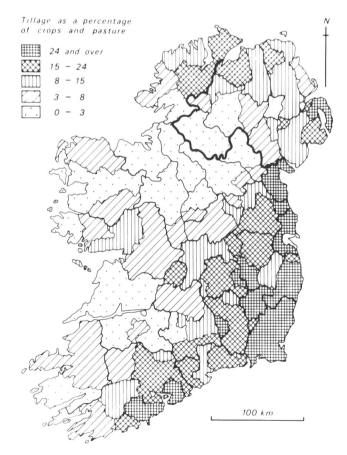

Tillage as a percentage
of crops and pasture

▦	24 and over
▨	15 – 24
▥	8 – 15
▧	3 – 8
⦂	0 – 3

N

100 km

Figure 6.2
Agricultural land

LAND OWNERSHIP

Control over land was a critical factor in Irish rural history and this still has a bearing on attitudes towards land. As in many other countries, originally communal ownership under a tribal control system gave way forcibly to individual private property rights. The inequities of the defective tenancy system which developed led to land conflict and to the transfer of ownership from the landlords to the tenant-purchasers in the late nineteenth and early twentieth centuries. In the resultant owner-occupancy system, control over land remains of major significance economically and socially in rural Ireland. Ownership is also of great importance because of the power which landowners have to affect the appearance of the countryside and the nature of the environment. It is growing concern about this which has led to the reassertion of communal interests and to the need for controls over land use.

The family farm is the basic unit of land ownership in Ireland, with little involvement by large business interests. There is a strong desire to own land and there is emotional attachment to specific tracts of land. Considerations of land ownership overshadow the use to be made of the land, so that much land is neglected despite its perceived importance. Many farms have remained in the same family for generations. Transfer of land is predominantly by inheritance, with only about one-fifth of it through the open market. This lack of mobility in land ownership, combined with the cost of land, limits the opportunities for acquiring land by young people without farms and by smallholders wishing to expand.

About one-tenth of land is let for use under the conacre or eleven months system by people who do not wish or are unable to work it themselves. The practice is most common in the north. Conacre provides a market in land use but the short term nature of the letting is a disincentive to land improvement. Longer term leasing had been discouraged as a reaction against the defects of the former tenancy system but it is now promoted as a means of access to land use for those who lack capital or opportunity for purchases.

Commonage is land on which more than one farmer has grazing rights, communal usage having been retained from early times. It is generally on mountain or bog. The number of livestock which members of the group have the right to graze is measured in units termed 'soums' in the north and 'collops' in the south. Joint ownership has been lessened through purchase of shares and by inheritance. The desire to increase the productivity of commonage has led to some subdivision and fencing of land.

Irish farms are predominantly of medium and small size. The average extent is 25 hectares (about 60 acres) but there are major regional variations. The average area of improved land per farm in Kildare is nearly three times that in Mayo. Size tends to diminish northwestwards and small holdings are a feature of the west but local variation occurs everywhere. The small farm problem is accentuated by the tendency for such holdings to be on the poorer land, so that their land resources are limited both in quantity and in quality.

There are two fundamentally contrasting attitudes towards land ownership. One views land as a commodity to be traded at will and as personal property whose ownership and use should be determined by the free play of market forces. The other sees the ownership of land incorporating a sense of stewardship, in which there is a responsibility towards the recognised interests of the wider community and of succeeding generations. This contrast affects the way in which land is used and it is involved in many land issues. As community interests have become acknowledged, the need for public controls over the use of land has been recognised increasingly. For private owners to suggest that they have the right to do what they wish with the basic resource on which the whole of society depends seems selfish and irresponsible. It is unfortunate in this respect that the constitution of the Republic of Ireland and interpretations of it attach an excessive and outdated importance to private property rights, though it allows for reconciliation with the interests of the common good.

EMPLOYMENT

Even though the availability of employment is vital to the life of the countryside, there is little precise information about the total extent and distribution of rural employment. This is because in the censuses of population most of the areas for which statistics are given include urban and rural places and also people are recorded according to where they live rather than by workplace. Furthermore, it is difficult to distinguish clearly between rural and urban employment. Agriculture, forestry, fishing and mining may be regarded as the traditional countryside industries involved in the production of food and raw materials. The processing of this output is intimately related to the rural sources of the materials but a substantial amount of it is located in the towns. This applies also to the manufacture of fertilisers and equipment for the primary industries, to the marketing of their produce and to the financing, administration and other servicing of the rural activities. Other employment associated with the countryside in craft industries and in tourism cannot be distinguished separately in the statistics. Employment in the shopping, transport, educational, medical and other services used by rural people is located mainly in towns but also in the countryside. The distributions and relationships of employment indicate the extent to which the welfare of town and country are interconnected.

Rural employment is clearly dominated by farming and the trends in the agricultural labour force have had profound effects on the life of the countryside. The number of people who regard themselves as being engaged principally in agriculture is only one-quarter that of the 1920s. Many factors have contributed to this huge decline but the main influences have been the better incomes, opportunities and working conditions in non-agricultural employment in Ireland and abroad and the reduced need for labour on the farms because of modern technology. The number of those who own farms has declined much less than relatives assisting on farms or agricultural labourers. Thus farmers now comprise four-fifths of the agricultural workforce and the one-person farm has become predominant. The role of agriculture in the total economy has declined to the extent that it accounts for only 5 per cent of employment in Northern Ireland and 15 per cent in the Republic of Ireland, the difference in status having originated with the industrialisation and urbanisation of the northeast.

In addition to those engaged fully in agriculture, part-time farming has become an important feature of the rural employment scene. More than one-quarter of Irish farms are worked on a part-time basis. Growth has been mainly because many smallholders availed of the increased alternative employment opportunities to achieve much higher living standards than they would have from farming alone. Some part-time farming results from the acquisition of land, which often includes a residence in the countryside, by people in business, professional or other non-agricultural occupations. This may be termed 'hobby farming'. The growth in the role of part-time farming may be seen as a development of a practice of multiple job holding and income earning which have for long been a feature of rural areas.

The establishment of new manufacturing industry throughout much of the Republic of Ireland from the 1950s afforded major employment oppor-tunities for residents of the countryside and has been an important promoter of change in rural society. The previous tendency in industrial location had been for further increase in the already high degree of concentration in Dublin and the major ports. This was because of access to imported raw materials, industrial labour and markets. The reversal of this tendency was the outcome of both a state policy of industrial dispersion and also the nature and locational choice of modern manufacturing. State measures included the payment of higher grants for western and rural locations, the provision of advance factories and industrial sites, and the advice and encouragement given by the Industrial Development Authority. Dispersion was possible because much of the new development was of light industry with compara-tively low transport costs and industrialists were attracted towards the less urbanised areas by labour, community and environmental considerations. The outcome has been factories in many towns, villages and even some open country locations, making industrial employment much more accessible to rural people. Nearly one-half of the manufacturing employment in the state had been in Co. Dublin in 1960 but the proportion has fallen towards one-quarter. Dispersion has been much weaker in Northern Ireland, where there was less new development and a greater tendency to locate in the east. It is fortunate that most modern rural industrialisation involves factories that have little or no detrimental environmental effect, provided there is proper siting, design and landscaping.

The revival of craft activity has been a significant aspect of rural industrialisation. The decline in traditional craft industry had represented a major loss not only of rural employment but also of indigenous skills and sense of pride in work. The resurgence of interest in traditional crafts and also the development of many new craft activities in recent decades have been the result of a growing appreciation of craft articles, greater affluence and the search for new and fulfilling forms of employment. Much skilled work is being done in wool, clay, stone, metal, wood, rush, straw, leather, turf, glass and other materials. Pottery, knitting, weaving and basket making are amongst the most popular handcrafts. Many craftspeople and artists choose to live and work in the countryside and their products may be seen at an increasing number of studios and craft shops.

Almost all rural people traditionally lived at or close to their place of work but commuting has become a major feature of life in the countryside. Commuting has been made possible by the growth in private car ownership and to a much lesser extent by public transport. The journey may be to employment elsewhere in the open country or a village but the bulk of commuting is to towns and cities. It has grown both as more rural people have taken urban employment but retained country residence, and also as more people from towns and cities with urban employment have chosen to live in the countryside. As commuting has increased, so the occupations of residents of the countryside have become much more diversified, as they are no longer restricted to the employment available in rural areas.

Inadequate employment in quantity and type is a basic problem of the Irish countryside. The new employment in manufacturing and in services has fallen far short of the decline in agriculture, traditional handcrafts, general labouring and domestic service. For those living close to towns and cities, there is the possibility of access to employment in manufacturing and in the much larger service sector which has concentrated in urban areas. Elsewhere long commuting journeys may be necessitated and even this may not be a possibility for those who do not own cars. In the more remote areas the range of job opportunities may be very limited. This is even more acute for women because the primary industries which predominate in the countryside are traditionally male employing. Thus rural areas tend to have an unbalanced employment structure with high rates of unemployment and underemployment.

AGRICULTURAL LANDSCAPES

Farming is not only the major business of rural areas but also it has been the most powerful force in shaping the countryside. Much of the appearance and character of the Irish countryside is the result of the past and present activities of farmers. Thus an appreciation of agriculture adds greatly to an understanding of the countryside. Farm activities put life into the rural scene and add to its interest, from the farmer and dog herding sheep to the combine harvester cutting grain. Most visitors to the countryside get more pleasure from livestock than from rare species of animals.

Even in the small area of Ireland there is considerable regional variation in the nature of agriculture. This is reflected strongly in the appearance of the countryside and comprises the main element in the regional diversity of the Irish human landscape. Farm size is one important factor for it has an influence on the sizes of fields and farmsteads. The type of farming is indicated by the nature and numbers of the different livestock, by the extent and variety of arable crops, by the forms of the farm buildings and by the work being done in the fields. It is possible to distinguish different agricultural regions, each having its associated distinctive type of landscape. Even the driver who is blind to the surrounding countryside may be aware of the regionally varying effects along the roads of features such as farm machinery in arable areas and mud at sugar beet harvest time, cows at milking time in the dairying areas and sheep going to and from the hills, and the smell of slurry associated with pig and poultry production which is common in Northern Ireland.

The agricultural landscape is partitioned amongst many thousands of farmers and its patterns of farming are the result of the decisions made by these individuals. The decisions are influenced by the personal character and social circumstances of the individual. For example, a farmer who is old or has another occupation is more likely than others to concentrate on cattle production. This is because it involves less work than other farm enterprises and its lower financial returns are not as important a consideration for that person. Family circumstances, education, past experience and personality are other socio-personal factors which affect decision making. Individuals

Arterial drainage work on the river Boyne. (photo: An Teagasc)

Modern milking parlour. (photo: An Teagasc)

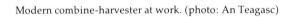

Modern combine-harvester at work. (photo: An Teagasc)

may differ greatly in the ways in which they perceive and respond to the general economic and physical environments in which they operate. Important economic considerations include the prices of different agricultural products and of materials purchased, the availability and costs of labour and capital, and ultimately the profitability of different farm enterprises. In these and other respects farmers' decisions are influenced strongly by political policies and measures. The amount and quality of land which the farmer owns and the relief, climatic and drainage conditions are vital considerations. Although each farmer and farm is different and there may be great contrasts between adjacent holdings, yet there is an overall tendency towards local and regional conformity and this reflects in particular common responses to the physical environment.

The distribution of arable crop production is influenced by climatic and soil suitability (Figure 6.3). Four-fifths of the tilled area is under cereals. Barley is the leading crop, being grown mainly for livestock feeding but also for malting for the brewing and distilling industries. The significance of wheat and sugar beet in the Republic of Ireland is related to the state protection given to them prior to entry to the European Community. Potatoes are proportionately more important in Northern Ireland, because of less favourable environmental conditions for cereals there, market support of potatoes within the United Kingdom and a strong tradition of potato growing in Ulster. Arable cropping is least and simplest in the west, where conditions tend to restrict it to small areas of feeding barley, potatoes and oats, mainly for use on the farm. Irish horticultural production is principally of field vegetables, protected crops of mushrooms, lettuce and tomatoes, and apples and soft fruit. Apple orchards are a distinctive feature of the landscape in north Armagh.

Dairy farming is concentrated in two regions, Munster and Kilkenny in the south and Ulster in the north, but occurs to a lesser extent in many parts. Irish conditions are very favourable for dairying and the south has the comparative advantage of a longer grass growing season. Milk production is mainly from grass in the summer but in Northern Ireland there is more feeding of cows to maintain winter supplies. Most of the output is processed for butter, cheese and other dairy products but supply of liquid milk is important around the cities.

Beef cattle production is the most widespread farm enterprise; it occurs on most holdings and is the leading enterprise on half of them. It is of greatest importance on the central lowland. The dairy herds and areas are the major sources of calves but there are also beef cows kept for suckling. Western farms tend to rear store cattle, while on the better land and larger farms of Leinster and east Ulster the emphasis is more on fattening cattle.

Sheep are most important in the farm economy of mountain areas, where they have a comparative advantage over other enterprises under the difficult environmental conditions. They tend to be a subsidiary enterprise on the lowlands but traditionally have been of major significance in east Galway and adjacent districts. Conditions are favourable in this area of dry limestone land, characterised by its stone walls.

Irish horse breeding is favoured by suitable land and traditional skills. Thoroughbreds are mainly on specialised stud farms, with the main concentration around the Curragh in Kildare and adjacent parts of Meath and Dublin. Other horses are more dispersed and are bred by many farmers who keep one or two mares.

The distribution of pigs and poultry is quite patchy because most are concentrated into a relatively small number of large production units. Both are most important in Northern Ireland, where expansion occurred under the advantage of cheap imported grain prior to accession to the European Community and with access to the British market. The main pig and poultry areas in the Irish Republic are also in Ulster, pigs in east Cavan and poultry in Monaghan. Other production units are principally in the east and south.

There are very pronounced disparities in the financial returns derived from the varying regional types of agriculture. Farm incomes are highest in the south, followed by the east and north. This pattern is mainly the result of the influences of farm enterprise, size of holding and land quality. The profitability of dairying is the main contributor to the high incomes of southern counties. It is significant in the north with pigs and poultry. The returns from arable crops are important in the east. The very low incomes of western areas are partly attributable to the reliance on cattle and sheep production but also to the major effects of the small size of holdings and the lower quality of the land. Attempts by national governments and the European Community to assist farming in these disadvantaged areas through a variety of measures give some recognition to the severity of the problem but have fallen far short of requirements.

CHANGES IN FARMING

Despite the apparent stability of the countryside and the importance of tradition in farming, profound changes have occurred in Irish agriculture in recent decades. It is often said that farming has changed from being a way of life to being a business; it may be preferable to consider it as both but there has been a major shift in emphasis and attitudes. It has become much more commercialised and practices have been transformed through the application of new technology. Agricultural output doubled over a period when the labour force halved, indicating the huge growth in productivity and the extent of development.

One aspect of change which has affected most others has been the greatly increased influence of government. This involvement is most obvious in the huge financial support given to agriculture. It is also evident in the ways in which government policies and advice to farmers have shaped the form of development. The volume of support and the range of state measures grew first in Northern Ireland within the context of the United Kingdom and later in the Irish Republic as its economy developed. Since accession of both to the European Community in 1973, farming differences have lessened within the framework of the Common Agricultural Policy.

Mechanisation has been the most obvious feature of farm modernisation, with mechanical means of production replacing much of the labour of people and horses. Huge growth in the number and size of tractors has been an important part of this trend. The work of the combine harvester is perhaps the most striking illustration, in its replacement of the formerly separate operations of reaping, binding, stooking, gathering and threshing. The many tasks of haymaking done by hand and horse have been superseded by the tractor and the end products are generally rectangular or circular bales, rather than the haycocks and haystacks which once dotted the countryside. Milking machines and the storage and transport of milk in tanks have altered dairying. Farm mechanisation has taken much of the spirit and social occasion out of haymaking and harvest and it has removed picturesque features from the landscape and life of the countryside. Despite such nostalgia, it has generally speeded up many farm operations and lessened the amount of hard work and tedium, making possible huge increases in labour productivity.

The construction of new farm buildings and modernisation of some old ones have been conspicuous features of agricultural change. Much has been done on dairy farms, where modern milking parlours facilitate the handling of large numbers of cows. Many of the farm buildings are associated with the winter housing and fodder provision for cows, beef cattle and, to a lesser extent, sheep. Others represent major changes in the structure of poultry and pig production, the farmyard flock of poultry and the small pigsty having been largely replaced by big intensive production units.

Other inputs which have increased greatly as part of the growth in the capitalisation of Irish agriculture include purchases of fertilisers and lime for land improvement, of compound feedingstuffs for livestock and of chemicals for the control of pests, weeds and diseases. As the investment needs of farmers have increased with capitalisation, so their attitudes towards seeking credit have changed and the indebtedness of the industry has risen greatly. Yet the level of capitalisation remains lower than in many of the more developed countries. It is higher in Northern Ireland than in the Republic, as indicated by levels of mechanisation, fertiliser use and purchase of feedstuffs. Within the Republic of Ireland, dairy and arable farms are the most highly capitalised and levels are lowest on the small farms of the west.

There has been major advancement in the standard of farm management, though great variation occurs between farms and much land remains underutilised. Improvement has been related to the development of applied research and formal education, to the work of the farm advisory services and to the influence of the mass media. One change in farm practice which was actively promoted and has had a considerable impact in the countryside was the substitution of silage for hay in much of the conservation of grass for winter fodder. Silage is favoured over hay because of its greater suitability to the uncertain weather conditions as it does not require drying, because of its lower labour requirements and because of its feeding value. The grass is cut and stored in the green state as silage and generally livestock are given access to it under a self-feed arrangement.

There has been a pronounced trend towards greater concentration and specialisation in Irish agriculture. This was partly through a slow increase in size of holdings as the number of farm owners declined. More striking has been the tendency for farms to streamline their production by reducing the number of enterprises, so that each enterprise is practised on a smaller proportion of farms but at a larger scale on those where it occurs. Thus the traditionally mixed nature of Irish agriculture has diminished. The popular perception of a farm with all varieties of livestock and crops differs from the reality of most farms today. Many farmers now produce few of the food requirements of their own households. The trend towards greater specialisation at the farm level reflects in part that which has occurred in the country as a whole, as the concentration on milk and beef has increased to the extent that they account for almost three-quarters of the value of total Irish agricultural output.

Some of the changes which have been occurring in farming are reflected in the numbers and types of livestock and crops to be seen in the countryside. Because of the increased intensification and specialisation, there are more dairy and beef cattle in the fields in summer but many are now housed during winter. Few poultry and pigs are visible as almost all are now permanently indoors under controlled environments. Working horses have practically disappeared from the scene, releasing a large area of land for other purposes. The search for higher yields and better quality has led to new varieties of livestock and crops. This has involved changes in cattle breeds, which are a distinctive feature of the countryside. Cows had been predominantly Shorthorn and the Hereford and Aberdeen Angus were favoured for beef. These remain but the dual-purpose Friesian has risen to predominance, especially in dairy herds, and continental breeds such as the Charolais and Simmental have been introduced in response to the demand for leaner meat. The area of arable crops has declined and it is increasingly dominated by cereals, mainly because of the work associated with root crops and changing feeding practices. Conversely, some new crops have appeared, most prominently the striking yellow oil seed rape.

The extent of modernisation and its effects have varied greatly between farms. As much of the government support was related to levels of output and investment, the large producers benefited most and dairy farmers in particular were favoured. The large farms contributed an increasing share of the output, especially in the more profitable enterprises. In contrast, there were many farms where there was little change and few of the benefits of modernisation. These were most likely to be smallholdings and on poor quality land and many of the owners were old or unmarried. The outcome is that there remains a large number of farmers who have unacceptably low incomes.

AGRICULTURE AND THE ENVIRONMENT

The changes and development in agriculture, guided by state support, have been of economic benefit to the farming community and to the country as a whole but there have been disadvantageous side-effects on the quality of the rural environment. The large proportion of land used by farmers means that the implications have critical importance for the countryside. Environmental change has occurred since earliest times but it is the accelerated pace and magnitude of change which prompt concern. Many would feel that the outcome is a more polluted and less diversified countryside which has suffered reductions in wildlife content, visual attraction and historical interest. Yet the extent of deterioration has been small compared with agriculturally more developed countries, especially those with much more capitalised, intensified and arable farming systems.

The increased use of chemical fertilisers, pesticides and herbicides has been a cause of environmental pollution and has had detrimental effects on wildlife. The impacts could be lessened by judicious use, giving attention to the type of products and to the level and methods of application. More concentrated and serious sources of pollution are large intensive livestock production units and silage storage facilities. The effects are evident in the pollution of lakes in the north midlands by the waste from pig farms and in fish kills in rivers caused by silage effluent. Proper siting, design and operation of livestock housing and silage layouts and recycling of waste by careful spreading on the land are essential in order to minimise environmental damage.

Land drainage and clearance have huge environmental implications. Poor drainage is a major problem in Irish agriculture but the deepening, straightening and widening of river channels through arterial drainage works on the lowlands is of great harm to wildlife habitat and amenity value. Full consideration should be given to all the costs, and the benefits of further major schemes would be questionable. Hill reclamation encroaches upon the upland environment and the desirability of undertakings should be given due consideration where the threats to wildlife, scenery, soil and recreation are greatest. There has been some removal of field boundaries to facilitate the operation of machinery and increase the efficiency of land use. The loss has not reached critical proportions but it is of concern because hedgerows and trees are such a vital aesthetic component of the Irish landscape and a major sanctuary for wildlife. Also they serve as livestock fences, shelter belts and timber reserves.

Damage has been caused by farming both in structures destroyed and in some created. Sites and buildings of archaeological, historical and scientific value have been damaged or removed in agricultural and associated work. Many modern farm buildings are a visual intrusion in the countryside with regard to scale, shape and composition. While buildings must satisfy the technical needs of agriculture, greater attention should be given to siting, design, building materials and colour and to screening by trees.

The countryside serves as the factory floor of agriculture but also farmers may be regarded as the custodians of much of the countryside and there is often conflict between these two functions. A financially successful agriculture is necessary for the maintenance of the rural landscape and community but maximisation of productivity is environmentally damaging to the countryside. Compromise between the economic and conservation goals is necessary, not only in farming practices but also in government policy and measures relating to agriculture. Some practical guidelines were given in Northern Ireland in the expansion of production in accordance with good conservation practices on a research hill farm at Glenwherry in Co. Antrim and in the encouragement of measures to promote environmentally sensitive farming which was initiated in the Mourne area of Co. Down. Reconciliation makes all the greater sense in the context of surplus agricultural production. From the viewpoint of farming itself, it is vital that a high quality environment should be maintained, so that Ireland's great potential in the production and marketing of pure food can be exploited. Conservation agriculture is in the best interests of the future of the countryside and its people.

FORESTRY

Because of the tiny amount of natural woodland which survives, forestry in Ireland relates almost entirely to planted trees. The first phase of planting was that by landlords on their estates in the eighteenth and nineteenth centuries, initially mainly for landscaping purposes and later with commercial motives. The second and dominant phase has been in the twentieth century for timber production, principally by the state but with some private planting. The impacts of the two phases on the landscape of the countryside were in marked contrast, for the first was mainly of deciduous broadleaved trees and the second predominantly coniferous.

State forestry began effectively in 1904, when the Avondale estate in Co. Wicklow was acquired for a forestry centre. Planting expanded over subsequent decades but greatly increased targets were set in the late 1940s. This thrust was prompted by the timber shortages of the second world war. The rate of new state afforestation has fallen from the peak levels of the 1960s because of the cost and difficulty of land acquisition and financial curtailment, and because an increasing proportion of planting involves reforestation of land after felling.

State development to rectify the dearth of forestry has aimed to achieve certain benefits. The main objective has been to provide a home supply of timber, initially as a strategic reserve but more to replace imports and later contribute to export earnings. Forestry was intended to be a profitable form of land use but, in order to minimise competition with farming, it has been confined mainly to land of low agricultural potential. The provision of rural employment in forestry and timber processing has always been an important consideration. Direct employment in state forestry is less than 3,000, having fallen by more than one-half from a peak about 1960 because of increased labour productivity and reduced planting. Indirect employment is now greater and increasing as the forests mature. Provision for recreation has become an important objective of forestry and there is also some wildlife habitat development.

State planting is almost entirely coniferous because broadleaved trees would not grow satisfactorily on much of the land available, because coniferous trees grow much faster and yield a quicker return on investment and because of the large demand for softwood. European conifers were used at first but species from western North America proved more successful. Sitka

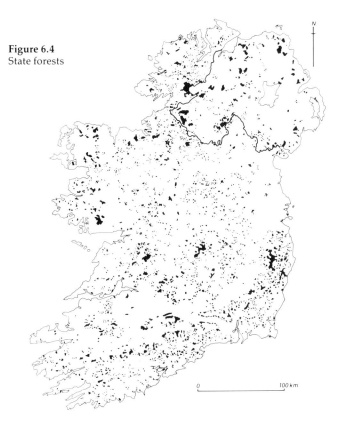

Figure 6.4
State forests

0   100 km

Top: Devil's Glen, Co. Wicklow. *Right*: Blue Pool, Killarney. (photos: Jan de Fouw)

● Forest parks
• Other forest recreation sites
■ National parks
▲ Country parks

Figure 6.5
Recreation sites

0   100 km

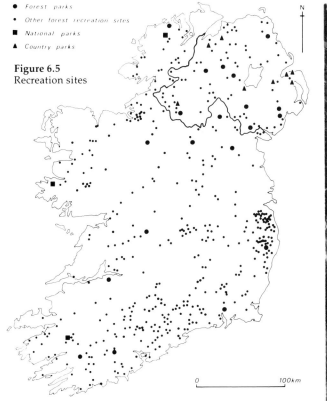

spruce is dominant but lodgepole pine is used on the poorer and more exposed land. Growth rates under the mild and moist Irish conditions are far above those of mainland Europe. The potential is greatest on wet lowland soils, especially those of the drumlin belt.

The two state forest authorities together own over 500,000 hectares, making them by far the largest landowners in the country. The association of forest land with areas of mountain, hill and bog is the main influence on its distribution (Figure 6.4). Much of the early planting was on the more favourable hill slopes of the eastern half of the country and on former estates on the lowlands. From about 1950 there was a major shift in afforestation onto poorer and more exposed land, mainly westwards but also higher up the mountains. This was made possible by the introduction of new machinery, fertilisers and trees species. It resulted from the easier acquisition of poor land and its greater extent in the west and from increased attention to promoting development in disadvantaged areas.

Irish forestry is unique in western Europe, not only because of its small extent but also in that only one-fifth is under private ownership. Landowners have been reluctant to plant trees because of the long-term nature of the investment, the small size of holdings and the lack of a forest consciousness. Most of the private forests comprise deciduous woodland of old or former estates and small woodland plots on farms. These are a very important amenity but much is old and in deteriorated condition. Modern private forestry is predominantly coniferous. Planting expanded in the 1980s in response to government promotion with generous grants and to development of commercial forestry and financial institutional interests.

The environmental effects of forestry and attitudes towards them vary. Commercial forestry may be viewed at its extreme as the imposition of large monotonous tracts of alien even-aged sombre spruce in geometric layout within straight boundaries, damaging scenery, wildlife and soils. The aesthetic aspects of forestry have been given consideration only since the 1960s and more could be done. Much can be achieved through careful location and design, with the overall need being to introduce greater diversification and sensitivity. Measures used include adapting the shape and layout of plantations to the topography, varying the species and ages of trees, using some deciduous varieties where feasible, leaving small areas and strips unplanted in order to preserve views, promote wildlife and add diversity, and proper management of felling operations. Forestry can add variety and beauty to the scene and conservation forestry on even a small part of the total area can have a considerable impact. The visual effects of forestry are accentuated by much of it being on sloping land in areas of high scenic quality.

FISHING

The fishing industry is intimately associated with rural areas as most of the catch is landed at small towns, villages and isolated harbours around the coast and the fishermen live in these settlements or in the open countryside. There are over 9,000 people engaged directly in the sea fisheries, more than half of them on a part-time basis. These are the most widely dispersed sector, especially along the west coast, many being farmer-fishermen. Most of the rural areas where fishing occurs have few alternative employment opportunities, so that the industry has great local significance, especially in Co. Donegal. There are also commercial fisheries on the major rivers. People associated with the fisheries often form tightly-knit communities. The fishery harbours, being places of activity, interest and visual attraction, add much to the character and tourist appeal of the coastal areas where they occur.

Huge growth in the Irish fish catch occurred with development of the industry from the 1950s. Provision of government grants and credit facilities for the purchase of boats and fishing gear did much to encourage expansion and modernisation of the fleet, with a trend towards larger and better equipped vessels. There was major harbour and industrial development to improve landing and processing of the catch and servicing of the fleet. Training schemes were provided to counteract the lack of skills and reluctance to adopt fishing as a livelihood which had existed. The establishment of fish farming was actively encouraged. Substantial improvements in the transport and marketing of fish were effected, with promotion of markets at home and abroad. Despite such overall development, the majority of participants operate on a small scale in inshore waters.

The expansion of Irish fish landings, combined with the even greater effect of increased takings by the fleets of other countries off the Irish coast, led to the curtailment of catches from the 1970s by resource supply problems. Landings of the main species were controlled under the Common Fisheries Policy of the European Community. Conflicts over scarce resources developed, even between Irish fishermen. The salmon is a prime example of conflicting interests, as huge growth in drift netting at sea greatly reduced the supply of fish available to anglers and commercial fisheries on the rivers. Drift netting is an important source of income to the owners of small boats in coastal communities but the revenue per salmon caught is much higher from angling through tourism. The difficulties are accentuated by widespread illegal fishing and some associated violence. The problems of the fishing industry clearly illustrate the critical need for proper management of resources.

Left: Sport fishing. (photo: Bord Failte)

Right: Fish farming, Co. Donegal. (photo: Jan de Fouw)

Below: The harbour at Burtonport. Co. Donegal. (photo: George Morrison, courtesy of Bord Iascaigh Mhara)

EXTRACTIVE INDUSTRIES

The extractive industries involve the removal of products from the earth through mining, quarrying and peat production. Mining of metals has often attracted much public attention and coal, barytes, gypsum and salt are also produced at a small number of locations. Of much greater importance, both in terms of their more widespread occurrence and the employment involved, are the quarrying of stone, sand and gravel and the production of peat. The extractive industries are located almost entirely in the open countryside as the small area of urban land is practically sterilised for such development.

The extractive industries are prominent examples of how there are benefits and disadvantages associated with development and consequent conflicts of interest. They yield materials which are essential to society and benefit the economy of the country. Locally they provide important employment and income and they stimulate services. They may even add diversity to landscapes and create new habitats for wildlife, and historical features of mining may contribute much to the character and interest of an area. Yet there may be many and varied disadvantages to the environment and society. These include destruction of scenery, land dereliction, loss of agricultural potential, pollution of water and air, noise and inconvenience, health hazards, damage to wildlife and historical features, truck traffic on country roads, and social disruption. It is fortunate that much of the extractive industry in the Irish countryside has been in areas which are not considered to be of prime scenic quality, copper mining in the Vale of Avoca in Co. Wicklow having been a major exception. It is of fundamental importance that extractive activity is by its nature temporary, so that the areas concerned face economic and social difficulties when it ceases but also that many of the disdavantages will terminate. It is now technically possible to rehabilitate much of the land for purposes such as agriculture, housing, recreation, conservation and waste disposal. The extractive industries should be organised so as to minimise the disadvantages while achieving the benefits.

The production of sand, gravel and crushed stone as aggregate for buildings and roads is a major activity. About 4,000 are employed in quarrying and many rural people also work in the associated construction industry. One important feature is that deposits are generally shallow, so that large areas of land are involved in supplying the huge volume of material required. Another is that, because of high transport costs on the heavy and bulky aggregate, much quarrying is close to urban areas, where there is most competition for land and the environmental effects are strongly felt. The landscape impact of quarrying is evident around Dublin and Belfast.

Large parts of Ireland's extensive cover of peat bogs traditionally had been cut by hand for domestic fuel. This declined because of its laborious nature and as other sources of energy became available. One unusual occurrence is the cutting of turf by a considerable number of Dublin residents on the adjacent mountains. Private production of peat revived in the early 1980s with the introduction and grant-aiding of small machines which have caused environmental damage in places.

Large scale mechanised production of peat, in which Ireland ranks second to the Soviet Union, began effectively with the establishment of the semistate company Bord na Móna in 1946. It has become one of the largest owners of rural land, with over 80,000 hectares, and it employs 5,000 people. Activity is concentrated on the raised bogs of the midlands, which are suitably large, flat and deep. The peat workings and associated electricity power stations have a huge impact on rural development and population in the midlands. Thus the future exhaustion of the peat resources raises major problems relating to employment and to the appropriate uses and ownership of the cutover bog, whether for forestry, pasture, arable crops, recreation, conservation or other purposes.

RECREATION

The countryside has assumed a major new role as leisure has become an increasingly important aspect of life and the tendency to spend leisure time in a rural setting has grown rapidly. No longer does the countryside function for society only as a place of work and of residence. As many of those using the countryside for outdoor recreation live in urban areas, it represents an important new relationship between town and country.

Recreation is a human need but provision for it also involves work and land use. Employment and income are generated in many recreational and related services but the impacts are most obvious in tourism, which is that component of recreation involving a stay of at least one night away from home. Over two million people visit Ireland annually and the countryside constitutes the dominant attraction for them. Domestic tourism is also of major significance. Although business is seasonal and most incomes are moderate or low, recreation has become a supplementary or main source of revenue for a large number of rural people and many rural areas. One advantageous aspect is that much tourism is oriented towards those areas which most need the benefits, especially the west. The fact that recreation has become a major industry affords a strong economic rationale for conservation of those features of the countryside which constitute its appeal.

The huge growth of recreation in the countryside has been a feature

Tara, Co. Meath. These great earthworks were once the seat of the High Kings of Ireland. They are slightly elevated above some of the most fertile agricultural lands in Leinster.

Clonmacnoise, on the banks of the River Shannon, was one of the greatest ecclesiastical and monastic centres of rural Ireland. To this date they act as a magnet for both foreign and Irish visitors.

A rural scene from just east of the mouth of the River Nore, Co. Waterford. The remains of castles, monastic sites and great houses sit easily on the present Irish landscape.

Left: Among the most challenged and hardiest people of rural Ireland are our island dwellers. Few would argue that Tory Island, Co. Donegal, presents the greatest challenge of all.

Below: North Donegal coastline. Ireland's location astride the Atlantic ocean and a climatic belt along which cyclonic depressions freely move, generates an ever-changing skyscape.

mainly of the twentieth century and especially of its second half. It has been
the outcome of many interrelated factors. There is much more time for leisure
because of more holidays, longer weekends and shorter working days and as
a result of longer retirement. Greater affluence promotes much higher recreational spending. Improvements in transport have facilitated movement to
Ireland and the countryside. The introduction of car ferries and greatly
increased car ownership and rental have been particularly important. This is
because the personal and family mobility which the car provides enables
freedom of choice and penetration of much of the countryside which would
not be accessible otherwise. Improved education and the media have
promoted travel and led to greater awareness of and interest in the
countryside. Participation has increased greatly in outdoor activities for
which rural areas provide a setting, including angling, horse riding and
sailing. The growth of urbanisation at home and overseas has been of fundamental importance, because of the extent to which the space, naturalness and
tranquillity of the countryside are perceived by many as a desirable contrast
and change from the built-up environment and pressures of urban life.

Recreational activities
There is a very wide range of recreational activities in the countryside,
varying with the resources and accessibility of different areas and with the
personal characteristics, perceptions and preferences of people. It is evident,
however, that most visitors to the countryside engage in comparatively
passive informal pursuits. Pleasure driving is the most widespread activity,
involving viewing of the landscape and experiencing the countryside while
travelling or stopping occasionally at vantage points or other places. At such
stops people sit in or outside of the car, many go for walks and picnic and the
children play but the great majority of people remain within relative proximity to the vehicle. The orientation of much traffic towards scenic areas
indicates the importance of landscape in pleasure outings.

   Water is a major recreational resource, both as a component in landscape
attraction and as a basis for aquatic activities. The lure of water is indicated
in the extent to which the coastal zone is the prime recreational area, despite
climatic conditions being less than ideal for beach activities. Ireland is fortunate in the relative accessibility of all parts of the country to the lengthy coast
and to the network of rivers and lakes and some canals and reservoirs.
Another advantage is the comparatively low levels of pollution in most
waters. There is major scope for angling for game, coarse and sea fish; it is
one of the most popular activities amongst residents and an important attraction for overseas visitors. Sailing has grown rapidly and other aquatic
activities include outdoor swimming, motor cruising, power boating, canoe-

Above: Mechanised peat production on a midland bog. (photo: Bord Failte)

Right: Turf bank. (photo: Jan de Fouw)

Quarrying. (photo: Cement Roadstone)

ing, rowing, water skiing, windsurfing, surfing and subaqua sports. The Shannon and Lough Erne are unique resources for inland cruising and are used by many European visitors.

Walking affords intimate contact with the countryside in addition to physical exercise. Activity ranges in type and volume from the popular casual stroll in the country to endurance hikes for several days over rugged terrain. The extensive upland areas provide considerable opportunities for hillwalking, mountaineering and rock climbing. Activity is most concentrated in the Wicklow and Mourne Mountains because of accessibility to urban populations but conditions are more rugged in the west. Forested land provides the best conditions for participants in orienteering to find their way across country using map and compass. Caving is most common in the limestone of Clare and Fermanagh. The dense road network of the Irish countryside and the comparatively small volume of traffic afford conditions which are very suitable for cycling and walking. There are several motor sports and minority activities above ground are hang gliding, gliding and flying.

With the reputation which Ireland has for horses, there is a strong local following for equestrian pursuits in the countryside and considerable participation by tourists. Activities include tuition, dressage, jumping, racing, hunting, trekking and horse-drawn caravanning. Hunting occurs over much of the lowlands and generally involves foxhunting but there are some harriers and stag hunts. There is rough shooting for varied birds and some animals and there is higher quality shooting for pheasant and grouse and for wildfowl on lakes and estuaries. Much of the access for fieldsports is based on the goodwill of landowners.

Visits to specific places because of their historical, cultural or natural heritage are a major feature of recreation in the countryside. They are an important reason for tourists choosing to visit Ireland and historical features appeal to North Americans in particular. Most of the popular monastic sites, mansions and gardens are located in the countryside. There are more than one million visits annually to those sites which are owned by members of the Historic Irish Tourist Houses and Gardens Association. Most of the properties open to the public in Northern Ireland are owned by the National Trust. Sites of scientific interest have much lesser appeal, except where there is a unique element as at the Giants' Causeway and in caves, but nature trails have become more common and popular. Historical and nature outings to different sites are organised by local societies and by special interest groups for activities such as birdwatching.

Parks and forest recreation
There are three national parks in the Republic of Ireland, comprising Killarney in Co. Kerry, Connemara in Co. Galway and Glenveagh in Co. Donegal, and a fourth is being developed in the Burren in Co. Clare. The purposes of the national parks are to conserve the wildlife, landscapes and other features of the parks and to provide for public appreciation of them. They are located in areas of high environmental quality. There are park centres and nature trails, with interpretative displays, publications and programmes designed to enhance the experience of visitors.

The country parks of Northern Ireland also have conservation and recreational roles but they cater more specifically for recreation. They provide facilities for informal outdoor recreation in a rural setting. The most popular country park is Crawfordsburn on the southern shore of Belfast Lough with over half a million visits annually.

The opening of state forest land to the public has been the most significant development in provision for recreation in the Irish countryside. The first forest park was established at Tollymore in Co. Down in 1955 and most of the development has been only from the 1960s. There are about three million visits annually to the five hundred forest recreation sites. Facilities range from just forest paths and parking space at many sites to quite a high level of provision at the twenty forest parks. Use is mainly by family groups for informal walking and relaxation in the forest environment and people express a high degree of satisfaction. Forests offer the advantage that they can absorb more people than other types of land without detracting from the recreational experience. The distribution of sites reflects that of the state forests, so that they are mainly in upland areas and many are in scenic settings (Figure 6.5). It is particularly fortunate that there is extensive forest and over sixty open sites in south Dublin and Wicklow accessible to the Dublin population concentration.

Some problems in recreation
The huge growth and variety of recreation must not conceal the major problem of access to the countryside for many people. Activity is predominantly car-oriented and there is proportionately lower participation by the poor, the elderly and the disabled and by inner city residents as a whole. Lack of mobility may not be the only influence, as in the disinterest of some youths, but there is a need to provide greater opportunity through improved accessibility. This might be done through organisation of group travel to the countryside, through provision of public and private transport services, and through taking accessibility to existing services and to the cities into account in the planning of recreational provision. There is a general need to provide

more parks in urban fringe areas accessible to city residents. These should be varied in catering for different tastes, ranging from simple provision for an afternoon outing to leisure parks with many outdoor and some covered facilities.

A different accessibility problem relates to the lack of formal provision for movement off roads within the countryside. Ireland is very poorly served in this respect compared with other European countries. The contrast is most striking when made with the dense though diminished network of footpaths and bridleways in England and Wales, and the acceptance of recreational use of private land in Norway and Sweden. There are few public footpaths, most rights of way have been neglected and there are complications in relation to trespass, liabilities and compensation. Even recognisable routes such as canal towpaths, disused railways and the old green roads have often been blocked off. Public rights of way are regulated in Northern Ireland by the district councils but the legal and administrative situation is worse in the Republic. The major development has been the establishment of long-distance walking routes such as the Ulster, Wicklow and Kerry Ways. Over much of the countryside if walkers leave the winding country roads and lanes and the forest walks, they are dependent on the favourable attitudes of individual landowners. It is desirable that there should be developed throughout the country a system of public footpaths through registration of existing rights of way, creation of new paths and signposting. Although access to sea and lake shore is better than in some countries, it needs to be protected against encroachment and to be extended. More coastal paths, such as that developed by the National Trust in the Mourne country, would be a wonderful asset. Conversely, restriction on access is desirable in some remote areas, particularly in relation to motorised transport, so that the wilderness character of these places may be conserved for those who value and seek it.

Recreational needs are important in the countryside but recreation itself can cause damage. Examples include the effect of trampling on vegetation, soils and sand dunes, the danger of forest fire, the disturbance or destruction of wildlife, the damage to farm property, the pollution of land and water, the landscape effect of unsightly development and some social and cultural impacts of tourism. Only a minority of people misbehave, some wilfully but more through ignorance. Even though the density of countryside recreation is low in Ireland, numbers may cause problems because of the concentration into particular places and at specific times. Thus traffic congestion and parking difficulties relate mainly to movement around urban areas and especially to seaside visits and they occur on summer weekends and particu-larly on the few sunny Sundays and public holidays.

An important concept with regard to numbers of people is the recreational carrying capacity of a place. This refers to the level of use which an area can sustain without an unacceptable deterioration of the character and quality of the resources or of the recreation experience of the users; thus it has ecological and psychological dimensions. As more people come into the countryside it becomes less easy to find the solitude which some of them seek, though much of Ireland is far from its carrying capacity in this respect.

Co-ordinated recreational management of the Irish countryside is largely lacking but highly desirable. This relates both to provision for recreation and also to its regulation. Leisure should be provided for, just as are medical and educational services. This includes basic facilities such as car parks, picnic sites, playgrounds, toilets, signposting and scenic routes but also in other ways. General education for leisure is needed and interpretation in the countryside enhances the recreational experience. Better organisation would help to lessen antagonism with farming and other uses of rural land. Regulation could reduce the conflicts between different recreational uses, as would follow from the separation in space and time of motor sports and horse riding from other activities. Much could be done to regulate usage levels through road and parking control and through signposting and promotion. Balancing supply and demand would be a major objective of organisation. Positive management would aim to facilitate recreational use of the countryside and maximise the satisfaction of those participating, while minimising damage to the countryside which they have come to visit and to those who live and work there.

Top: State Forest and Recreation site in the Slieve Bloom Mountains, Co. Laois. (photo: Desmond Gillmor)

Above: Carragh River Valley, Co. Kerry. (photo: Jan de Fouw)

Left: Hill-walking in the Mournes. (photo: Northern Ireland Tourist Board)

Rural People and Services

THE CHANGING COUNTRYSIDE

MARY CAWLEY

oundaries between rural and urban areas and people in Ireland, as in many other countries of western Europe, have become increasingly blurred in the years since the second world war. There are many manifestations of this blurring apparent in the landscape, most notably in the gradual physical extension of towns and cities into the surrounding countryside, often with severely negative aesthetic effects. A blurring of boundaries is apparent also in the popular conception of who constitute rural people in Ireland. The ranks of farmers, fishermen, foresters and the craftsmen, shopkeepers, clergy, teachers and police who care for their spiritual and temporal welfare have been enlarged by the addition of a growing band of newcomers who actively seek rural residence for aesthetic, social and economic reasons. These include new suburbanites whose incomes permit them to move to the countryside to live and who travel to work daily in nearby towns and cities. Immigrants also include 'pastoralists' who, individually or as groups, seek alternative life-styles, varying from economic self-sufficiency to the practice of religious cults in remote locations.

The arrival of newcomers to the countryside serves to diversify the structure of the society to which they move and to modify the physical appearance of the landscape. The retention of members of the indigenous population who in the past would have migrated elsewhere in Ireland or overseas in search of employment, and the return of former outmigrants, became possible during the 1970s because of improved occupational opportunities within commuting distance of their home localities. The presence of these two groups has contributed to economic change in the countryside but its effect has been less socially disruptive than has immigration. The emergence of a 'six o'clock' and 'weekend' variant of part-time farming is closely associated with the decision of members of farm families to adopt urban-based employment while remaining resident on the family farm holding. Their increased incomes contribute to improvements in housing, living standards and agriculture, although not necessarily in that order. Because of close family ties with their area of residence and their involvement in agriculture, this group is both 'in' and 'of' the countryside, a circumstance which distinguishes them clearly from recent immigrants. Together with the latter, however, they form an important component in the daily flow of commuters from countryside to town.

Urban encroachment on rural land is a feature of most towns and cities in Ireland today, notably in the Republic of Ireland where controls on urban-related residential development have tended to be less stringent than in Northern Ireland. Few parts of the island have escaped urban influence; even less scenically attractive remote upland and agriculturally depressed areas inland are sought as second-home locations. Small numbers of people, including immigrants from mainland Europe, have moved to such areas in recent years to embrace a life of economic self-sufficiency as an antidote to the pressurised existence of the contemporary urban environment.

The integration of urban and rural areas and people that is currently taking place in Ireland involves highly complex processes which are not fully revealed by tracing urban-generated housing and recreational areas on maps, or by identifying changing occupational structures from census data. These processes of change are a product of and are moulded by a series of economic events that have been particularly marked since the 1960s. Included are the widely-spread pattern of industrial development that was fostered in the Republic by the Industrial Development Authority (IDA), Údarás na Gaeltachta (The Gaeltacht Authority) and its predecessor Gaeltarra Éireann, and in Northern Ireland by the Industrial Development Board and the Local Enterprise Development Unit (LEDU). Important changes in the distribution of population have been associated with industrial development, involving migration to the environs of towns and villages and continued decline in the less accessible parts of the countryside. This redistribution of population is bringing about new needs for social and consumer services in the countryside and creating novel problems with regard to their provision. Service needs and aspects of delivery vary very markedly between urban fringe and remote localities.

A 'sense of community' is actively sought by some urban incomers to the countryside as a social construct which will provide a feeling of belonging, of face-to-face relations, as an antidote to the increasing anomie of urban society. The social bonds of community are assuming renewed economic importance also in relation to community development. In this context, the unity engendered by common interests and problems forms the basis for self-help movements. Such movements are gaining momentum notably, but not exclusively, in locations where state-funded industrial development is lacking or where such initiatives are not considered adequate to meet local

Above: Rent-a-Cottage, Puckane, Co. Tipperary. *Right*:
Fishing. *Below*: Shannon cruising. (photos: Bord Failte).
Left: The Irish coast is ideal for scuba-diving. (photo: Bord
Failte)

needs. With state help, community co-operatives have burgeoned in many rural areas in recent years, fostering a range of agricultural, industrial and service activities including tourism.

A series of new residential and occupational forms is being grafted on to the countryside to a varying extent in different locations. Strong underlying dimensions of an older long-established rural identity persist, within which countryfolk have organised their social and economic activities for generations. Of major importance are parish structures which form one of the most basic territorial units in rural Ireland, serving as a focus not only in religious affairs but also in primary education and for a wide range of voluntary organisations. The strong sense of place identity associated with parochial structures is actively sought by some newcomers to the countryside. Others, whose social contacts are viewed as an extension of their occupational position, lack this sense of place identity and are 'in' rather than 'of' the countryside.

RURAL POPULATION CHANGE

Many areas of the countryside have experienced population growth in recent decades. Yet, for more than a century after the Great Famine of the 1840s, rural decrease through migration overseas was the major factor contributing to a net loss of population in the twenty-six counties that now comprise the Irish Republic. In the six counties of Northern Ireland, population growth recommenced at the end of the nineteenth century but in upland areas west of the River Bann low rates of growth or decline persisted. The difficulties of agricultural cultivation associated with upland and poorly drained lowland environments, combined with a predominance of small-farm structures and the absence of substantial employment opportunities outside agriculture were the main factors contributing to rural out-migration. The younger better-educated members of communities dominated among those who left the countryside, as did females for whom local employment opportunities were even more limited than for males. Prolonged age and sex selective outmigration had inevitable consequences for the structure of residual populations of more remote localities: marriage rates fell and the incidence of bachelorhood among middle-aged farmers increased. Such men possessed little interest in farm improvement. Furthermore, at a community level, the pool of potential leaders in social and economic affairs became severely diminished, thereby serving to inhibit social and economic advance. The areas of the countryside that have suffered most severely from outmigration and its associated problems have a broad western distribution (Figure 7.1).

Within this region, however, some notable reversals of past trends have taken place in recent years.

Using a conservative definition of 'rural' as referring to areas outside settlements of 250 inhabitants or more, approximately one-quarter (400,000) of the population of Northern Ireland and nearly two-fifths (1,300,000) of the population of the Republic can be so defined. This rural population increased during the 1970s, although not necessarily in the more remote localities. Recent growth has been greatest in the vicinities of the towns, as a result of the overspill of population into the surrounding countryside. Because the rates of rural increase were less than those in urban areas, the share of Ireland's total population in rural areas declined. For this reason, it is questionable if the term 'population turnaround', which has been applied to rates of rural population growth which exceed urban rates in parts of the United States, Canada and the more developed countries of western Europe, is truly appropriate to explain recent changes in Ireland.

By the 1960s, decline or stagnation characterised demographic structures in remote rural areas of Northern Ireland with slow growth being the predominant pattern elsewhere, except in areas fringing Belfast where rapid urban overspill was occurring. Little change has occurred in the total rural population since 1970. At a sub-county level, growth was most marked in north Down, reflecting suburbanisation from Belfast. Growth took place in the vicinity of most large urban centres but was least apparent in mid and south-east Ulster. Decreases occurred in extensive areas of the west and south and in the Antrim uplands. Nevertheless, the rural component constitutes one-half or more of the total population throughout much of the west of the province and in the uplands of north Antrim and mid Down. It is in these latter areas that the most severe problems of rural underdevelopment currently exist (Figure 7.1).

From the end of the nineteenth century until 1960, rural decline was the main factor contributing to population loss in the Republic of Ireland. During the 1960s, when increased levels of state investment in industrial development served to retain large numbers of young people and attracted immigrants from overseas, growth occurred in the environs of the larger cities of Dublin, Cork, Limerick, Waterford and Galway. This pattern of increase became more widespread during the 1970s, and the early 1980s as more extensive areas came within the ambit of acceptable commuting distances from urban-based employment. Only remote coastal districts of the west, many of which are dominated by inhospitable mountain masses and by low quality agricultural land, together with equally depressed areas of east Connaught and south Ulster, have failed to take part in population growth, due mainly to a dearth of off-farm employment (Figure 7.1).

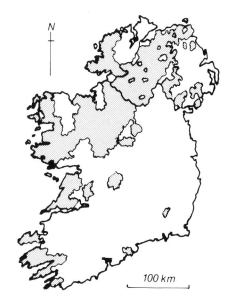

Figure 7.1
Rural problem areas.

Where population growth has occurred, a number of underlying contributory factors may be identified. Rural immigration of professional, managerial and retired households has been particularly marked in the environs of cities and large towns. Smaller towns and villages have experienced this phenomenon on a lesser scale. Limited movement of working-class households to public authority housing estates has occurred on the margins of the major urban-industrial centres. Proximity to urban-based employment is undoubtedly of major importance in explaining population retention in areas of open countryside since 1970; occupational outmigration from agriculture continued as a corollary of the increased capitalisation and mechanisation of farming following accession to membership of the European Community. More remote localities experienced localised population growth as a result of the employment creation activities of the Gaeltacht development agencies. Local co-operative initiatives based on fishing, agriculture or craft enterprises have further contributed to produce pockets of rural population increase, as have tourist developments such as holiday cottage schemes.

Contrasting policies have operated in relation to the location of industry in the countryside in Northern Ireland and the Irish Republic. Such contrasts have had implications for patterns of rural population increase. The strict application of a key settlement policy in the wake of the *Northern Ireland Development Programme* of 1970 placed an effective limit on development outside selected urban locations. It was in fact hoped that the chosen key settlements would act as destinations for rural outmigrants. The industrial base in selected villages was to be strengthened through the work of LEDU, established in 1970. This organisation was committed with the task of stimulating enterpreneurship and economic development in more remote areas which had proved unattractive to investment under existing industrial policy. The LEDU scheme has been less successful in rural areas than was initially hoped, because of the need to channel much of its efforts into the greater Belfast area to offset high levels of unemployment. A commitment to rural industry, having due regard to avoiding deleterious environmental effects, has been a central element in development policy in the Republic of Ireland, as pursued by the IDA, the Shannon Free Airport Development Company (SFADCO) and the County Development Teams since the early 1970s. Few limits have operated on the choice of locations for investment, however, with the result that associated residential growth is more widespread than in Northern Ireland.

During the 1970s, the rural exodus was considerably reduced and indeed reversed in areas within acceptable commuting distances of urban-based employment. Marriage rates increased, contributing to an annual average birth rate in excess of 20 per 1,000 in the Irish Republic, with the result that one-half of the state's population is under 25 years of age. The inability of the national economy to absorb the growing workforce due to both international and national retrenchment means that increasing numbers of young people are seeking employment overseas. Rural outmigration has recommenced.

PHYSICAL PLANNING IN THE COUNTRYSIDE

Patterns of contemporary settlement and housing differ markedly between Northern Ireland and the Republic. Sir Robert Matthew's *Survey and Plan* of 1963 for the Belfast Region had an important, although not overriding, influence on subsequent physical planning in Northern Ireland. Essentially, Matthew wished to curtail the growth of Belfast and to direct development and population to six growth centres elsewhere in the province. Rural areas were viewed as having a passive role to play against which these changes would occur. Further restrictions on physical development in the countryside were introduced by regulations relating to rural subsidy housing in 1964 which formed the keystone of housing policy for the following fifteen years. A key settlement strategy was recommended as a means of preventing ribbonisation and dispersed housing and with a view to reducing the costs of service provision. Permission to build outside nucleated settlements was restricted to defined groups of farmers and rural workers.

These regulations were partially revised in 1973, but it was not until after the publication in 1978 of a *Review of Rural Planning Policy*, prepared under the chairmanship of Dr. W. H. Cockroft, that a relaxation of the restrictions occurred. It was decided then to permit development outside certain specified areas which are to be preserved with a view to preventing urban sprawl and protecting locations of high amenity. In consequence, greater flexibility of control emerged in approaches to rural residential development in Northern Ireland during the early 1980s.

Widespread urban encroachment on the countryside in the Republic of Ireland provides ample evidence of the markedly different attitudes that have prevailed towards rural residential growth by comparison with Northern Ireland. Physical planning in the Republic lies within the responsibility of local authorities (county councils and borough councils) under the provisions of Local Government Acts of 1963, 1976 and 1982. The concept of restricting permission for private house construction to members of the farm population and others with a clear need for rural residence was inherent in physical planning policy in the Republic since its inception but it has not been strictly adhered to by planning authorities. Suggested reasons for nonadherence include the long tradition of the individual homestead in rural Ireland and the individuality of the Irish character. A ministerial circular of 1973 which urged that 'proposals for residential development in rural areas (one house or a small group) should be granted if at all possible' reflected a generally held attitude of tolerance towards new house construction in areas previously experiencing population decline.

A further limit on the ability of professional planners to implement stringent policy proposals relates to the overriding role of county councils in decision making under the provisions of Section Four of the City and County Management (Amendment) Act of 1955. This Act was designed initially to provide for council house allocation but it has been used in a discretionary way by some county councils to permit private residential development in locations scheduled for conservation as amenity areas, notably along the west coast. Apart from the negative aesthetic consequences of ribbon and open-country residential development, the attendant costs of providing public water, sewerage, refuse collection and postal services are estimated to be three times the levels pertaining in nucleated settlements. Contamination of wells and the possibility of pollution through seepage to lakes and rivers are emerging in areas where large numbers of houses are located on individual sites and dependence on underground tanks for waste disposal is high. Traffic hazards and high transport costs are other disadvantages of dispersed housing development.

Some of the modern private residences constructed in rural Ireland lack sympathy with their immediate environment in terms of design, siting and building materials. Less strict planning regulations have contributed to more severe problems in this regard in the Irish Republic than in Northern Ireland. In general, new housing development in the Republic is characterised by basic bungalow or two storey designs, modified to produce individuality. House plans are frequently derived from mass-produced manuals, a practice which is neither new nor confined to Ireland since many of the manuals are produced for the British market. Original architect-designed dwellings are less numerous but frequently reflect borrowings from many cultures and time periods, rather than seeking compatibility with the landscapes and culture in which they are located. Thus, Spanish arches, classical porticos, Tudor half-timbering and curb roofs are appearing with increasing frequency in the Irish countryside.

The visual impact of many new dwellings is heightened by their newness and by the immaturity of their surrounding grounds which do not yet temper the impact of the dwelling. In scenic locations, sites have sometimes been chosen to maximise on panoramic views, with the result that the integrity of skylines and lake and sea shores is interrupted by new dwellings. The building materials used in contemporary structures, notably the excessive use of concrete to the neglect of local stone, have been criticised by many observers. Clearly steps could be taken to ensure that new dwellings blend more effectively with their environment in terms of siting, elevation and use of building materials and enclosures. Planning authorities operate guidelines in these respects but with varying levels of success as the evidence demonstrates.

An awareness of the desirability of preserving older dwellings of traditional design and materials is emerging in the Irish countryside. Costs are often high, in repairing and maintaining thatched roofs for example, and many of these roofs have been replaced by cheaper asbestos sheeting or by tiles or slates. As a result, the intrinsic character of many traditional buildings has been lost. In response to this loss, the need for conservation is being emphasised by An Taisce (The National Trust for Ireland) and by Bord Fáilte (Irish Tourist Board) through its annual Tidy Towns and Villages competition. In many of the more remote areas of the countryside, however, issues other than conservation assume prime importance in the public consciousness. Major problems pertaining to rural welfare have been highlighted in recent years.

WELFARE ISSUES

Within the realm of rural welfare, as reflected in income levels and the broad standards of living experienced, two groups emerge as being in deprived positions relative to national norms in both Northern Ireland and the Republic. These are small-farm households and the elderly. Both are strongly represented in areas of poor agricultural potential along the west coast and in upland locations inland. Indeed, these groups may be viewed as those who *par excellence* have become trapped within a cycle of cumulative deprivation in personal and locational terms. They include the sons of small farmers who remained with their parents to work the family holding while their brothers and sisters migrated to live and work elsewhere in Ireland, or more commonly, overseas. When some of these men inherited the farm in their father's old age or on his death, any initiative for farm improvement or enlargement had been lost and old systems and structures persisted.

Because of distance from urban centres, few opportunities for off-farm employment existed and outmigration of the young and better educated persisted. Continuing population decline in turn contributed to the contraction of service facilities. The potential for attracting and retaining a young working population was further reduced, with the result that residual demographic structures in remote and upland locations tend to have above average proportions of less well-off and elderly persons present. Many farmers in such locations have experienced considerable difficulty in breaking the economic constraints imposed by small farms and they have gradually become dependent upon supplementary sources of income, including state transfer payments and part-time employment. The elderly, among whom bachelors living alone form a large component, commonly lack the physical ability or the motivation to work their farms. They have become almost totally dependent on their state pensions as a source of income and frequently they live in substandard housing conditions.

Small-farm structures and their negative influence on family farm income have for long been issues of concern in rural Ireland but agricultural measures have singularly failed to erode the relative disparity that exists between large and small farm categories. A state sponsored income support measure has been specifically designed for the owners of small uneconomic farm holdings in the Republic of Ireland in the form of a Smallholders Unemployment Assistance Scheme, introduced in 1965. All farmers, the valuation of whose land falls below a fixed threshold figure, are eligible for support. A farmer may also qualify for financial support on the basis of a factual assessment of income. Dependence on Smallholders Assistance and on other forms of state transfer payments has increased to a stage where such payments account for 40 per cent of gross income among farmers with holdings less than 12 hectares in size. In Northern Ireland, farm families with one or more dependent children whose resources are insufficient to meet their needs are eligible to apply for a means tested family income supplement.

The rural elderly form a second major group whose welfare is the subject of particular attention, notably aspects of income and housing. Persons over 65 years of age comprise 11 per cent of the total population of the Republic of Ireland and 12 per cent of the total in Northern Ireland. In areas where off-farm employment opportunities have been limited in the past, many of the elderly are dependent almost exclusively on their state pensions as a source of income. Fuel and electricity allowances, free television licences and free travel permits for public transport in the Republic, and on payment of a small fee in Northern Ireland, are designed to ensure that the elderly experience a basic standard of living. However, a physical disability, such as arthritis, or distance from bus stops in remote areas may prevent use being made of free travel concessions. As a result, where a family member is not available to provide transport, elderly men and women may have to spend substantial sums of money on essential trips to a town to collect their old age pension or to visit their doctor's surgery.

Home ownership levels among the rural elderly are higher than among their urban counterparts. House structures tend to be older in the countryside, dampness is a frequent problem and piped water and indoor sanitation may be absent. Research by the National Council for the Elderly in the Republic has highlighted the existence of such problems on a localised basis. Essential repairs, including the replacement of roofs, doors and windows, are carried out by local authorities, who also provide temporary dwellings in cases of need. In both the Republic and Northern Ireland, local authorities, Health Boards, voluntary organisations and the Northern Ireland Housing Executive are becoming involved in providing purpose-built and sheltered housing with resident wardens, for the elderly. Schemes for bringing essential services to the elderly in their homes or at points near their homes are also receiving additional attention. Such schemes involve the provision of additional chiropody services and increased numbers of nursing staff and health visitors. The needs of the elderly are, of course, part of a broader problem relating to rural service provision in general.

While residual groups who experience below average living conditions certainly persist among rural populations, standards of living in general have improved markedly in the countryside in recent decades. Initially, this involved the extension of electricity supplies to all rural homes, a task that was substantially completed by the 1960s. Enhanced subsidies were made available for the construction of new homes in the countryside during the 1960s and additional numbers of local authority dwellings were provided for less well-off families. The development of public water supplies was financially aided by the Department of the Environment in the Irish Republic during the 1970s in joint schemes with local communities. Prior to that time, many rural homes had been dependent on artesian wells for their water supply and some still lacked indoor sanitation because of the high costs associated with developing such wells. Increased farm incomes following on membership of the European Community also facilitated many improvements in the standard of farm housing.

Higher incomes from both farm and non-farm sources have contributed to increased ownership of consumer durables among rural populations. Levels of motor car and television ownership have increased in recent decades, as has the range of labour saving devices in farm homes. Recreational facilities for young rural people have improved markedly also. These include playing fields as well as indoor sports' facilities which are frequently funded jointly from state and community sources. In common with many other developed economies, major disparities in living conditions between town and countryside have been eroded gradually in Ireland although deprived areas and groups certainly persist.

Top left: Gate – recycled! (photo: Jan de Fouw). *Above*: Modern ribbon-development along an Irish road. (photo: Desmond Gillmor). *Below*: Cottage Co. Wexford. *Left*: Thatcher at work, Donegal. (photos: Jan de Fouw)

SERVICE NEEDS AND PROVISION

Major advances have taken place in the levels of social and welfare services provided by state agencies in Northern Ireland and the Republic of Ireland. This applied, for instance, to the increased numbers of people who were brought within the ambit of the state health sector and the free secondary education system in the Republic from about 1970. Yet, in terms of the access to fixed service points that they experienced, the populations of remote rural areas began to lag seriously behind national norms. Low population densities and continued demographic decline had for long contributed to relatively low levels of facilities being available in the countryside. Centralisation policies, designed with a view to gaining economies of scale as well as improving the standard of service provided, served to exacerbate the problem of accessibility.

Many rural residents now live substantially greater distances from primary schools, general practitioners' surgeries and grocery shops than do their urban counterparts. Public transport provision, which would help to overcome the problem of distance to fixed-point facilities, is generally characterised by low route densities and by infrequent schedules in the open countryside. Some localities have only a once weekly service to a large town while many people live several miles from a bus stop. The elderly, low-income households in general and housewives with young children who do not have access to a car while their husbands are at work are particularly severely affected.

The large scale closure of one and two-teacher rural primary schools dates to the mid 1960s in both Northern Ireland and the Republic. The expansion of the school curriculum to include art, environmental studies and physical education, subjects which required specially trained teachers who could be economically employed only in large schools, was a major contributory factor. Falling school rolls in areas which had experienced prolonged outmigration, the need to replace outmoded buildings and the increasing difficulty of attracting highly qualified teachers to remote locations were involved also. The policy of closure was made more acceptable in the Republic by the introduction in 1967 of a free transport service for children living more than two miles from a primary school.

Over 300 schools were closed in Northern Ireland between 1960 and 1980. Almost 2,000 closures took place in the Republic between 1966 and 1977, when the policy was officially abandoned, partly at least because of the increasing cost of transport. The role of the local primary school in maintaining community cohesion and in socialising young children within a familiar environment has been forwarded as a key reason for its retention in recent years. The long distances and protracted periods of time that young children may spend travelling to and from schools in towns and villages are also considered to be undesirable.

Centralisation within the primary health sector dates to the early 1970s too, although proposals for health centre development to replace single-handed surgeries predate that period in Northern Ireland. The reorganisation of primary care and community health services in Northern Ireland in 1973 resulted in the establishment of a large number of health centres, mainly in town and village locations. In the Republic in 1971 a 'choice of doctor' scheme was introduced to offset one of the major disadvantages of the dispensary system which dated from 1851. The closure of many rural dispensaries followed, although a doctor may still attend for a number of hours per week. Medical card holders who are eligible for free medical treatment in Health Board areas along the west coast now live substantially greater distances from their doctor's surgery than do their counterparts in eastern Health Board areas. A major effect of centralisation, designed in part at least to improve the quality of care provided, has been to increase the cost incurred by some rural patients in using a basic welfare service.

The local grocery shop, often with a public house attached, functioned both as an economic and a social focus in rural Ireland in the past. It provided a wide range of goods and served as a locus for meeting friends and neighbours. The number of such shops has declined continuously since the 1960s in response to falling population levels and to increased competition posed by supermarket chains and multiples in towns and villages. The closure of the rural shop results in considerable hardship for people without easy access to transport, including the elderly and low income households. Mobile shops compensate for the loss of fixed facilities in part but they circulate at infrequent intervals, provide a limited range of goods and charge relatively high prices because of the need to allow for additional transport costs.

Public transport provision, which would help offset the problems associated with declining levels of accessibility to fixed service facilities, is notoriously low in rural areas of dispersed population. The total rail network in Ireland has shrunk to 2,300 km, less than one-half of its former extent. Rail services function mainly as links between the major centres of population. Rural bus services consist of two elements: an expressway service between large towns and cities and a fare stage service in the countryside. The latter functions as a social rather than an economic facility and is heavily subsidised.

Strategies to offset the problems associated with accessibility to basic social and welfare services currently in operation or under consideration include home visits to the elderly, meals on wheels in the vicinity of towns and villages, community-run buses and a postbus in Co. Clare. Mobile banks and mobile libraries are also familiar to many rural residents in remote locations, but their value to persons without easy access to public or private transport is not always fully appreciated by the public at large. Banking facilities are particularly important for the elderly because of the risk of assault associated with keeping large sums of money in their homes. The pursuit of non-conventional strategies to meet rural service problems is apparent also in more general approaches adopted to rural development.

COMMUNITY DEVELOPMENT

The concept of community development has deep roots in Ireland, stretching back into the late nineteenth century when the Irish Agricultural Organisation Society (IAOS) was established by Sir Horace Plunkett. Creamery societies involved in the collection of milk for processing into butter and in the sale of farm inputs to shareholding members formed the main co-operative enterprise during the early part of the twentieth century. In recent times some of the farmer co-operatives have expanded into multi-million pound corporations through mergers and takeovers. Kerry Co-operative and the North Connaught Farmers Co-operative are two notable examples of expansion in this way. The product range of the new organisations has been extended from milk processing and butter production to embrace a wide variety of dairy-based items, including specialty cheeses, yogurt and cream-based liqueurs.

While recent trends in the traditional agricultural co-operative system have been towards the development of corporate structures with public shareholding, co-operative enterprise has revived under another guise in other economic sectors on a widespread basis throughout the Republic of Ireland in particular. The activities engaged in range from fish farming and forestry to a broad spectrum of industrial and craft enterprises. The emergence of community-led activities is attributed to the failure of state policy in the years since the second world war to meet the economic needs of rural populations through conventional methods. A general disillusionment with centralised planning has been expressed by the populations of some more remote areas.

Father James McDyer, a Roman Catholic priest, established one of the first modern experiments in co-operative community enterprise at Glencolumbcille, Co. Donegal in 1952. His initial efforts were orientated towards improving the basic quality of life for his parishioners by expedit-

Old and new community development. Muintir na Tire Hall (1945), showing new sports and recreation centre (1985) at rear (photo: John Gough)

Mobile Bank. (photo: Bank of Ireland)

Local GAA hurling match. (photo: *Cork Examiner*)

Waiting for the school bus, Connemara. (photo: IDA)

ing the electrification of the area, constructing a parish hall and introducing a piped water scheme. Vegetable and fish processing and knitwear production followed. The Glencolumbcille Development Society subsequently diversified into other activities, including handcrafts, the development of a holiday cottage scheme and the management of a hotel. Partly because of over-expansion and because of increasing competition from other producers, the co-operative began to experience financial difficulties by the late 1970s and it sold its assets in 1981. In its early years, the Glencolumbcille Development Society made very important contributions to improving living standards in the Slieve League area of Co. Donegal and provided an example which many other communities sought to emulate.

The Gaeltacht areas produced a social movement seeking economic and political independence during the 1960s. The Cearta Sibhialta na Gaeltachta (Civil Rights for the Gaeltacht) movement was particularly active in Connemara in west Galway. It was influential in having an Irish language broadcasting service, Raidió na Gaeltachta, established at Costello in 1972. Local representation on the statutory body responsible for Gaeltacht affairs, Údarás na Gaeltachta, followed in 1982.

Small scale community development efforts receive considerable financial support from Údarás na Gaeltachta, because of their potential for retaining population at a local level and so contributing to the maintenance of the Irish language. Land reclamation projects in Corca Dhuibhne, Co. Kerry, afforestation and shellfish farming in Connemara, and the provision of vital services such as electricity supply in the Aran Islands and piped water supplies in Connemara and Donegal have all received aid from Údarás na Gaeltachta. Approximately twenty community co-operatives currently function in Gaeltacht areas but dependence on state support is high.

Outside the Irish-speaking areas of the Republic of Ireland, co-operative initiatives have enjoyed some notable successes in the Killala Community Council in Co. Mayo and Connemara West Limited in Co. Galway. The former group has expanded local recreational facilities and has attracted substantial industrial investment. The latter has developed a craft centre for woodworkers, potters and fabric designers in a former juvenile detention school at Letterfrack, as well as establishing a holiday cottage scheme. Since 1982, the Rural Resource Organisation (RRO) based at Shannon, Co. Clare has assisted, with advice and financial support, a range of small scale community enterprises. State and European Community financial aid is also provided to many community groups. In Northern Ireland, the Rural Action Project which is funded from both sources acts as a co-ordinating body for rural-based development initiatives in a number of locations throughout the territory.

A series of Pilot Schemes to Combat Poverty operated in the Republic in the 1970s has now become part of a European Community scheme. Much of the work of the Irish programme was concerned with raising levels of consciousness of marginalisation among socially and economically deprived groups in urban and rural locations. Education, involving fundamental questioning of existing structures, was therefore a central element in its activities. The groups worked with included small-boat fishermen in Kenmare, Co. Kerry who wished to have a ban on drift net fishing lifted, and householders in west Galway who sought to have electricity installed in their homes but were unable to pay the required fee to the Electricity Supply Board.

Community development efforts undoubtedly have an important role to play in improving social and economic conditions in rural Ireland. A number of major obstacles currently inhibit progress. The necessity of consulting a large number of separate state agencies to obtain information and financial aid is both time consuming and economically expensive. What is viewed as an excessive concentration of administrative and executive power at central level is also cited as seriously inhibiting local initiatives. A reorganisation of power structures involving devolution of authority to regional and local level is sought by some community leaders. Notwithstanding the absence of any significant measures for economic self-determination, local communities in rural Ireland possess a long experience of social organisation.

RURAL SOCIAL ORGANISATIONS

A noteworthy experience of voluntary endeavour in the spheres of recreation, self-help and economic and social development exists in rural Ireland, dating back to the end of the nineteenth century. Indeed, some of the major national organisations of the present day had rural origins and their public images reflect that heritage very strongly. The Gaelic Athletic Association (GAA), the largest sporting organisation in contemporary Ireland, provides a prime example. The Association was founded in 1884 at Thurles, Co. Tipperary, with the expressed aim of preserving and cultivating national sports, including athletics, handball, hurling and football. In its origins, the GAA had close links with the Irish nationalist movement and promoting the cause of the Irish language has always been one of its objectives.

The GAA is represented in all thirty-two counties of Ireland and organises the playing of Gaelic games from parochial to national level, notably the games of hurling and football. The annual provincial and national championship matches command widespread attention and receive extensive coverage from television, newspaper and radio media. Competition on the football or hurling field has contributed to long-standing rivalries between counties and triumph or defeat for a junior team can enhance or deflate the prestige of a community. Membership of a national champion-ship team has provided an entrée for many men into areas of public life, including politics.

Like the GAA, the Irish Countrywomen's Association (ICA), the main women's voluntary organisation in the Republic, had its origins in rural Ireland but is now represented in both town and countryside. It was founded in 1910 and now has approximately a thousand guilds or branches and 29,000 members. The basic objective of the ICA relates to improving social and economic conditions in rural communities. Some of its most sustained efforts from the 1950s onwards related to extending rural electrification to homes which remained outside the network.

The commercial activities of the ICA include Country Markets Ltd., formed in 1946 as a co-operative society of small-scale producers and craftworkers which is now widely represented throughout the Republic. The Slieve Bawn Handcraft Market at Strokestown, Co. Roscommon was one of its most successful co-operatives during the 1970s. As part of its general educational role, the ICA organises residential courses on a wide range of craft and leisure activities at its headquarters 'An Grianán' (The Solarium) at Termonfechin, Co. Louth. Handcrafts play a central role in branch activities, but the Associ-ation is represented in many aspects of national social and economic life.

The ICA's counterpart in Northern Ireland, the Women's Institute (WI), is a federal organisation consisting of more than two hundred branches divided into twenty-four area groups and is affiliated with its British parent body. The WI is, like the ICA, a non-political non-sectarian organisation. Its stated aim is 'To unite in promoting any work which makes for the better-ment of our homes and the development and improvement of conditions of rural life'. This aim is to be achieved through providing facilities for educa-tion and social interaction.

Muintir na Tíre (The People of the Country), founded by Canon John Hayes in Co. Tipperary in 1937, is undoubtedly one of the voluntary bodies that has contributed most to improving the quality of rural life in the Repub-lic of Ireland. The parish was the basic organisational unit chosen, although Muintir na Tíre was not promoted as an exclusively Catholic body. Its found-ing philosophy was based on Christian Social principles of placing the communal good above self-interest and in that spirit many community projects were undertaken. Since 1973, the work of Muintir na Tíre has assumed greater professionalism with the establishment of a Development and Service Unit to meet the training needs of community development workers and to provide them with the necessary information for their work. A representative Community Council has replaced the Parish Council as the basic administrative unit of the organisation.

Conservation groups have been active in rural as well as urban areas for many decades. Their role has been enhanced in recent years because of the growing threats to natural landscapes and architectural monuments. The National Trust for Northern Ireland is a statutory body financed by endowments, membership subscriptions, gifts, legacies and admission fees to its properties. The Trust owns several architecturally important buildings, two twentieth century gardens and owns or holds rights of way to 60 km of coastline in Counties Antrim and Down. Its conservation activities include the protection of wildlife in Murlough Nature Reserve, Co. Down and the creation of Northern Ireland's first Education Nature Reserve in an area of worked-out clay pits near Galstry, Co. Down. The villages of Cushendun, Co. Antrim and Kearney, Co. Down are in its possession also.

An Taisce was founded in the Republic as a voluntary organisation in 1948. It has statutory rights to make representations relating to physical planning proposals where it feels aspects of the environment are under threat. The aims of An Taisce relate to the conservation and development of the physical heritage of land, air and water, places of outstanding beauty, sites of historical or scientific interest, buildings, and wildlife. Its most valuable contributions have been its efforts to ensure conservation of landscapes under threat from physical development and pollution.

TERRITORIALITY IN RURAL IRELAND

A wealth of anthropological and sociological literature attests to the importance of identity with locality in the folk consciousness of rural Ireland. The family farm has been the primary reference point for a majority of rural residents until very recently. Continuity of occupation by particular families for a century or more is commonplace and 'keeping the name on the land' has always been perceived as a major duty of the farm family. The close psychological attachment to land and the independence which it represents has both positive and negative attributes. This attachment was a major influence in giving a sense of continuity to rural life. The practice of inheritance which accompanied family occupations of land has, however, operated strongly against the enlargement of farm holdings through purchase. In consequence, small and uneconomic structures have persisted over time, especially in western coastal and upland districts. Attachment to land is reinforced by a religious dimension in Northern Ireland where strong social pressures, including sanctions, operate to prevent sales across the religious divide.

The townland is the second most important geographical reference framework in rural Ireland. It is the smallest administrative division in the island, most being between 80 and 200 hectares. About 62,000 exist, many of them dating back to Celtic times. Close kin relationships frequently existed between families within particular townlands, as a result of the system of partible subdivision of land among heirs on the death of their father. Co-operative performance of farm tasks and sharing of agricultural equipment was also usually organised on a townland basis, before mechanisation replaced animal and manual labour as a major factor of production. Although its social and administrative significance has diminished, the townland remains the primary postal address in the Republic of Ireland. It is also the context within which the Roman Catholic Church practice of celebrating Mass in private housholds, known as the 'station' and dating back to the seventeenth century, is organised.

After the townland, the parish, as the visible territorial expression of church authority, assumes special importance as the arena within which not only religious affairs but a wide range of other social activities are organised, including primary education. The GAA and Muintir na Tíre both chose the Catholic parish as their basic organisational unit in recognition of its central role in local social and cultural life. Parish structures assume relatively less importance for the populace at large in Northern Ireland where non-Anglican Protestant denominations form a sizeable proportion of the total population. Catholic and Church of Ireland parish structures exist, of course, in Northern Ireland and church affiliation is known to have a strong influence in determining the schools attended by children and in the organisation of a wide range of leisure activities. Church of Ireland and Roman Catholic parishes do not correspond; the former date from Anglo-Norman times onwards and the pattern of Catholic parishes developed since the seventeenth century.

Parish structures have been identified as playing an important role in influencing the distances over which marriages were contracted in rural Ireland in the past. Such was the case in particular among the small-farm and cottier classes, whose network of social contacts was more geographically circumscribed than that of larger farmers, shopkeepers or professional families. In the era before daily travel to work and to secondary schools in towns, few opportunities existed for establishing social contacts outside the local community, so that marriages among the lower economic groups were usually contracted within the confines of the parish of residence or even within the townland of residence. In this way, local ties were strengthened continuously between small-farm families.

As social status increased, so also did the geographical distance over which marriage partners were chosen. This pattern was especially marked in the commercial farming zones of the south and east of Ireland but it was not confined to those areas. Social position in general, however, overrode propinquity in the contraction of marriage in rural Ireland in the past as it does today. Nevertheless, females tended to move greater geographical distances on marriage than did males who inherited farms. This movement was often associated with enhanced social status.

The ties established through marriage alliances served to reinforce the interrelations between families in any particular locality. This had implications for a wide range of social and economic activities, including the patronage of shops. It has been suggested in the latter context that the sons of urban shopkeepers sometimes contracted marriages with the daughters of rural farmers with a view to extending their clientele through the social contacts established in that way.

In Northern Ireland, religious affiliation has strong cultural and political overtones which lend further complexity to patterns of social interaction. Anthropological research reveals that some of these patterns have persisted in broad outline during recent decades. A basic dichotomy exists between Catholic and Protestant, which has important political implications relating to opposition to or support for the Union with Great Britain. Political affiliation with Loyalist or Unionist, Nationalist or Republican cause, influences local commercial transactions, with each group tending to support shopkeepers and businessmen of their own political persuasion. Public houses are also generally known to have affinities with one political side or another, although class is thought to possess equal significance with religion in differentiating between the clientele of different bars.

Notwithstanding broad political and religious divisions, strong feelings of local community identity exist in Northern Ireland, as documented in recent research findings. Unity and cohesion are most marked and most readily expressed in face of outside opposition, notably in the case of sporting fixtures where the 'honour' of the community as a whole is at stake. When political violence occurs the sense of community may result in blame being apportioned to outsiders. However, a class dimension has been identified here, whereby working-class groups are more likely to engage in open criticism of their political opponents than are their professional middle-class co-religionists.

Old patterns live on. Gradually, however, rural populations in Ireland are becoming more cosmopolitan in composition and in outlook because of changing patterns of migration, journeys to work and to school, and the ubiquitous influence of television. The broader context of social life in the countryside, as reflected in the adoption of urban behavioural norms and the access to leisure activities experienced, has been diversified considerably also. A wide variety of special interest groups exists for young rural people. The increasing professionalisation of farming has further served to integrate the agricultural population at large within a wide range of national organisations. Attendance at formal meetings and lobbying to promote particular policies and issues have therefore become a normal feature of life for the contemporary farmer. Formal and informal social outings have replaced the traditional practice of visiting neighbours and friends in their homes as a form of entertainment for most farmers and their wives.

IMPACTS OF CHANGE

Rural Ireland has been subject to a complex series of social and economic changes in the years since the second world war which have had the effect of integrating the countryside more fully into national and international structures. The influence of the communications media, in particular television, has been central to this process of integration. So too has membership of the European Community, which since 1973 has broadened the horizon within which Irish economic affairs are viewed. Widespread industrial development since the 1960s has played its part in introducing urban work patterns to off-farm commuters. Changing population movements in the wake of regional industrial development have, however, been a major force in bringing about the process of integration. A number of components to this movement may be recognised involving the retention, within their home localities, of members of farm families who in the past would have migrated elsewhere in search of employment, the attraction of former outmigrants, and inmigration of urbanites in quest of the environmental ambience of rural residence.

Population growth in the countryside has had many benefits for rural services and social life. Declining enrolments in primary schools have been arrested and reversed. Rural shops, garages and public houses have gained through an increase in their clientele, with many of the latter undergoing a metamorphosis from country pub to 'singing lounge' where commercial entertainment is provided. Former country shops in dormitory villages on the urban fringe have become part of independent retailer grocery chains in response to demographic expansion. Small speciality restaurants have also become a feature of urban fringe villages in recent years.

The emergence of craft workshops involved in pottery production, weaving, knitwear and woodworking is associated with repopulation in more remote locations. Philosophical commitments to principles of small scale and alternative technology, which motivate many craftworkers, have influenced their movement to peninsular areas of the south and west coasts. The availability of preferential grant funding from government agencies in such locations was undoubtedly involved also. The relatively unpolluted environment of the west coast has proved attractive to small numbers of specialty food producers, some of whom practice methods of organic farming.

The alternative lifestyle movement, which gained momentum in North America and Great Britain during the 1970s, is less strongly developed in Ireland. Its proponents include serious advocates of agricultural self-sufficiency who have documented their progress, as well as a number of cult groups who seek rural isolation. The psychological as well as the practical benefits of agricultural labour are being used in a therapeutic way on a number of farms in Northern Ireland. These properties have been acquired by groups involved in the peace movement to provide young urban people with an opportunity to experience for a short time an alternative lifestyle to that of violence and confrontation.

Some problems ensue on rural population growth. In Gaeltacht areas, an increased use of English in schools and factories is associated with return migration, inmigration and industrialisation. Within the countryside in general, some of the most marked changes ensuing on inmigration occur within commuting distance of large urban centres and involve substantial numbers of people, many of whom possess no previous connection with the area to which they move. Residential segregation often emphasises the division between new and established residents and contributes to difficulties of integration. The strength of existing community cohesion emerges as playing a major role in the ease with which newcomers, usually characterised as 'blow-ins' in the Republic and 'interlopers' in Northern Ireland, can be absorbed.

Where a strong local leadership structure exists, usually consisting of businesspeople, professionals and owners of large farms, newcomers may be integrated into existing social organisations without any great difficulty. By contrast, where prolonged outmigration has impoverished the local pool of social leaders, the arrival of middle-class newcomers almost invariably creates fears of being 'taken over'. The latters' tendency to work through formal organisational structures and to seek leadership in existing voluntary societies and groups comes into conflict with established patterns. These depend upon face-to-face relations and on ascribed positions in a status hierarchy which is not solely class based and which has evolved over a prolonged period of time. Such communities are described as 'closed and disintegrating' by comparison with 'open integrated' communities which can absorb newcomers. Intermediate types exist also which reflect the extent of inmigration and the strength of existing social structures.

Many aspects of rural family and community life have changed since the 1960s. The extended three generation family, occupying one farmhouse, is less common now. Many farmers' wives have pursued non-farm occupations prior to their marriage and continue to do so after they have children. A certain secularisation of social values has taken place also, as evidence of declining levels of religious belief and church attendance reveals. Nonetheless, strong adherence to traditional values remains among certain sectors of the population. Indeed, the overwhelming defeat in a referendum in 1986 of a proposal to permit divorce in the Republic, illustrated very clearly the dominance of what many observers viewed as a rural ethos on a widespread level outside the greater Dublin area.

Management of the Countryside

DESMOND GILLMOR

t is evident from preceding chapters that the Irish country-side is one of great interest and importance because of the character of its physical landscape and wildlife content, because of its heritage of historical features and folk traditions and because of its contemporary economic and social features. The richness and diversity of the countryside add greatly to the quality of life of the people of Ireland, both rural and urban.

There are deficiencies and dangers in any idyllic perception of the countryside as a place of happy contentment and unchanging tranquillity – the rustic image of the pictorial calendar or the chocolate box. There are distinctly beneficial features for those living in a countryside environment and rural community; yet country life for many people may involve some problems such as inaccessibility to services, inadequate employment opportunities, low and uncertain incomes, and long hours of hard work or travel.

Despite strong elements of continuity, the countryside is a dynamic system in which change has been an inherent feature of its long evolution. The pace of this change has fluctuated over time but it quickened dramatically in recent decades in response to technological, economic and social circumstances. The countryside must, as in the past, adapt to changing conditions and cannot be fossilised. The impacts on the landscape have not all been harmful but the gradual nature of some of the change has tended to conceal its effects. The outcome has been a distinct reduction in the quality of the countryside environment with a trend towards homogeneity and loss of valuable components. The material welfare of rural residents has improved greatly but the benefits have been distributed very unevenly, so that there are many deprived groups and individuals. Thus there is a need for guided change; it is essential that there should be both development and conservation.

RURAL DEVELOPMENT

There is a strong case for promoting rural development. Even if conservation of the countryside were to be the only objective, it would be necessary to have flourishing communities based on prosperous rural economies. People who wish to remain in the countryside have a right to expect a secure livelihood and acceptable quality of life. Also it is in the interests of the country as a whole that the best use should be made of all the physical and human resources of the countryside through a self-reliant thriving rural economy and society. There are major weaknesses in the present situation and the problems vary with the degree of rurality and from place to place but there is a general need to increase and widen socio-economic opportunities through rural development.

Most of the development effort and finance directed specifically at rural areas has gone to promote agriculture. This reflects the vital role which farming plays in the countryside but the emphasis has probably been excessive as agriculture itself cannot support a viable economy. Also, aid has been accompanied by a huge exodus of people from farming and much of the assistance has gone to those who are least in need. Greater income support is necessary for small farmers with low living standards. There remains a considerable potential within Irish farming and the marketing of its output could be improved greatly. Substantial development has occurred also in forestry and fishing, there being much scope for more tree planting and fish farming in appropriate locations. An important agribusiness sector has developed but in all the primary industries there is the capacity for much more downstream processing which would enhance greatly the employment and income to be derived from their output.

General regional development is important to the countryside because much of the area to which it relates outside of the few main urban centres in Ireland is predominantly rural. Much interest in regional development occurred in the 1960s, especially in the Republic of Ireland, but the momentum diminished subsequently. Manufacturing industry has been seen as the centrepiece of regional development and its dispersal throughout the country has had a huge impact on rural areas. Much more is needed. Two projects in west Galway are examples of commendable efforts to promote the type of manufacturing appropriate to small communities; they comprise small industries and craft activities on an Industrial Development Authority park at Roundstone and a village of handcraft workshops built by Údarás na Gaeltachta at Spiddal.

The service sector, which is becoming increasingly dominant in developed national economies, has received inadequate attention in Irish regional and rural development. Tourism has been the main focus and there remains considerable potential for recreational and tourist development of the appropriate types. Office activities have shown a strong tendency to concentrate in the major urban centres but the development of modern

Top left: Cushendun Bay from Torr Road. (photo: The National Trust)

Centre left: Cushendun Village. (photo: Desmond Gillmor)

Above: Granite stone walls, Mourne Mountains, Co. Down. (photo: Conservation Volunteers, Northern Ireland)

Left: Sheep on the road at Glenveagh Castle, Co. Donegal. (photo: Bord Failte)

technology should enable more service activities to be performed in dispersed premises and in people's homes. The attractions of country living should lead to the growth of such service and other activities which are not tied to central locations.

Another aspect of the service sector and one which is fundamentally important to residents of the countryside, is the maintenance and provision of access to shopping, educational, medical, entertainment and other services and facilities. Transport considerations are significant to everyone and in all forms of rural development. Housing is another important component and there has been substantial provision by public authorities. The economic and social infrastructure in general is critical to rural development.

Rural development efforts have been characterised by a narrowly sectoral and uncoordinated approach, in which individual activities or features are promoted in almost total isolation from all other components of the socioeconomic structure of the countryside. This results mainly from the structure of government administration, in which there are separate organisations and agencies with jealously guarded responsibilities for individual activities. Exceptions have been the broader perspectives of the Congested Districts Board in the west from 1891 to 1923, the Shannon Free Airport Development Authority in the midwest region of the Irish Republic and Údarás na Gaeltachta in the Irish-speaking areas. The sectoral approach leads to compartmentalised thinking in which there may be duplication and conflict between the objectives and policies of the different organisations and there are inefficiencies in the allocation and use of resources. It is essential that as a minimum there should be a major shift in emphasis towards a more cohesive approach. It is difficult to achieve effective coordination between organisations, however, so that there should be investigation of the feasibility of the total policy reformulation involving the adoption of truly integrated rural development.

An important component of such integrated rural development would be much more active participation by the affected populations of the countryside in the decisions and measures relating to their development. This is termed the bottom-up approach, as compared with the top-down approach in which central agencies have the main responsibility for formulating policies. Integration seems more likely to be attainable at the community level than would the merging of government agency interests. Local people should be in a better position to identify the diverse local potentials and needs, so that such community development should be more efficient and equable in the use of resources and the promotion of appropriate development. Indigenous promotion avoids some of the alienation associated with centralised external direction but problems related to varied

divisions within local communities cannot be ignored. Innovative self-help schemes have been devised but the capacity of local enterprise varies and external advice and funding are also needed, so that appropriate blendings of the bottom-up and top-down approaches seem desirable.

OPPOSITE PAGE:
Fiddler at Doolin, Co. Clare.
(photo: Bord Failte)

COUNTRYSIDE CONSERVATION

Compared with rural development, conservation of the countryside has received little attention in Ireland. This reflects the low levels of environmental awareness and concern that exist in general, though some improvement has begun. The rural landscape, including its wildlife and historical resources content, has a low priority and often displays poor senses of responsibility and taste. This is reflected in the scandals of litter, refuse disposal and discarded cars and of modern scattered housing in the Republic of Ireland, both commented upon unfavourably by many overseas visitors. In the context of such strong nationalistic feelings of whatever orientation and the marked local identity and pride which exist, it is difficult to understand how little concern there is about conservation of the great heritage of scenery, wildlife and historical features in the Irish countryside. Furthermore, conservation is much more than sentimental preservation, for in a wider sense it involves wise use of a resource which has a major economic role.

The countryside conservation movement is small and fragmented and there is limited public and political support for planning, the situation being at its worst in the Republic of Ireland. In it there is no organisation concerned specifically with general countryside conservation, compared with the voluntary Ulster Society for the Preservation of the Countryside and the state Ulster Countryside Committee in Northern Ireland. The most comparable voluntary body is An Taisce, which includes urban interests, and its resources are very limited compared with The National Trust in Northern Ireland. State responsibilities in Northern Ireland for landscape, wildlife and historical conservation and for physical planning are within different sections of the Department of the Environment. Even there countryside conservation has inadequate status and resources and many would favour a semi-autonomous body such as the Countryside Commissions in Britain. In the Republic of Ireland, responsibilities are split between several departments and many different agencies and the government commitment is low.

Landscape conservation in the countryside as a whole is largely through the development control exercised in physical planning, which has developed mainly from the 1960s. Planning has a largely urban orientation, partly because much building development occurs in urban areas. More important is the fact that the rural activities of agriculture, forestry and peat extraction are unlike the other land use activities in being favoured through exemption from development control by society, as are certain government agencies. Apart from this, planning policies are generally appropriate but major difficulties and deficiencies arise in their implementation. This is most evident in the extent to which scattered housing has marred the countryside of the Irish Republic and added to the costs of public services. Here firmer control, combined with positive measures such as advice on location, design and materials and provision of sites in towns and villages, would be beneficial.

The other main form of countryside conservation in Ireland is through the designation of certain buildings, sites and larger areas as having special importance and protection. The level of protection ranges from those owned by the state or voluntary conservation organisations, through those under private ownership but with specific preservation controls which vary in their effectiveness, to those which have just been designated as important but without any measure of protection. The protection is in part through physical planning, especially in relation to buildings. Wildlife and its habitats are conserved through the establishment of nature reserves, though there is also general specification of some protected species. Reserves are better developed in Northern Ireland, where there are national nature reserves, forest nature reserves and areas of special scientific interest. More might be added and there are needs for enlarged areas to promote effective conservation and for more management. Existing nature reserves in the Republic of Ireland have been established in a generally piecemeal fashion and it is important that there should be systematic provision of additional sites incorporating representatives of the different wildlife habitats and physical features.

The establishment of large landscape conservation areas can be a contentious issue. There was a proposal in Northern Ireland in 1947 to establish five national parks, centred on the Antrim glens and coast, the Mourne Mountains and adjacent coast in Down, the Sperrin Mountains in Tyrone and Derry, Upper and Lower Lough Erne in Fermanagh and Slieve Gullion in south Armagh. The power to designate national parks remains but the proposal was not implemented, apparently because of local opposition, mainly from farming interests which feared restrictions on their activities, together with political and administrative considerations. Instead there were established eight areas of outstanding natural beauty, which involve special controls on development but lack the positive conservation measures which should characterise a national park. These areas are extended tracts based on the national park proposals, with the omission of Lough Erne, and the addition of part of north Derry, the Lagan valley between Lisburn and Belfast, the shores of Strangford Lough in Co. Down and the nearby Lecale coastal area.

The national parks proposed for Northern Ireland were envisaged as being similar to those in England and Wales, in that much of the land would be under private ownership and that economic activities would continue to function. The model followed in the Republic of Ireland is that developed initially in the United States of America. It accords with the national park definition of the International Union for the Conservation of Nature and Natural Resources in being under direct state control and operated primarily for conservation. This is the most effective means but it is unlikely that such state ownership would extend over more than a small part of the country. Thus there have been varying suggestions for designation of different areas, generally envisaging arrangements involving park authorities similar to those in England and Wales. Because of confusion with the form of national parks already established in Ireland and for other reasons, it is seems preferable to use alternative terms such as heritage areas. The two types could coexist within a particular locality. A very strong case can be made for designation of the most cherished landscapes and especially for those under the greatest pressure, such as the Dublin and Wicklow Mountains and the Mourne Mountains. An inherent danger in any form of designation is that it may lead to polarisation, focusing conservation effort and resources on elitist areas to the detriment of the remainder of the countryside, where the impression may be given that there is little worth conserving and that the unfettered exploitation is possible. Ideally designation would be unnecessary because appropriate conservation would be practised throughout the whole countryside.

In area designation and in countryside conservation in general it is desirable that there should be a more integrated approach to conservation, incorporating landscape quality, wildlife values and historical heritage. In each aspect and in countryside conservation as a whole there are needs not only for more state commitment but also for better general education and greater voluntary effort. Attitudes favourable towards conservation are much more likely when people are informed of the need for it and understand the benefits to be derived from it. Field studies in schools, outdoor pursuits centres and the youth hostelling organisations play vital roles in introducing young people to the countryside, encouraging them to understand, appreciate, enjoy and respect it. Much useful conservation work can be done through employment provision schemes and on a voluntary basis; the rehabilitation of old buildings is an effective example of the former and tree planting of the latter. Voluntary organisations and individuals have important roles to play in the conservation of the Irish countryside, both in practical measures and in exerting pressures.

INTEGRATED MANAGEMENT

The potentials for both integrated rural development and comprehensive countryside conservation have been stressed in the preceding sections but a highly desirable further step in co-ordination would be the bringing of the two together in total management of the whole countryside of Ireland. This might seem paradoxical in that development and conservation so often seem to be at variance, and developers and conservationists even more so. What is necessary is not only attainment of the right balance between the two but also recognition of the extent to which they are interrelated. These relationships may be seen in how a good quality environment is a major economic asset in forming the basis for tourism and providing attractive living conditions for those working in all types of industries, thus promoting development. Countryside conservation can no longer be regarded as a luxury, for it has a place in all activities and it is an essential component in the broad perspective of comprehensive rural management. This incorporates sustainable development which provides a basis for the maintenance of stable rural communities into the future, rather than short-term exploitive development which destroys irreplaceable resources. A coherent policy for management in an integrated or holistic fashion would aim to conserve and enhance the environment of the countryside while promoting the economic vitality and social fabric of rural areas.

Adoption of the comprehensive countryside management approach would involve integration of physical planning with economic and social planning. Development control is essential but the focus of physical planning almost entirely on restrictive measures has resulted in its negative public image. Intervention by planning to initiate and promote improvements and socio-economic development would give it a much more constructive role in positive countryside management.

Agriculture affords a prime example of how countryside management might involve the integration of development and conservation policies and also the use of a variety of co-ordinated measures. There has been much discussion in some countries concerning the relative merits of planning control as against voluntary approaches in effecting conservation in farming. They need not be mutually exclusive as each can play a part, combined with placement of the main focus on the incorporation of conservation criteria into all aspects of agricultural development policy, which might be regarded as an intermediate but potentially more effective approach. Thus state support of agriculture would be orientated so that good conservation practice would be an integral and requisite component of all grants, subsidies, tax incentives, farm advice and farm development plans. This would be supplemented by persuasion and education to instill the conservation ethic and by use where appropriate of the type of voluntary management agreements with farmers which have had some limited successes elsewhere. Selective planning control would apply to developments such as buildings, roads and reclamation, providing the necessary backup to other measures with respect to major changes and objectionable proposals. Total regulatory control of all farming activity would be cumbersome and unduly restrictive and it should not be necessary.

The case for fuller control could be made more readily with respect to forestry and it increases with growing private participation and commercial orientation in the industry. The planting of trees on sizeable tracts is a long-term change in land use with considerable impacts. Substantial further afforestation is feasible and desirable but there are areas which should not be planted for reasons of landscape and wildlife. Planning would provide the regulatory framework but voluntary adoption of amenity standards and the inclusion of conservation in state support measures would be of major importance. Thus private afforestation should be grant-aided only if done on approved land and in accordance with specified conservation and social objectives. Planting of broadleaf trees should be encouraged more actively.

A prime aim of integrated management would be to resolve the demands and needs of the various land uses and interests which exist within the countryside or affect it. As the pressures on the countryside increase in number and intensify, clashes of interest become inevitable. The levels of conflict which have been reached in some countries might be avoided in Ireland by earlier attempts at reconciliation. The ideal of total consensus would be difficult to achieve but considerable benefits could follow from improvements in understanding, appreciation and co-operation in the inter-relationships between interests and from compromises between them. In any one area the relative priorities to be given to the different demands might be established but these would vary from place to place. Thus recreation would be given a higher rating close to urban areas and in the coastal zone and scenic places than in other parts of the countryside.

One general conflict of interests and values which is commonly seen to exist is that between town and country. More specifically, this may often be between non-agricultural and agricultural interests, as in the extent to which disagreements over tax obligations unfortunately have widened the gap in the Republic of Ireland. The two groups are interrelated through production and consumption but also through the countryside being a recreation area for urban populations and through the state financial support of farming being derived from people in other occupations. These people thus have a legitimate interest in what happens in agriculture and in the countryside which is a resource of society as a whole. By having access to the countryside, urban residents are more likely to understand and be sympathetic towards the problems and needs of those who work and live in rural areas. Farm holidays play an important role in this respect. The interests of the countryside have to be acknowledged with regard to certain facilities designed to meet largely urban requirements, such as waste disposal sites, major roads, high tension electricity transmission lines, power stations, reservoirs, quarries and telecommunication installations. The interrelationships between town and country reinforce the need for integrated management.

Reference to the interests of the population as a whole raises the concept of stewardship; there is need for a much wider recognition and acceptance by the owners and users of the countryside that they have responsibilities or trusteeship to contemporary society and to future generations. This stewardship ethic and its implications should receive appropriate emphasis in the training and continuing education of those entering and in agriculture and other activities concerned with the countryside. Greater balance would involve both consideration of ecological matters in vocational training and adequate recognition of the economic and social dimensions in all environmental education. The mass media have important roles to play in presentation of the multidimensional nature of rural matters and of the need for integrated management of the countryside. Two appropriate specific contexts in which such ideas concerning development and conservation might be presented would be at agricultural shows and on demonstration farms. These would be promoted not just for the rural community but also to appeal to urban people, introducing them to the realities of life in the countryside and helping to bridge the gap between town and country.

The diversity of the Irish countryside, in which each area has a unique combination of physical and human characteristics, ensures that policies and measures would not be uniformly applicable throughout the country. The relative development and conservation needs are very different in remote rural areas which lag behind in socio-economic development and suffer population loss, from those in places which are under pressure from urban expansion, tourist development or agricultural intensification. Policies would have to be flexible enough to accommodate the diversity. Highly centralised administrative structures tend to be out of touch with local needs, whereas a high level of decentralisation might lead to extreme fragmentation and lack of coherence. Thus a proper regional planning and management framework could provide the forum through which local diversity and needs could be balanced with the wider national goals.

Decisions concerning appropriate administrative structures and integrated management policies for the Irish countryside must be essentially political processes. Major entrenched institutional constraints would hinder a more coherent approach in practice. Organisational possibilities to effect co-ordination would include a department for rural affairs, an inter-departmental committee or an autonomous agency. For those people interested in the Irish countryside, there would seem to be scope for a voluntary society encompassing all aspects of rural areas. Such a broadly based society could make useful contributions to the improvement of information about the countryside and the formulation of policy. Popular support and in particular political will are necessary for the derivation of a coherent set of positive and workable policies which would both enhance the environment of the countryside and effect rural economic and social development. It is a duty to future generations to ensure that there is integrated management of the Irish countryside.

SELECTED FURTHER READING

F. H. A. Aalen, *Man and the landscape in Ireland*, Academic Press, London, 1978.

F. H. A. Aalen (ed.), *The future of the Irish rural landscape*, Department of Geography, Trinity College Dublin, 1985.

C. M. Arensburg and S. T. Kimball, *Family and community in Ireland*, Harvard University Press, Cambridge, 1968.

R. P. O. Beach (ed.), *AA touring guide to Ireland*, Automobile Association, Basingstoke, 1976.

J. Bell and M. Watson, *Irish farming implements and techniques 1750-1900*, Donald, Edinburgh, 1986.

D. Bellamy, *The wild boglands, Bellamy's Ireland*, Country House, Dublin, 1986.

J. Blackwell and F. J. Convery (eds.), *Promise and performance: Irish environmental policies analysed*, Resource and Environmental Policy Centre, University College Dublin, 1983.

H. Bohan, *Ireland green*, Veritas, Dublin, 1979.

Book of the Irish countryside, Blackstaff Press, Belfast, 1987.

H. Brody, *Inishkillane, change and decline in the west of Ireland*, Penguin, Harmondsworth, 1974.

B. Breathnach, *Folk music and dances of Ireland*, Mercier, Cork, 1977.

P. Breathnach and M. Cawley (eds.), *Change and development in rural Ireland*, Geographical Society of Ireland, Maynooth, 1986.

D. Cabot (ed.), *The state of the environment*, An Foras Forbartha, Dublin, 1985.

J. G. Cruickshank and D. N. Wilcock (eds.), *Northern Ireland environment and natural resources*, The Queen's University of Belfast and The New University of Ulster, 1982.

L. M. Cullen, *Life in Ireland*, Batsford, London, 1968.

K. Danaher, *The year in Ireland*, Mercier, Cork, 1972.

K. Danaher, *Irish country people*, Mercier, Cork, 1976.

K. Danaher, *The hearth and stool and all!*, Mercier, Cork, 1985.

G. D'Arcy, *The guide to the birds of Ireland*, Irish Wildlife Publications, Dublin, 1981.

E. de Buitléar (ed.), *Wild Ireland*, Amach Faoin Aer, Dublin, 1984.

E. de Buitléar (ed.), *Irish rivers*, Country House, Dublin, 1985.

J. de Courcy Ireland, *Ireland's sea fisheries: a history*, Glendale, Dublin, 1981.

E. E. Evans, *Irish folk ways*, Routledge and Kegan Paul, London, 1957.

E. E. Evans, *Mourne country*, Dundalgan, Dundalk, 1978.

E. E. Evans, *The personality of Ireland, habitat, heritage and history*, Blackstaff, Belfast, 1981.

J. Fairley, *An Irish beast book*, Blackstaff, Belfast, 1984.

J. Feehan, *The landscape of Slieve Bloom*, Blackwater, Dublin, 1979.

J. FitzMaurice Mills, *The noble dwellings of Ireland*, Thames and Hudson, London, 1987.

H. M. FitzPatrick, *Ireland's countryside*, Trees for Ireland, Dublin.

J. Forsyth and D. E. K. Boyd, *Conservation in the development of Northern Ireland*, Department of Extra-Mural Studies, Queen's University of Belfast, 1970.

J. Forsyth and R. H. Buchanan (eds.), *The Ulster countryside in the 1980s*, Institute of Irish Studies, Queen's University of Belfast, 1983.

T. W. Freeman, *Ireland, a general and regional geography*, Methuen, London, 1969.

A. Gailey, *Rural houses of the north of Ireland*, Donald, Edinburgh, 1984.

A. Gailey and D. Ó hÓgáin (eds.), *Gold under the furze, studies in folk tradition*, Glendale, Dublin.

L. Gallagher and D. Rogers, *Castle, coast and cottage: the National Trust in Northern Ireland*, Blackstaff, Belfast, 1986.

D. A. Gillmor, *Agriculture in the Republic of Ireland*, Akadémiai Kiadó, Budapest, 1977.

D. A. Gillmor (ed.), *Irish resources and land use*, Institute of Public Administration, Dublin, 1979.

D. A. Gillmor, *Economic activities in the Republic of Ireland: a geographical perspective*, Gill and Macmillan, Dublin, 1985.

H. Glassie, *Passing the time, folklore and history of an Ulster community*, O'Brien, Dublin, 1982.

S. Gmelch (ed.), *Irish life*, O'Brien, Dublin, 1979.

D. F. Hannan, *Rural exodus*, Chapman, London, 1970.

P. Harbison, *Guide to the national monuments in the Republic of Ireland*, Gill and Macmillan, Dublin, 1970.

A. Hebbert and B. Sheldrick (eds.), *Ordnance Survey leisure guide Ireland*, Automobile Association, Ordnance Survey of Ireland and Ordnance Survey of Northern Ireland, 1987.

M. Herity and G. Eogan, *Ireland in prehistory*, Routledge and Kegan Paul, London, 1977.

G. L. Herries Davies and N. Stephens, *Ireland*, The geomorphology of the British Isles series, Methuen, London, 1978.

N. Hicken, *Irish nature*, O'Brien, Dublin, 1986.

Historic monuments of Northern Ireland: an introduction and guide, HMSO, Belfast, 1983.

C. H. Holland (ed.), *A geology of Ireland*, Scottish Academic Press, Edinburgh, 1981.

A. A. Horner, J. A. Walsh and J. A. Williams, *Agriculture in Ireland, a census atlas*, Department of Geography, University College, Dublin, 1984.

Irish Environmental Library Series, Folens, Dublin.

Irish Heritage Series, Eason, Dublin.

D. W. Jeffrey (ed.), *Nature conservation in Ireland, progress and problems*, Royal Irish Academy, Dublin, 1984.

P. M. Jess, J. V. Greer, R. H. Buchanan and W. J. Armstrong (eds.), *Planning and development in rural areas*, Institute of Irish Studies, Queen's University, Belfast, 1984.

P. Logan, *Irish country cures*, Appletree, Belfast, 1981.

P. Logan, *Fair day, the story of Irish fairs and markets*, Appletree, Belfast, 1986.

Lord Killanin and M. V. Duignan, *The Shell guide to Ireland*, Ebury, London, 1967.

J. Lynam, *Irish peaks*, Constable, London, 1982.

E. McCracken, *The Irish woods since Tudor times*, David and Charles, Newton Abbot, 1971.

F. Mitchell, *The Shell guide to reading the Irish landscape*, Country House, Dublin, 1986.

T. M. Mogey, *Rural life in Northern Ireland*, Oxford University Press, London, 1947.

C. Moriarty, *A natural history of Ireland*, Mercier, Cork.

E. C. Nelson and A. Brady, *Irish gardening and horticulture*, Royal Horticultural Society of Ireland.

W. E. Nevill, *Geology and Ireland*, Figgis, Dublin, 1969.

J. J. Newman (ed.), *The Limerick rural survey 1958-1964*, Muintir na Tíre, Tipperary.

W. Nolan (ed.), *The shaping of Ireland*, Mercier, Cork, 1986.

N. O'Carroll (ed.), *The forests of Ireland – history, distribution and silviculture*, Turoe, Dublin, 1984.

A. O'Dowd, *Meitheal, a study of co-operative labour in rural Ireland*, Comhairle Bhéaloideas Éireann, Dublin, 1981.

F. O'Gorman (ed.), *The Irish wildlife book*, Coughlan, Dublin, 1979.

T. P. O'Neill, *Life and tradition in rural Ireland*, Dent, London, 1977.

S. P. Ó Riordáin, *Antiquities of the Irish countryside* (fifth edition revised by R. de Valera), Methuen, London, 1979.

A. R. Orme, *Ireland*, Longman, London, 1970.

F. J. O'Rourke, *The fauna of Ireland*, Mercier, Cork, 1970.

R. L. Praeger, *The way that I went*, Figgis, Dublin, 1969.

E. Sandford, *Discover Northern Ireland*, Northern Ireland Tourist Board, Belfast, 1981.

P. and M. Shaffrey, *Irish countryside buildings*, O'Brien, Dublin, 1985.

M. J. Shiel, *The quiet revolution, the electrification of rural Ireland 1946-1976*, O'Brien, Dublin, 1984.

D. Shaw-Smith (ed.), *Ireland's traditional crafts*, Thames and Hudson, London, 1984.

L. Symons (ed.), *Land use in Northern Ireland*, University of London Press, 1963.

M. Viney, *Another life*, Irish Times, Dublin, 1979.

J. B. Whittow, *Geology and scenery in Ireland*, Penguin, Harmondsworth, 1974.

H. E. Wilson, *Regional geology of Northern Ireland*, HMSO, Belfast, 1972.

INDEX

Because of the diverse nature of the subject matter of this book, a very detailed index would be inappropriate and unduly long. Thus minor references, including those of one sentence and less, have been omitted.

Accessibility 173, 187, 188
Agriculture, see also
  Farming, 13, 61, 88-89,
  109-117, 146-148, 152,
  154-162, 184-198, 201,
  208-210
Aille 22
Algae 64
Alternative lifestyle 198
Anglo-Norman 83-87, 105
Animals 41-42, 44, 50,
  55-57, 60-61, 62-63, 66
An Taisce 194
Antrim 17, 36-37
Aonach 119
Aquatic activities 169-171
Arable crops, see also
  Tillage 156, 160
Arbutus 59
Archaeology 73, 106-107
Arctic-alpines 54
Areas of outstanding
  natural beauty 206
Baile 105
Badgers 61
Banks 189
Basalts 17
Baskets 140
Beaches 68
Bearberry 54
Beds 139
Benbulben 54
Birds 50, 57, 60-66,
  67-70
Blacksmiths 125-126
Bladderworts 48
Bog-flows 24, 50
Bogs 24, 43-44, 47-52,
  74-76, 167-168
Bord na Mona 50
Bray 36
Bread 138
Britain 118
Bronze Age 77
Building stone 17
Burren 21, 54, 59
Bus 188
Cabins 101
Cairns 76, 93
Calendar customs 132-135
Callows 66

Canals 97-98
Capitalisation 158
Carnivorous 48
Carrying capacity 174
Cashels 78-80
Castles 84
Catholic 103, 195-196
Cattle 156, 159-160
Caves 22-23
Céilí 126, 128
Celts 77-80, 87
Centralisation 187-188
Change 175-181, 197-200
Christianity 80-83, 128
Christmas 134
Churches 81-83, 103-105
Church of Ireland 103, 195
Cinclidotus 66
Cistercians 86
Cladonia 53
Cliffs 29-30, 32-33, 68
Climate 26, 41-45, 52
Clubmosses 54
Coal 96, 137
Coast 32-36, 66-70, 165, 169
Cockroft 181
Colour 41, 62, 68-69
Comhar 112
Commonage 150
Communications 97-98
Community development
  176, 189-192, 193-194,
  203
Commuting 153, 198
Conacre 150
Concentration 159
Cong 22
Congested Districts Board
  141
Conservation 37, 52, 62,
  70, 107, 161-162, 164,
  172, 194, 205-211
Cooking 137-139
Co-operation 117
Co-operatives 189-191, 193
Coopers 125
Copper 95-96
Cord grass 67
Corries 29
Costumes 133-135
Cottages 101

Country parks 172
County councils 182
Court tombs 76
Crafts 125-126, 139-141,
  153
Craftsmen, Craftworkers
  125-126, 197-198
Crannogs 78
Creameries 104
Creels 141
Croagh Patrick 132
Cuilcagh 21
Cultivation 111-114
Dairy farming 13, 156, 158
Dancing 128
Deer 55
Demesnes, see also
  Estates,
  58, 94-95
Development, see
  Community
  development,
  Industrial development,
  Regional development,
  Rural development
Domestic industry 96-97
Downslope movements
  23-24
Drainage 25, 93-94, 161
Drink 138-139
Driving 169
Drumlins 31
Dwellings, see also
  Houses,
  182-183
Ecosystem 41, 47-48
Elderly 183-185
Employment 151-154, 162,
  165, 180-181, 184
Enclosure 89-92
Environment, see also
  Physical landscape and
  Wildlife, 160-164, 167
Epiphytes 59
Erne 25, 31
Eskers 30-31
Estates, see also
  Demesnes,
  89, 94-95, 162
Estuary 66-68
Eutrophication 64, 66

Extractive industries
  167-168
Fairs 118-124
Farm buildings 101, 158,
  161
Farmers 61, 117, 152,
  154-156, 183-184
Farm implements 110-116
Farm machinery 110-117
Farm management 159
Farming, see also
  Agriculture, 74-77,
  154-160
Farm practices 109-117
Farms 89-92, 94, 150, 152,
  160, 184, 194
Farmscape 11
Farm size 150-151, 184
Farmsteads 87, 101
Farmwork 132
Farmyards 101
Fen 43, 66
Field boundaries 106, 161
Fields 74-76, 80, 84-86, 91,
  106
Fire 135
Fish 63-64, 165
Fishing 117-118, 165
Flood 24-25
Flushes 52
Folds 15
Folklife 109-145
Folkmusic 127-128
Folksongs 127-128
Folktales 126-127
Food 137-138
Footpaths 173
Forest parks, Forest
  recreation 172
Forestry 162-164, 209
Forests, see also
  Woodland 42-43, 55, 74,
  92-93, 148, 162-164, 172
Forts 78
Fossils 15-16
Fuel 135, 137
Furnishings 139-142
Furze 137
Gaelic 104-105
Gaelic Athletic
  Association 192-193

Gaeltacht 191
Gannet 70
Geese 67
Geography 10
Geological history 14-17
Giant Irish Deer 42
Glaciation 26-31, 35-37
Glenariff 36-37
Glencolumbcille 191
Glenmalure 35-36
Government 158
Granite 17, 35
Grass, Grassland 62, 74,
  147
Gravity 23-24
Grouse 57
Habitat 44, 45-47, 62
Hallowe'en 133-134
Hare 55
Harvest 114-117, 132,
  158
Hay 62, 116, 158, 159
Hazel 59
Health services 188
Heath, Heather 53-54
Hedgerows, Hedges 57,
  60-62, 89, 161
Herring 117-118
Hiring fairs 124
Historical heritage 8, 72,
  106-107, 171
History 72-107
Holy wells 128-129
Home life 135-142
Horses 157, 171
Houses, see also
  Dwellings, 94-95,
  98, 101, 103, 135,
  181-182, 185, 206
Ice 26-31, 42, 44
Igneous rocks 17
Immigration 175-176, 180,
  198-199
Incomes 157, 160, 183-184
Industrial development,
  see also Manufacturing,
  176, 180
Industries 124-126
Immigration, see
  Immigration
Insects 48-49, 57, 60-61

214

Integrated management 208-211
Integrated rural development 203
Invertebrates 57, 63, 67
Irish Countrywomen's Association 193
Irish Folklore commission 127
Iron 93, 95-96
Iron age 77
Islands 59-60, 78
Kames 30
Karstlands 21-23
Kilbride 129
Killarney 59
Labourers 114, 116, 118
Lakes 22, 29, 32, 43, 53, 59, 64-66, 78
Land 88-94, 146-151, 194-195
Landforms 13-37
Landlords 88-89, 91-92, 94-95
Land ownership 150-151
Landscape history 73, 105
Landslips 23
Land use 105, 146-148, 209
Lead 95-96
LEDU 180
Lent 133
Lichens 52-53, 69
Livestock 74, 85, 119, 124, 159-161
Living conditions 185
Limekilns 94
Limestone 15-24, 54, 66
Linen 96
Lough Derg 132
McDyer 189
Management (Countryside) 200-211
Manufacturing, see also Industrial development, 88, 152-153, 201
Marble Arch 21-22
Markets 119-124
Marram grass 68
Marriage 195-196
Marsh 66-67
Matthew 181
May Day 134-135
Meadows 62
Meath 36
Mechanisation 158
Medieval 83-87
Mediterranean 54, 59
Megaliths 74-77
Meitheal 117
Metamorphic rocks 16
Migration 118, 175-178, 198
Midlands 15, 43, 168
Milk 138-139, 156, 189

Mills 96, 97
Mining 95-96, 167-168
Monasteries 81, 86
Monuments 106-107
Moorland 74
Moraine 28
Moss 43, 49, 53-54, 66
Motte-and-bailey 84
Mowers, Mowing 116
Muckross 59
Mud flats 67
Muintir na Tíre 193-194
Multiple land use 147-148
Museums 145
National parks 40, 55, 59, 172, 206-207
National Trust for Northern Ireland 194
Nature reserves 206
Neolithic 74-77
Newcomers 175, 178, 198-199
Normans, see Anglo-Norman
Nutrients 44-45, 48-52, 54
Oak 58
Oenach 119
Ordnance Survey 106
Outmigration 178
Outshot 139
Oxygen 48, 64-66
Pale 86
Parish 84-86, 195
Parks 172-173
Part-time farming 152, 175-176
Passage tombs 76
Pasture 62
Patterns 128-132
Peat, see also Turf 43-44, 48, 50-52, 167-168
People 10, 175-197
Physical landscape 8, 13-37
Physical planning, see Planning
Pigs 157
Pilgrimages 128-132
Pitcher plants 48
Placenames 104-105
Planning 181-183, 205-206, 208-209
Plantation 88
Plants 41-70
Ploughing, Ploughs 111-114
Pollen analysis 73
Population 10, 77, 88, 93, 176-181, 183, 197-199
Porridge 138
Portal tombs 76
Potatoes 93, 137-138, 156
Pottery 126
Poultry 157
Poverty 192

Protestant 103
Quarrying 95-96, 167
Quartzite 16, 36
Racomitrium 53
Railways 98, 188
Raith 105
Raths 78-80
Reaping hooks 114-116
Reclamation 92-94, 148, 161
Recreation 168-174, 185
Recreational management 174
Regional development 201
Religion 196
Religious devotions 128-132
Rivers 21-25, 30, 35-37, 62-67
Roads 97
Rocks 14-20, 24-25, 30, 52-53, 63
Roman Catholic, see also Catholic 195
Ropes 141-142
Rural development 200-206, 208-211
Rurality 11
Rushes 43
Saints 128-134
Salmon 165
Salt marsh 67
Sand dunes 68
Sandstone 15-17
Scenery 13, 37, 164
Schools 104, 187-188
Scree 52-53
Scythe 114, 116
Sea 15, 32-33, 66-70
Seanchaí 127
Seaweeds 68-69
Sedimentary rocks 15
Services 89, 176, 185-189, 201-203
Settlement, Settlements 77-80, 89-91, 94-95, 97, 105, 181
Shannon 21, 25
Sheep 157
Shops 124, 188, 197
Sickle 114
Silage 159, 160
Skib 141
Sligo 24
Smallholders Unemployment Assistance Scheme 184
Social life 126-135, 197
Social organisations 192-194
Social values 199
Society 9

Soil 35, 44-45, 77, 147
Sowens 138-139
Spades 112
Spealadóir 116
Specialisation 159
Sphagnum 43, 49
Stalactites/Stalagmites 23
Stewardship 151, 210
Stonemasons 125
Storytelling 126-127
Straw 140-141
Strawberry tree 59
Streams, see Rivers
Swans 67
Tea 139
Teelin 129
Territoriality 194-197
Threshing 116-117
Tides 67-70
Tillage, see also Arable crops, 147, 156
Tills 30
Tombs, see Megaliths
Tourism 168
Townhland 195
Towns, see also Urban, 84, 95, 105, 119-124, 151-153, 175-176
Trades, Tradesmen, see Crafts, Craftsmen
Transport 172, 184-198
Turf, see also Peat 135, 137, 168
Turloughs 66
Udarás na Gaeltachta 191
Urban, see also Towns, 10-11, 84, 89, 148, 151, 175-176, 179-181, 210
Valleys 25, 29, 35-36
Vegetation 41-70, 74
Verrucaria 69
Village 86, 89, 94
Volcanic rocks 17
Walking 171, 173
Water 25, 49, 62-66, 69-70, 169
Wedge tombs 76
Welfare 183-185
Wildlife 8, 41-70
Wildscape 11
Wind 68
Women's Institute 193
Woodland, Woods, see also Forests, 42-43, 57-60, 92-93, 164
Woodturning 126
Woodworkers 125
Wren boys 134
Yew 59